BREATHLESS

beacon press · boston

an

asthma

journal

BREATHLESS

Louise DeSalvo

BEACON PRESS
25 Beacon Street
Boston, Massachusetts 02108-2892

BEACON PRESS BOOKS
are published under the auspices of
the Unitarian Universalist Association of Congregations.

03   02   01   00   99   98   97   8   7   6   5   4   3   2   1

Text design by Elizabeth Elsas
Composition by Wilsted & Taylor

Library of Congress Cataloging-in-Publication Data can be found on
page 154.

for

E D V I G E   G I U N T A

and

C A T H E R I N E   K L E I N P E T E R

(without whom this book could
not have been written)

It is in sickness that we are compelled to recognize that we do not live alone but are chained to a being from a different realm, from whom we are worlds apart, who has no knowledge of us and by whom it is impossible to make ourselves understood: our body.

Marcel Proust

Something should be said for the rush of bliss that floods an asthmatic whose bronchial muscles have unclenched. Of course: air, in, out: this is how people do it. How simple.

John Updike

The majority of literature is the outcome of ill men, and, though you might not know it, I am always very ill. Logically, that means I am producing, or am going to produce, literature.

Dylan Thomas

When Clara had emerged from her mother's womb,
Nana had cradled and washed her, and from that
time on she had felt a desperate love for this fragile
creature whose lungs were always full of phlegm, who
was always on the verge of losing her breath and
turning purple, and whom she had had to revive so
many times with the warmth of her huge breasts
because she knew that this was the only cure for
asthma, much more effective than Dr. Cuevas's
fortified syrups.

Isabel Allende, **The House of the Spirits**

I add my breath to your breath
That our days may be long on the Earth
That the days of our people may be long
That we may be one person . . .

Ancient Keres Song,
Translated by Paula Gunn Allen

1   I am alone, walking on my favorite beach in Sag
      Harbor, on the East End of Long Island. It is just
after sunset on a warm day in late spring in 1992, and I
want to enjoy myself.

I try to ignore the trouble I'm having breathing, the
coughing attack that has continued, unabated, for the past
two hours, the slamming inside my head, my fatigue. Tell
myself that maybe this illness I've had for seven months
now, which no doctor can diagnose, is all in my head. If
that's so, maybe it's something I can control. But even if I
can't control it, maybe I can work on my attitude.

For the next few seconds, I try to ignore this body I
inhabit that has declared war on me. Try to notice the
changing sky. Watch the pair of mallards davening for their
evening meal. Ignore the chronic cough, the pain in my

chest, the lump in my throat, the rasp in my breath. And can't. And blame myself. Sometimes I wonder whether I'm exaggerating how poorly I've been feeling, or if I really *am* feeling as poorly as I've been feeling. Tell myself I'm just too goddamned sensitive.

"The Princess and the Pea," my husband calls me, after the fairytale princess, so sensitive she could feel a tiny pea beneath a pile of mattresses. And he's right. But I can't help it, no matter how much I try. I'm hypersensitive. Always vigilant. Unusually aware of my surroundings. Bothered by everything. Noises. Smells. Heat. Cold. Sleeping with me, my husband Ernie tells friends jokingly, is quite an experience.

This is what I have to do so I can fall asleep. I put on my pajamas. But if it's cold, I wear long underwear, too. Sometimes gloves. Maybe even a hat. Make sure the sheets are perfectly flat. Line the blankets up precisely so there are no lumps. Put in earplugs so I won't be bothered by noise. Turn on the electric blanket, even in summer. Get into bed. Smooth out my pajamas (this takes quite some time). Do my rhythmic breathing.

Ernie says he feels sorry for me. He's glad he's not like that. He jumps into bed practically naked. Wouldn't notice if the roof were leaking on him (and it has, and he didn't). Sometimes I wish I didn't inhabit this body in the way I do—but hyperreactive as my body may be, it's the only one I've ever lived in.

"Why do you do this?" Ernie asks one night. He's exhausted, wants to fall asleep, and is exasperated by how long my nightly ritual is taking me.

His is a rhetorical question, for we have often talked

about the reasons for my bedtime rite, that it is rooted in the nighttime terror I often felt in childhood in my embattled household, where I could not fall asleep until everyone else was asleep.

So far, no doctor has found a name for this illness I have, much less a cure. Ernie, who has a medical degree but who no longer practices, is equally baffled. And I am trying to live with this illness, and fight it, and figure it out, alone.

Usually, when I walk, I feel better than I do the rest of the day. Sometimes, even my chronic cough disappears. Today, though, I'm aware of every breath I take. Inhale. Cough. Sputter. Exhale. Inhale. Exhale.

I have recently learned that every day each of us takes about 20,000 breaths. That's 834 breaths an hour, 14 breaths a minute, one breath every four or so seconds. If I continue to be painfully aware of every breath I take, I will labor through 13,344 breaths during each day's waking hours, and 4,870,560 breaths in the next year.

Inhale. (Can't get enough air into my lungs. Feels like I'm suffocating, feels like I have a tomcat sitting on my chest and that I'm breathing against its weight. Feel, too, like I'm drowning in mucus.) Clear my throat. Cough. Clear my throat. Swallow. Clear my throat. Choke. Exhale. Inhale. (Better this time; if it were always like this, I could take it.) Clear. Swallow. Exhale. Inhale. (Shit. Tomcat's back.) Drowning. Mayday. Mayday.

I gasp, walk along, wonder how much longer I can take this, look out over the bay toward Shelter Island, now a navy blue mass against a yellow-pink sky. If I'm lucky, I'll see the pair of swans who live in this bay in flight against the evening sky. If I'm lucky, this illness will go away as quickly as it began. If I'm lucky, I won't have to kill myself. Still, I have decided that I *will* kill myself if, in time, someone can't figure out what I have and cure it, if this illness that has invaded my body and turned me into someone I don't know, and don't want to know, lasts very much longer.

When my husband asks me why I'm in such despair, I can't find the language to explain. Can't let him see that laboring through 13,344 breaths a day, and coughing, constantly, means I can think of little else but how the next breath will feel. It's been hard to do anything (although I've been trying to do everything)—teach, think, read, write, make love, cook dinner, wash clothes, enjoy a view—when you feel like you're suffocating, when you think that the next breath you take might be your last.

I sink down onto the pebble beach. Put my head in my hands. Last year at this time, before I got sick, I took this beauty for granted, I took everything for granted. Like breathing. Something my body did without my acknowledging it for the miracle it is. Last year, I didn't know the meaning of the word "despair."

breath, noun. 1. the air inhaled and exhaled in respiration. 2. respiration, esp. as necessary to life. 3. life, vitality. 4. the ability to breathe easily and normally. 5. time to breathe, pause or respite.

breathless, adjective. 1. without breath or breathing with difficulty; gasping; panting. 2. with the breath held, as in suspense, astonishment, or fear. 3. causing loss of

breath, as from excitement, anticipation, or tension.
4. dead, lifeless. 5. motionless or still.

Sunday, November 2, 1991, Ernie and I go to see "Little Man Tate." The movie captures my interest, for I see something of myself in that little boy. My mother, like his, urged me to cultivate my talents and this, too, entailed our separation.

Recently, I have been feeling wonderful, finally, after several very difficult years, my sister's suicide, my mother's long, debilitating illness and her death, my son Justin's near-fatal bicycle accident, my father's open-heart surgery. And I've been working well. My teaching at Hunter College has never been more enjoyable. I am halfway through a booklength project, writing about one of Virginia Woolf's suicide attempts, and about how Djuna Barnes was abused as a child. I am in that hardwon place that comes after much uncertainty, where, suddenly, inexplicably, you instinctively know the work you need to do.

Ernie and I leave the movie theater, clasp hands. Walk down to the Hackensack River to see the waterbirds that fish at dusk. There is a reedy spot beyond the parking lot that I love to visit that the moviegoers ignore, a tiny remnant of what was once a huge watermeadow. As a girl, I sometimes played in the swamp where the movie theater now stands. It has almost been obliterated. I can remember its watery beauty (lost to me, lost to us all) before the factories and warehouses and the New Jersey Turnpike came and destroyed it all.

Change. Loss. Separation. Constant themes in my life.

•   •   •

As we make our way to the car, I find that I am very, very tired, that my legs are rubbery, that I'm having trouble walking, even breathing. When we get to the car, I'm shivering and my head is pounding. My throat hurts. I feel like I'm going to die. In the space of two or three minutes, I have come down with something awful.

"The flu," Ernie tells me, his skill at medical diagnosis undiminished. "You know it's the flu when it comes on that fast."

It is the end of April, six months later, and I'm still sick, although I no longer have a fever. Every day I wake up, hoping I'll be fine. By mid-morning, though, I start coughing. By lunchtime, I am exhausted. By afternoon, I have a whacking headache. A nap helps. By evening, the coughing abates somewhat, especially if I have a glass of red wine with dinner. Sometimes, I have two. The great temptation to drink myself into oblivion, I have resisted, especially because wine seems to inhibit my coughing. Exhausted, I collapse into bed by eight, and, blessedly, sleep, uninterrupted, through most of the night, though, several times a week, I awaken, throat tingling, in the middle of the night, and I start coughing—but I can usually fall back to sleep soon enough.

Since November, I have had but five symptom-free days, when I try to convince myself I am back to normal. Various doctors have ruled out AIDS, Lyme disease, heart disease, lung cancer, emphysema, whooping cough, sinusitis. Each specialist has rendered a different diagnosis with authority and assurance, and each has put me on a drug regimen that I have hoped would work, but hasn't. I have spent thousands of dollars on doctors, and on medications, and I am still sick. I have been on nine different drug regimens (including three rounds of potent antibiotics). My druggist and I are on a first-name basis; I talk to him almost as much as I talk to my best friend Kate. Despite the expensive drugs I have taken, one brand of cough drop helps me the most. I pop them into my mouth (stained blue from the dye) all day long, ignoring the warning label that says they can be dangerous if used for an undiagnosed, persistent cough.

This is what I've been told so far:

1. That what I'm experiencing is the aftermath of a very severe flu; I can feel like this for a year, maybe more.
2. That I have a chronic viral syndrome. It's incurable.
3. That what I have is most definitely bronchitis.
4. That I have chronic motor rhinitis. (A fancy way of saying a runny nose, my husband tells me.) When I protest that it's in my chest, too, the doctor ignores me, turns to his assistant, and dictates "Chronic motor rhinitis," which she scribbles into her notebook.
5. And finally, and inevitably, that I am an hysteric. This, from a pulmonary specialist in an emergency room who complains that he has a terrible cold and coughs in my face as he examines me.

I have come to the hospital because of a coughing attack so severe and prolonged I almost lost consciousness.

I have waited over an hour and a half to be seen, hunched over, head down, sucking air, counting my breaths to calm myself, muttering how medical care in the United States is starting to resemble Russia's, too weak to make a racket or to demand to see someone immediately. Still, I have fantasized that the waiting would be worth it, that some Doctor Kildare-type would figure out this disease and prescribe some medicine that would cure me.

"I think I have asthma," I tell him. For months, I've had a nagging suspicion that what I have is asthma.

"No wheezing," he says, "so it can't be asthma."

Long pause.

"Are you going through a bad time? Making yourself hyperventilate? Have you considered that this might be hysterical?"

In another time, or another place, I realize, this guy would have the power to lock me up. I get so enraged at him, though I don't say a word, that I feel an adrenaline rush. I want him dead. And, for the first time since I've gotten sick, my breathing eases completely, and, though I'm exhausted, I know that, right now, I'm fine. (I didn't know then, though I know now, that it was the adrenaline rush from my anger that has made me stop coughing.)

As I rage out of the emergency room, I tell myself that this is good to know—that whatever it is I have, if I get angry enough, I will feel better.

I leave the hospital. I snort the air.

Throughout this "hell," I continue teaching, continue writing, though I do very little else. If I don't work, I'm afraid I'll give in to this illness and that it will completely overtake me. And if I stop working, I'm afraid I'll die—for my work, I have always believed, has kept me alive. It has been a source of strength to me, a place where I forget my chronic fears, where I feel centered and in control. Now, working gives me the illusion that I'm connected with normal life as I used to know it.

Still, I nap every day and I do as much work as I can in bed. I've pared down my life, given up everything that is not absolutely required of me—socializing, answering mail, public speaking, talking on the telephone.

Each day, I write in my journal, for I have read that daily journal writing boosts the immune system. And I am doing everything I can to boost my immune system. I walk on the days I'm able; meditate; do breathing exercises and visualizations; read an entry from *One More Day: Daily Meditations for People with Chronic Illness*, whose wisdom I appreciate, but whose lessons I find it difficult to enact ("The reality of our lives is this: our health has changed. . . . We can wistfully look back to another time and place, or we can live in the here and now by making the best of a less than ideal situation").

At times, I think I could cohabit with this illness, that I must pay closer attention to it, understand what it's trying to tell me, allow it a central place in my life. Daily I hope that this will be the last time I'm sick, yet I live, too, in fear that I'll never be well again. Occasionally I see that, though I have changed my life drastically, I still haven't changed it enough. I haven't taken the time to allow myself to heal. I have assumed that I would heal if I lived a somewhat simplified version of my normal life.

.   .   .

"I can't breathe because I have no breathing space," I realize one day, as I'm gasping for air.

If I'm going to get better, I think, I must listen to what my body is telling me.

I have been a critic, a biographer. Studied other people's lives, but never, in any profound sense, my own. I decide that I will now take the skills I have developed in my professional life, and use them to study myself and this illness. I will have to become self-absorbed, I realize. Until now, I have led a reactive life. Though I am usually in the middle of doing something I consider important, if, on any given day, you were to ask me "But what do you really want?" I couldn't answer immediately. Yet I have assumed that I am doing what I want to do—though I have never stopped to reflect upon whether what I am doing has satisfied, not only my mind ("You can't get out of your head," Ernie has chided me often), but also, my body, my heart, my soul. Nor have I stopped to dream of what I might like to do or see in the next moment, the next day, or the next year of my life.

I never stopped in the middle of a day to ask myself how I felt, how my body felt, or what that tightness in my neck or chest might be telling me. I never asked myself what I might do to care for myself.

I never stopped. I never cared for myself.

One night I awaken, heart pounding, from a dream that I know is connected to my illness.

I am in a house that is being dismantled and the place is full of jagged glass and workers are stripping the interior so there is nowhere to sit, nowhere to sleep, nowhere to work, nowhere to cook (this is important). In this house, there are organisms with claws and they begin sticking to my arms, my legs, my back, my chest. I know I must pull them off, and that if I don't, they'll devour me, but when I can pry one off and throw it into what looks like the sea, it jumps back on me. Finally, finally, after much effort and energy, I remove them all. But now there are sores all over my body where these creatures have been, and colored streamers that grow longer and longer are coming out of these sores. They are very beautiful. I start pulling them out of my body.

As I do this, I see a man in a wheelchair who tells me he knows what I'm going through, he's had the same disease I have, and he warns me it's dangerous, that it can kill me, and that I have to go to the hospital. He tells his mother (who is with him) to write down the name of the disease for me on a piece of paper. She gives it to me. I put it in my pocket, but later, when I want to read it, it's not there. I've come so close to knowing what I have. But now, I fear, I will never find out.

On impulse, I have bought a copy of Thomas Moore's *Care of the Soul*. Two of his chapter headings have intrigued me: "Honoring Symptoms as a Voice of the Soul" and "The Body's Poetic of Illness."

I read the book slowly. This is the dignified self-help book I need. One of Moore's themes, that we "come to know the soul only in its complaints: when it stirs, disturbed by neglect and abuse, and causes us to feel pain," strikes me deeply. I attempt to initiate the kind of self-care Moore describes. I begin by trying to understand what this illness is trying to teach me.

"Observance places you deep within the feeling," I quote Moore, at the top of a page of my journal.

I begin writing.

Spring 1992

What I want to observe, over a ten-minute period, is when I need to take a deep breath and what happens to me when I do.

Right now, I am breathing through my nose and exhaling through my nose. I inhale deeply, feel I can't quite get to the end of the inhale, and need to clear out my throat. I think that I need to clear out old things. Now I can inhale as deeply as I want. I also realize I want to breathe more fully. This means I want to do much more exercise than I am now doing. I want to be more physically fit, physically active.

What comes to mind, too, is that my mother stopped my breathing—that is, she was always cautioning me not to do too much, not to exert myself. Was this because she feared for my safety? Or was it because she wanted me to stay close to her so that she could have me for a companion? I always get to a certain stage of being active and expansive, and then I pull back. Breathing as deeply and as effortlessly as I want entails going beyond what my mother wanted me to do.

As a girl, I loved sports. On a summer holiday, I remember swimming powerfully across Lake George, my father, in a rowboat beside me. I swam from one side of the lake to the other. My mother had put up a fight. Told me I shouldn't do it, it was too dangerous. Yet I swam the whole way and it is a high point in my life, for I learned that I was strong, had stamina, and could pace myself to finish a long, difficult task. My father prized my intrepid nature; my mother tried to squelch it.

Breathing freely, has something to do with leaving my mother, with following my father's adventurous spirit. Breathing poorly connects me to my mother. Breathing deeply, to my father. Maybe now that my mother is dead, I want her. Maybe this illness is my way of staying with her.

Still, this disease is telling me that I need more room to breathe, relax, do enjoyable things. Knitting, cooking, walking.

2 July 1992. I go to a health food store to buy a stash of Throat Coat Tea and I spy a copy of *Vegetarian Times.* For some reason, I get a powerful urge to buy the magazine, though I've never read it before. When I get home, open it, and begin to read, I notice an article, "A Breath of Fresh Air," by Lucy Moll, which, given my condition, captures my interest. It's about asthma.

"An attack can be mild or severe and can come on slowly or quickly. In a severe attack, breathing is extremely difficult. . . . Inside, the asthmatic is in terror of suffocating. If the amount of oxygen in the blood drops significantly, the person's lips and face may turn blue and the skin may become clammy. In such cases, the attack may be fatal if medical attention is not received immediately."

Moll also discusses the breakthrough that asthma experts have recently made in their understanding of asthma, about the important role inflammation plays in the disease. Inflammation "causes the lining of the bronchial tubes to swell and steps up the production of thick, sticky mucus that further plugs the narrow tubes. (Doctors previously believed asthma was a disease of constricting bronchial tubes that became inflamed rather than vice versa.) What's more, the inflamed airways become 'twitchy,' meaning that the slightest provocation can lead to an asthma attack. During an attack, the tiny muscles that wrap around the bronchial tubes constrict (or go into 'bronchospasm') and bring on the symptoms of asthma: wheezing, incessant coughing and shortness of breath."

Except for the wheezing, this is exactly what I experience. I am sure that what I have is asthma. What Moll describes as asthma is what I have described to every doctor I've visited. Incessant coughing. Thick, sticky mucus I can't clear fast enough, which makes me feel like I'm drowning, like I'm suffocating (like a cat is sitting on my chest). Twitchiness in my throat, tightness in my chest. Shortness of breath. Cold hands, cold feet.

"Thank you, Lucy Moll," I say to myself. "I think you've saved my life."

I call Ernie, tell him about the article, tell him I'm sure I have asthma, ask him to find me an asthma specialist. Wouldn't it be a hoot, I say, if, after spending all this money on fancy doctors, I figure out what I have by spending a couple of bucks on the *Vegetarian Times?*

Moll's article reports, too, that most asthmatics can be

helped, most "can take control of their illness" by learning about it, and by using a combination of drug and nondrug treatments.

When I read this, I start crying.

So, I think, there's hope.

Diary entry for July 30, 1992
I want to record that today a pulmonary specialist in New York diagnosed my illness as asthma.

"But I don't wheeze," I tell him, repeating what has continued to puzzle me, based upon what the emergency room physician told me some months before.

"You don't have to wheeze to have asthma," he responds.

I ask the doctor what, if anything, the flu I had in November had to do with getting asthma. He tells me that often, after a severe flu, someone can either develop asthma or their asthma (if they've had it before) can worsen.

I have a treatment protocol. Two inhalators. One, a bronchodilator, to open the airways. The other, a corticosteroid (used with a spacer), to treat the underlying inflammation. In all, I'll be taking twenty-eight doses of medicine a day to start. As I get better, I'll need less.

The doctor takes the time to show me how to use the inhalators properly. He tells me that I should take the bronchodilator well before the corticosteroid, that I must wait an appropriate amount of time (specified in the drug package insert, which I must read) between inhalations or the medicine itself and/or the propellant might make my symptoms worse. He tells me to stand, to tilt my head back, to exhale deeply, to begin inhaling before releasing the medication, to hold my breath for several seconds before exhaling, to rinse my mouth after the steroids so I won't get thrush (Candida albicans, a fungus—a possible side effect).

Asthma, he says, is eminently treatable in compliant patients. The trouble is that many patients don't use their medicines as they've been directed. (A later note I have penned in the margin of this diary entry reads: "I have since found this to be true; I am the *only* asthma patient, of the hundreds I've spoken to, who has followed my doctor's treatment plan exactly.") I shouldn't wait for a severe attack and then treat it (which is dangerous, yet this is what many asthma patients do), the doctor says. I should use my medications to prevent a severe attack.

The good news is that I can lead a completely normal life, he's sure, once the disease comes under control. But this will take six months to a year and I must be patient. My lung capacity test was very good, considering. And I must buy a meter to monitor my vital capacity several times a day. This will show me when I need to take more medication—something I can't determine without using it.

"Congratulations on staying alive," he says, after explaining that an undiagnosed case of asthma as bad as mine can kill you. I ask him if it's common for a case like mine to go undiagnosed this long. "All too common," he replies, and tells me about one patient, an engineer, in even worse shape than I, who went undiagnosed, despite countless trips to doctors, for more than two years. There are many people, he says, suffering from chronic asthma who haven't been diagnosed.

When I later ask Ernie why, despite his medical training, *he* couldn't figure out that I had asthma, why all those doctors I went to couldn't figure it out, and why asthma goes undiagnosed so often, given recent advances in medical knowledge about asthma, he tells me that when he went to medical school, he spent about ten minutes learning about asthma. General practitioners and internists, the doctors most likely to see such cases, Ernie tells me, probably don't know enough about asthma to make the diagnosis, or, if they make it, to plan an effective treatment protocol, based on current research, and, so, to treat the underlying inflammation (which absolutely must be treated), not merely the bronchoconstrictive component of the disease. (A later note: I have found this, too, to be true. Though many people with asthma whom I've met carry around and use— indeed, often overuse—bronchodilators, only a few also use inhaled steroids, and almost none use them on the required daily basis.)

"Let's face it," Ernie says, "what with all the paperwork involved in the modern practice of medicine, and with all the emphasis on cost-consciousness, it's gotten much more difficult for doctors to keep up with research and with new and effective treatments. And it's become close to impossible for doctors to take the kind of time you must spend with a patient to make an accurate diagnosis."

Before I go, the doctor asks me what I've done to take such good care of myself, and I tell him about my exercise and meditation practice. "Since it's obviously been working, keep it up," he advises. He gives me an information sheet, "On the Nature and Cure of Asthma." It warns me that asthma, though treatable, is potentially fatal. It describes, in greater detail, the medications he has prescribed and their potential side effects.

I give myself a jacuzzi when I come home.

Asthma. I can't take it in yet, can't imagine what impact it will have on my life.

How do I feel about knowing that I have asthma? Since November, I've been living in a nightmare. It's good to have a name for what I have. I've been saying it feels like asthma for months. So, by paying attention, I helped figure this out.

I'm sure I'll do well because I have become active in the pursuit of my well-being.

I decide, though, that I will not let asthma rule my life. I expect, someday, to be back to normal.

3 After I am diagnosed, I decide to learn as much about asthma and about breathing as I can. I read Geri Harrington, *The Asthma Self-Care Book*; M. Eric Gershwin, M.D., and E. L. Klingelhoffer, Ph.D., *Asthma: Stop Suffering, Start Living—New Strategies for Controlling Your Asthma Including Diet, Meditation, Exercise, Self-Care*; Andrew Weil, *Natural Health, Natural Medicine*. (And I continue reading: *Mind/Body Medicine*, edited by Daniel Goleman, Ph.D., and Joel Gurin; *The Asthma Sourcebook*, by Frances V. Adams, M. D.; *Conscious Breathing: Breathwork for Health, Stress Release, and Personal Mastery*, by Gay Hendricks, Ph.D.)

At first, though, what I learn is confusing, often terrifying. Sometimes I have an asthma attack simply because of what I'm reading.

Asthma, I learn, is the only treatable disease that is becoming more fatal—and it is becoming more prevalent and severe. Asthma is incurable, though manageable. It can be fatal: 1 to 2 percent of people with severe asthma eventually die of it. The incidence of asthma is increasing, especially in inner cities (upwards of 10 million Americans currently have diagnosed asthma). It is especially increasing among children (7 in 100 have asthma; 14 in 100 have asthmatic episodes). And the number of hospitalizations and deaths from asthma attacks is rising dramatically.

No one knows definitively what causes asthma, though, in the past, psychological factors were considered paramount. Now, however, asthma is believed to be caused by a complex interaction among several factors—genetic predisposition, reaction to allergens or triggers (smoke, exhaust or chemical fumes, pollutants), stress, a hyperreactive nervous system.

David A. Mrazek, M. D., and his associates have found that "intense, early family stress" (parents unable to cope; baby allowed to experience prolonged periods of acute distress) is a "basic risk factor" for developing asthma. Conversely, parents who are responsive to their babies' needs, and who help babies manage distress, help them minimize the arousal that could lead to hyperreactive airways. Asthma, then, is a signal that a child has not been helped to learn to regulate a physiological state of arousal.

Asthma is described (by Mrazek) as the response of a

hyperreactive autonomic nervous system. Muscles that line the airways tighten (constricting the route through which air travels), the lining of the bronchial tubes swells and becomes inflamed (blocking air passage further), lubricating mucus becomes thick and sticky and may plug up the airways, and breathing out becomes increasingly more difficult so that air depleted of oxygen is trapped in the lungs, leaving no room for oxygen-rich air to enter. Asthma essentially is a disease of exhalation. In fatal attacks, the person suffocates.

Treatment protocols are not fixed or rigid, and it can take months to find one that works for a given patient. Many people with asthma use a combination of drugs, some inhaled, some taken internally (all with possible serious side effects—among them, seizures, elevated blood pressure, tremors, ulcers, blurred vision, heart attack, stroke, osteoporosis, obesity, insanity, cataracts, skin fragility, muscle weakness). Drugs are used to dilate the airways (theophylline or drugs derived from adrenaline or atropine), manage the secretion of mucus, and reduce inflammation (corticosteroids). A study published in *The New England Journal of Medicine*, though, has suggested that overuse of bronchodilators may be a primary reason why deaths from asthma are increasing.

Other approaches to asthma management use psychotherapy, herbal remedies (ephedra, for example), homeopathy, stress reduction, and relaxation techniques, meditation (which, in studies, has proved to alleviate symptoms), yoga, conscious breathing techniques, aerobic exercise (which can induce attacks), dietary and nutritional changes (macrobi-

otic or vegan diet, vitamin therapy, avoiding foods trig-
gering attacks), and acupuncture.

4 *Diary entry for Friday, August 7, 1992*
Today, I went to the Guggenheim Museum in Manhattan. It was the first day devoted to pleasure I've
spent in New York since the onset of my illness, and it was
wonderful. I didn't cough. I came home tired and euphoric,
feeling that I was getting my life back.

I will devote this month to figuring out my asthma medicine. One day at a time and all that.

I have so many lists to make—times when I must take
each medication, charts listing doses of medicines I've taken
(in case of an emergency), dates when I must buy new medication. It's daunting.

I had a crying jag last night about all this. I am mourning the loss of my old, healthy self. I don't know yet who
this new self is.

Because I know that clutter causes stress, and because I
have decided to reduce stress, I decide I will go through the
house and chuck away tons of stuff. I buy a couple of books
about organizing.

When Ernie walks into my study one morning, he
laughs. A copy of *Clutter Control* teeters precariously atop a
small mountain of books on my extremely cluttered desk.

"Looks like you're losing the battle," he says.

"Streamline, streamline, streamline," I tell him, "will,
in time, become my motto."

I go through the closet in my bathroom and throw out seven bottles of nail polish. The days of wearing nail polish are gone forever. Ernie has saved five shower caps from his business trips to fancy hotels and, since neither of us uses shower caps, out they go.

"Are you sure," Ernie asks at dinner, "that trying to get yourself organized to reduce your stress isn't making you even more stressed?"

He has a point, I concede. And stop my anti-clutter campaign.

In another of my asthma books, I learn that self-reliance is a behavior that asthmatics must cultivate. Apparently, there's an increase in some blood something-or-other in people who feel helpless. Do I feel helpless because I have asthma, or do I have asthma because I feel helpless?

Now, helplessness is a complicated issue with me. I rarely feel helpless in my professional life. But there are lots of little foolish things I struggle with. When I want to do something, such as go to New York for a movie by myself, I put stumbling blocks in my way by imagining that there'll be traffic or that I won't find a parking space. So instead of doing what I want, I think about how hard it will be for me to do what I want, and I talk myself out of it and don't go. This makes me feel helpless. I need to work on this.

At dinner, I tell Ernie I am going to work on self-reliance. He gives me a look.

"Okay, Ralph Waldo Emerson," he says, "tell me what you're going to do."

Although he is joking, I get the message. What with

my clutter control rampage and my newly instituted self-reliance kick, I see that I am trying to whip my poor, imperfect self into shape.

Diary entry for August 27, 1992
One-month visit to check on my progress. And I'm doing better than the doctor expected. When I told him how much I've been coughing, he told me the secret is to anticipate what I'll be experiencing and to medicate before, not to wait until I'm in distress.

And this is what I must learn from having this disease. To anticipate. To plan. To prepare myself in advance. To thereby cut down on the possibility of distress. Something I haven't been good at, but that I absolutely must learn.

I understand, since I've been using my medication, and since I've been breathing more freely, why I've been so tired. I've been starving for air all these months. Wouldn't it be amazing if my listlessness, my past "depression," is linked to my difficult breathing, to my undiagnosed asthma?

Today I had lots of energy. Bounded through the house joyfully. Drove Ernie crazy.

Oh, won't it be wonderful if this could come completely under control? How happy I will be!

I've had such ups and downs since I've found out. Days when I've been very frustrated, when I just lost it because I couldn't breathe. But, on those days, I probably wasn't taking enough medicine. I'm afraid of taking too much medicine. But my doctor reminds me that it will take months before I see real improvement. Even so, the improvement will be very gradual. And, so, I have to be patient.

Patience? I ask myself. What's that?

Diary entry for September 5, 1992

It's been a very difficult time. Two nights this week I burst into tears, then started screaming, raging at what I've been living with.

Once I coughed *all day*. And then became furious at myself for not describing to the doctor how absolutely awful I feel for much of the time.

"How are you doing?" he asks.

"Pretty well," I answer. It isn't that I'm lying. It's that I haven't yet learned how to communicate to him what he must know if he is to help me.

One day I had suicidal urges and finally banged on the kitchen table in frustration after coughing for six hours straight. Then, I had lightheadedness and extreme fatigue. Still, I go to work. Still, I teach. Still, I try to write.

September 19, 1992

I am really tired today. But from my reading, I learned about Atrovent, an inhaler for cough and mucus that my doctor agrees I should try. It seems to help. Since I've been using it, I haven't had a coughing attack—a blessing. Instead, yesterday, I coughed up mucus plugs for an hour-long period that eased the congestion in my chest considerably. It was disgusting.

My relaxation tape helps me enormously and I need to listen to it daily. I must do more work with relaxation, pleasure, and stress management. And I need to air my feelings in here.

I feel as if I've been beaten up. I feel as if I have post-traumatic stress disorder from my fear of suffocating.

I wonder if I had asthma as a young child. I used to "faint" a lot, for no apparent reason. I have memories of feeling I was suffocating every summer. I hated summer vacation, loved when school started.

From my reading about asthma, this is what I've learned I must do: 1. Exercise regularly. 2. Talk about my feelings; express myself; rage; cry, if necessary. (I've already seen that if I can get myself to cry, or get angry during a bad asthma attack, it usually goes away.) 3. Get enough rest. 4. Manage my time; drop inessential activities; don't take on more work than I can manage. 5. Experience, and appreciate, simple pleasures. (I've started making a daily list—the little curly blond-headed kid wearing tiny hiking boots I saw on my walk; listening to Vivaldi's Sonata for 2 Violins #12.) 6. Visualize, daydream, bring yourself to a peaceful place from your past (like the view from the window of my sleazy hotel in Barcelona). 7. Believe in your ability to make changes in your life.

Mid-September, 1992

My coughing is so bad that I have finally called my doctor, telling him I can't stand it anymore. My inclination has been not to describe how severe and disabling my symptoms are, but, instead, to try to tolerate them. The truth is that I've forgotten what wellness feels like. I have become so used to living with discomfort that I realize I must learn to be more explicit about what I'm suffering.

When I told him that I've coughed hundreds of times without stopping (once, I gave up counting at 347—counting my coughs was making me as crazy as the coughing), he put me on a short course of oral steroids—burst therapy—to treat the underlying inflammation that apparently isn't responding to the inhaled steroids. I'm afraid of the side effects of taking steroids long-term (weight gain, induced psychosis). But I'm told that a short course won't harm me and almost surely will help. I hope so. I must take the steroids *exactly* as prescribed, tapering the dose down gradually. Stopping them too suddenly is very dangerous.

Since I've been on steroids, though, I've been having strange dreams. Most of them are of my nearly drowning, of trying to climb into a lifeboat, of trying to keep my head above enormous breaking waves—like those that terrified me when I stayed at my aunt's on Long Island.

For a couple of days, I took theophylline to relax the bronchial wall, to ease my breathing. But I had side effects so severe—stomach cramps, nausea, tremors, severe heart palpitations—that I spent the whole time in bed. I have decided to endure the symptoms of my disease until the medicines with fewer side effects begin to work. So far, thank goodness, the others haven't caused any that I can't tolerate—occasional heart palpitations, tremors in my legs, some anxiety, and a dry mouth—though who knows what the long-term effects of inhaling bronchodilators and oral steroids several times a day will be.

I have decided that I can't, and won't, take medicines that prevent me from writing. And so I choose drugs that won't impede my creative life, rather than ones that will alleviate my symptoms completely but that will also prevent me from doing productive work.

And so I sit at my desk for the three hours that I require myself to write every day, coughing and writing, writing and coughing. I set a timer for thirty minutes and stop and get up and do some breathing exercises—mostly forced exhalations, some relaxing breaths, then some invigorating ones. I tend to sit hunched over my computer, I've noticed, which is not good for me. I also hold my breath. I've recently posted a sign above my desk—"Breathe," it says.

When I work, I'm often oblivious to my body; it doesn't exist. This has all changed since I've been sick, and my body now makes me aware of itself with every stroke of my pen, every strike of the keys. I'm writing through my body in a way I haven't before. I wonder what this will mean? If my work will change?

In the old days, before asthma (my life now divides into "the time before asthma" and "the time after asthma"), I could sit working for five or six hours straight, breaking only for a cup of tea, or to fix a quick lunch that I would eat at my desk. I was so completely intoxicated by my work that I scribbled through workmen renovating the house, through the dog chasing the cats, the cleaning people vacuuming around me, and two different kinds of rock music blaring from the kids' rooms. (Much to the amusement of my family, I outfitted myself with a pair of sound-deadening earmuffs, the kind used at airports by the ground crew who direct aircraft on the tarmac—my inexpensive and portable equivalent of Marcel Proust's cork-lined room.) My son Jason once quipped that if he came up to me while I was working and told me that he was bleeding to death, so deeply engrossed was I that I would respond, "That's nice, dear, fix yourself a snack, I'll be with you when I finish this paragraph."

I miss the deep concentration of those long sojourns at my desk. I miss how the world dropped away. Now I am forced to learn a new way of working—one that requires me to repeatedly leave and then reenter the trance of writing.

This isn't easy, because I have a before-work routine that I know helps me focus—straightening the house, doing a load of laundry, fixing myself a cup of tea (which I take with just one Crabtree and Evelyn orange cookie), arranging the papers on my desk, filling my fountain pen. This routine, I can't possibly repeat each time I break, so I must learn some new habits. Rereading the page I was working on before now seems to help me refocus.

Amazingly, I think I am writing better than before. My work is looser. Freer. After I finish this biographical project, I think I might write a memoir. Maybe that's because I'm aware, now, of time passing.

I'm newly aware, too, of the limited time I have left to write. Before asthma, though I didn't squander my time, I surely didn't treasure it. Now I cannot take time for granted. I must do what I can to enable myself to be fit enough to work. The time I have at the desk now feels sweeter than before, yet also deeply poignant—like the time one spends with a perfect lover who will nevertheless soon depart.

Certainly, my understanding of the writers whose lives I have been describing (D. H. Lawrence, Virginia Woolf)—

struggling to write despite their ill health)—has deepened because I, too, have become a storyteller whose body has betrayed me, as, eventually, I know, all bodies will. The truth is, that before I got sick, I never recognized their heroism in continuing to work under adverse circumstances. This is something that I will study systematically. Now that I am sick, I want to learn about how other writers faced illness.

Virginia Woolf, in her fifties, worked steadily to finish *The Years*—despite disabling headaches and an awful menopause that sent her pulse racing, made her heart beat wildly, and gave her anxiety attacks so severe she mistook them for insanity. When I read her diary accounts before I myself became sick (and before I myself was going through menopause), I thought that she exaggerated. I see now that her diaries recount her heroic struggle with illness, her reluctance to stop working though she is barely able to lift her head from her pillow. In her diary she wonders, always, not when she'll be well, but when she'll be well enough to work—an essential difference, I understand now that I myself have a chronic illness. For what I learned from Woolf's diaries is that if one works despite illness, and through illness, then one can restore one's sense of self-worth, so deeply challenged by the experience of illness.

When I first worked on Lawrence's *Women in Love*, I barely noticed that, for much of the novel's composition, Lawrence was desperately ill, often bedridden, too weak to arise. I knew that he suffered from tuberculosis, but I ignored its consequences, as many other able-bodied biographers ignore (or, worse still, interpret as neurotic) the impact of illness on their subjects' lives and works. I know I must go back over this time in Lawrence's life and pay careful attention to what he says about his body—something I paid scant attention to before.

Lawrence was always changing residences, moving from city to countryside, from country to country, continent to continent, in search of clear, untainted air that he could breathe freely. I thought that he was restless, neurotic, unable to stay in one place for any length of time—that he wanted to get away from where he was because he was trying to bury his past. Now I realize I may have been wrong. Though he surely was troubled, I believe it was because he couldn't breathe, because he was so often so sick. What must it have been like to struggle for air, without much hope for a cure?

I only began to understand why Lawrence moved about so often after I myself was told by a doctor to move away from my home. This was before I was diagnosed with asthma and this doctor conjectured that I was having a profound allergic reaction to automobile exhaust—he knew I lived close to a major highway. He suggested I move to where the air was pure to see if I got better. If, after four or five days in a pollution-free environment, I stopped coughing and choking, then his diagnosis would be confirmed, and, he said, I should move permanently.

It was the end of May, and I had been having coughing fits for seven months. The term at Hunter College was finished. Unlike Lawrence, who was often so poor that he had to beg friends to house him, I was lucky enough to have a little summer house in Sag Harbor where I could stay.

I went there alone. Ernie stayed back home in New Jersey to work and care for our son Justin, still living at home. And I wondered if I'd have to change my life completely—live alone, quit my teaching job—if the doctor was right.

After a few days, I was somewhat, though not entirely, better. Rather than being grateful, I was enraged. I felt that I was in exile. I believed I had lost my freedom to live where I chose. I had become a prisoner of my disease.

People with environmental illness, the doctor had told me, seem to have especially sensitive nervous systems that react to stimuli that don't affect other people. How does this happen? I ask. No one really knows, he replies. But early trauma, he says, sometimes permanently alters the nervous system.

After a month and a half in Sag Harbor, my symptoms came back, and I returned home.

Our family remembers this as a most difficult time in our lives. I paid no attention to them. Didn't care about them. I wanted to die. I had become someone they (and I) didn't know. Humorless. Willful. Short-tempered. Nasty. Imperious. Self-centered. Mean-spirited. Ungrateful. Any attempt on Ernie's part to cheer me up, I brusquely and rudely rebuffed. I know others have described how they have become better people because of their illness. Like Lawrence, I did not. Like him, I was a tyrannical, unlikable despot.

Before my illness, I minimized Woolf's despair and despised Lawrence. Now that I had suffered as Woolf had, and despised myself as I despised Lawrence, I believed I could meet them on common ground. For, like Woolf, I

wanted, more than anything, to work, and I understood
the compelling urgency of her desire. And, like Lawrence,
because I believed I had an illness with no cure, I had
come close to his kind of madness—one that, I now understood, could be born from lifelong physical affliction, helplessness, and desperation.

5 *September 27, 1992*
Ernie and I were supposed to go to Les Roches
Blanches in Cassis, France, for my fiftieth birthday. I
have been looking forward to this holiday for a year, studying, almost daily, the brochure of the beautiful hotel overlooking the Mediterranean. I have imagined myself on its
patio, drinking my coffee, eating my breakfast of French
bread and preserves, peacefully staring at the water. I have
dreamed of the special fish dishes I would eat (steamed mus-
sels in wine and bouillabaisse, of course), and the local
wines I would drink.

But I awaken in a panic one night, a week before we
are to leave, afraid that I will have a bad asthma attack on
the airplane, which, I know, permits smoking. My asthma
is not yet under control, and I am afraid, too, to be away
from my doctor, for I don't know if I could get the help I
might need in an emergency.

Late in the night, worrying about going to France for my
birthday, I start crying because of how my life has changed,
because I can no longer act unthinkingly, because I now
must consider the consequences of what I do.

My sobbing awakens Ern.

The next morning, he cancels our holiday and arranges instead to take me to a health spa, where there is medical care if I need it, where we can hike and swim, and where I can find out more about asthma.

And so I unexpectedly find myself in Tucson, Arizona, in the Sonoran desert, sitting beside a pool, looking across at the mountains that ring this desert city (whose air is nowhere near pure, for it sits in a bowl ringed by mountains), in an unfamiliar landscape covered with saguaro cactuses.

I'm still coughing. But I'm glad to be away. I'm lucky to be here.

I take classes in conscious breathing, and learn some physiology and a few important techniques I start using immediately. I learn it's dangerous for asthmatics to try to take deep breaths when they're in difficulty. When you're in trouble, you should forcibly exhale as much air as you can; the inhale that follows will be deep and full. I learn that when I'm hyperventilating, which can cause fainting, I should hold my breath, then shift to relaxing breaths— making oceanic sounds as you inhale and exhale; or I can count my exhales (one to five, and then repeat), which is also relaxing.

An exercise physiologist has explained why I must walk or exercise daily. It will strengthen my lungs, force more oxygen into my system, and help me expel mucus from my lungs. I also learn that I haven't been walking fast enough. I buy a heart monitor so that when I walk, I can set the required pace. He tells me, too, that I should build up the musculature supporting my lungs, and he gives me weight lifting exercises (with free weights) that I must do every other day.

I learn how to lose weight by eating far more fruits, vegetables, and grains, and far less fat and animal protein than before. The less I weigh, the less trouble I'll have breathing. It takes a year, but I drop off about twenty-five pounds. One morning I call Ernie into the bathroom. I am terrified at the two huge lumps I see protruding under my breasts. "They're your ribs," he says. "You haven't seen them in twenty-five years."

I learn a simple yoga routine that will help my posture and help me breathe better. I learn one special yoga posture for asthma—lying on my back, supporting my back with my hands, and lifting my legs in the air.

The idea is to build my muscles, improve my flexibility, increase my lung capacity, and the efficiency of my cardio-vascular system—which will help my breathing and, at the same time, relieve stress.

I am enjoying myself. I find that I am focusing on my body, but in a different way. I feel myself reentering my body. I wonder if I'm too old to become a female jock.

When I get home, I vow to continue this program. I think about how much I've learned about what I can do for myself. Though I'm educated, I have needed the help of specialists. We can afford it. But such help should also be freely available to poor people with asthma and should become a national priority.

I discuss my asthma with a counsellor, who suggests that because of all I've lived through over the last few years, I must be tired of being the caregiver in the family. I've given myself this illness, he suggests, so that I can be cared for. He urges me to start taking care of myself. He insists that my asthma is caused by repressed anger, and he pulls a book off his shelf that proves his point. I read it, but it strikes me as pop-psych bullshit. Sure, I think to myself, but don't say to him, blame me. Everyone I know is angry about something, but not everyone I know has asthma. It's true that I *have* been very angry that the serene life I long for has been invaded by family obligations. But family life also gives me the love and support I need to do my work.

I will think about what he's said about anger and asthma, though it's likely I'll disagree.

That night, I have a dream in which I see myself taking care of myself. In the dream, I realize that focusing on my wellness is different from focusing on my illness. Since November, when I got sick, I have been concentrating on my illness. I want to take control over what I *can* change (my physical fitness and what I eat, using techniques that can help bring an attack under control). I can learn about my relationship to my illness by going back into therapy. And I can try to accept what I can't control (that I have this disease and that I might have it for the rest of my life). This particular advice from the counsellor—that I must focus, now, on taking care of myself—I will heed.

September 29, 1996
Today, for the first time in my life, I've had acupuncture.

First, the acupuncturist took a medical and emotional history, during which she was extremely attentive. Then she did a pressure-point analysis of my body. It was extraordinary. When she touched certain points, I felt nothing. When she touched others, the pain was so intense that I recoiled and cried out.

She said that the pressure-point analysis showed that I had bottled up grief and tremendous fear. This is very different from the counsellor's idea that my asthma is related to anger. Grief and fear sound more like it to me.

I told the acupuncturist that, though I'm brave, and have done many things that I have wanted to do, including things others might not do—like scuba diving and giving speeches in public—I'm often terrified *in anticipation* of those activities. Once I start doing something, though, I'm fine. It's getting myself to start that's hard. I'm afraid of travel before I get to the airport, not when I'm on the airplane.

Where, she asked me, did this fear come from? I tell her that I really don't know. I don't want to discuss this now.

And grief, what about grief? Have I ever cried for my mother? my sister? Not really. And what would happen if I started to cry? Once I start, I say, I won't ever stop.

When she inserts the acupuncture needles, I experience strange bodily sensations. How to explain them? I see pulsing lights behind my eyelids. I feel fields of electrical energy waves in my head—as if my brain is being repolarized. I start crying without knowing that I am going to cry. I become very afraid of being alone. I don't want to her to leave the room, but she does. Soon, I settle down.

I feel an enormous amount of tension in my neck. I tell myself to relax the back of my neck, to let it sink into the table. I feel a melting sensation there. I feel my bronchi drying out. And I have a vision of myself coming down off a cross, jumping into a swimming pool, and swimming, powerfully, for a great distance.

September 30, 1996

When I ask myself who I want to be now, I see myself as a woman who can be free to mourn my sister. I haven't realized that I've never grieved for her. I start to cry for her and can't stop. I think that something about the way my breath catches when I can't take in a breath has to do with how my sister died. She stopped her breath by hanging herself.

I will always wonder what happened to her and what made her kill herself. Perhaps I really have felt guilt these past years for being unable to stop her. My breathing disorder—the mucus that blocks my breath—might be connected to all those tears I haven't shed for her, all the tears I've held inside.

After she died, I remember living my life as if nothing had happened. But I soon broke out in gigantic hives. And nearly lost my breath, nearly fainted, often.

Jill killed herself about ten years ago. She was almost thirty-seven. And I think the acute stage of my asthma started then, though I am certain that I've had it since I was a girl. I remember being sick in the summers, when it was humid. I remember coughing uncontrollably during the winters, when I breathed in cold air, and having long bouts of what the doctors called "chronic bronchitis" several times a year throughout my life. And, yes, since her death, I have gotten sick each year (though never as severely as this past year), and at the same time of year as she killed herself.

I want to remember her, to remember us together, as children, heads bent over some small task that pleases us both, like cutting out clothes for the paper dolls we kept in shoe boxes covered with shiny gold paper. I want to imagine us breathing together. Effortlessly. In synchrony.

A friend asks, "Do you think your asthma flared after your sister's death as a way of keeping you connected to her?"

My first impulse is to say no, emphatically, no. But I know that if *I* heard my own story, it is the conclusion I would inevitably come to.

My sister and I lived our lives in what was to me an all-too-close proximity. When I was a child, my mother consigned my sister to my care, and, at first, I hovered over her, unsuccessfully trying to keep her out of harm's way. Then later, when I was a teenager, and too old, I thought, to have a shadow sister, I tried to ignore her and deliberately outpaced her as she trotted unhappily after me. At seven, ten, thirteen, fifteen, I felt too young to be someone's mother.

My most complicated memories of Jill are those of sharing a bed with her from when I was seven until I left to marry. Though four years separated us, I often told friends that, in sharing that bed, we became twins, *ex utero*. There was something comforting, and troubling, in her closeness, in our togetherness. I wanted my own bed, my own space; yet I wasn't comfortable unless she was near, couldn't fall off to sleep until after she had.

I made elaborate rules for how she had to behave in bed if I were to continue to tolerate her existence. (In truth, I had no choice. We shared the double bed my mother had bought to save money. No matter how much I protested, there would never be twin beds, and it never occurred to me to sleep on the floor.) She had to sleep with her back to me, so that I wouldn't have to breathe the air she exhaled. She couldn't hog the covers, cross over to my side, or raise her legs (which made air pockets).

So, did my asthma flare as a way of keeping me bound to my sister beyond her death? And, yes, I must answer, to my friend, and to myself, yes, as, in memory, I see myself reach across our bed to pull the covers over my sister's slender shoulders during her fitful sleep, turn my back to her, and try to relax, as I listen to make sure she is still breathing, listen to make sure she is still alive.

6 *Diary entry, early October, 1996*
I am back in therapy.

Something prompted me to get up in the middle of the night to read Leonard Shengold's *Soul Murder: The Effects of Childhood Abuse and Deprivation*, and I came upon his statement that fainting is a symptom of "too muchness," from too much early stimulation, or terror.

I remember now—though these memories did not come until a few years ago, when I was writing about how Virginia Woolf had been molested as a child—being fondled against my will, in the bathtub, and when I was put to sleep, by my aunt on Long Island, when I spent the summers there, and how confusing it was, because I liked her and liked being there, and because she often disguised her actions as play. I remember holding my breath, and waiting patiently for it all to end, and looking up at the pattern made by the light coming through the blinds, as I tried to disconnect myself from what I was experiencing. I remember being terrified from growing up in wartime (from seeing the newsreels at the local movie theater where my mother often took me) and how angry my father was when he came back from the war, and being afraid, always, that he would kill me.

7 When I got asthma, but didn't know it was asthma, I was researching the life of Djuna Barnes, who suffered from asthma (and a host of other ailments—emphysema and arthritis, among them). As I struggled to work each day, if only for a few hours—though I could hardly breathe—as I took notes from Barnes's letters to her friend Emily Coleman, while lying in bed (for I coughed much less when lying down), or as I scribbled still incomprehensible sentences on a yellow pad, I learned that Barnes, living in her tiny Patchin Place apartment in New York City, was disabled by coughing fits, the result of asthma. I learned that she, too, wrote lying down. But I did not connect my illness with hers, did not realize, at least not consciously, that I had asthma, though I felt an affinity with her struggle.

I was working on a book describing how Barnes wrote her autobiographical play, *The Antiphon*, which graphically depicted the horrific abuse she had endured as a child and young woman—how she was sexually abused by her grandmother (and probably by her father), how she was beaten and sold into sexual slavery by her father, and how her mother complied. Barnes believed that writing this play was just payback for how her family had damaged her. She described her motive for writing it as justice, not revenge.

Able to understand and describe the relationship between the pernicious effects of Barnes's childhood and her various illnesses (including asthma), and how she used her work to right the wrongs in her life, I was still unable to comprehend the meaning of my illness. Working on Barnes's life, though, I now realize, provided me with information and understanding that I could later apply to understanding myself.

After my diagnosis, when I tell a friend about the odd coincidence that I was working on Barnes when I got sick, she asks me if I think I got sick *because* I was working on her. Secretly, I myself have worried that because I've been so moved by the tragedy of Barnes's life, because I feel so sorry about how crippled she was, emotionally and physically, in her old age because of her abuse, I have given *myself* asthma because Barnes had asthma. I know, though, that this is ridiculous, that I tend to put the most pathological spin on something that is normal.

But Ernie and I have always joked about what he calls my "loose boundaries," about how I can slip into a fictional or nonfictional account so completely that I feel I'm sharing the experience with the narrator, and about my inability to wrap myself in a self-protective mantle when I learn of a tragedy.

I don't think my boundaries are as loose as he does, though sometimes I feel that I need to station troops to guard my borders. As a biographer, I know I've been drawn to write about authors whose lives have strangely paralleled mine—Virginia Woolf fought lifelong depression and eventually committed suicide; my mother was hospitalized for severe depression, my sister killed herself, and, when younger, I, too, battled depression. I believe I can slip into the skin of my subjects, though now, blessedly, because I know what I must do to care for myself (walk, work, meditate, cook, and lead a quiet life) and because I've received excellent treatment, I no longer am depressed. I believe I have used this identification with my subjects—the ability to imagine what they've felt, to think what they've thought, to slip into their skins, as it were—without self-harm.

I don't believe I've ever overidentified with my subjects, though I know this is the occupational hazard of biographers. Over the years, I have known many biographers. Some, who have started eating what their subjects ate, wearing what their subjects wore, sounding like their subjects sounded, drinking what their subjects drank (and as much, which is dangerous), and doing what their subjects did (this can be risky, for it often involves sleeping around). I have even known a biographer or two who have come to look like their subjects. (This is creepy to watch.)

But after a writing day, when I emerge from the trance of working, I am sure that I know that I am who I am and that who I am is not who my subject was, though our lives may overlap in certain ways, though I may have taken up what I see as some of their better habits. Like buying a pair of hiking boots the same color as Virginia Woolf's (chocolate brown) and hiking the Sussex South Downs.

So, no, I don't really believe that I "gave myself" asthma because Barnes had asthma, and I tell my friend that I think I've had a form of asthma all my life, and that its virulence waxed and waned, and that, without realizing it overtly, I have become alert to the possibility that what I have is asthma by reading about Barnes. For it has always been easier for me to understand my own life by first trying ✓ to understand someone else's.

8 When I next visit my doctor, he tells me that it's important to be alert to what triggers my asthma.

Asthma is an idiosyncratic disease, he reminds me. What bothers me might not bother someone else. If I can determine what causes my attacks, I will feel less helpless and this will be beneficial.

I like this idea. So I go out and buy a special diary. "My Asthma Diary," I call it. Soon, I tell myself, I'll have this figured out. Soon, I'll be back to normal.

Day One. Morning.

I wake up, I get up, I'm fine, I'm not coughing (thank the Lord). I hope that maybe today I'll have a good day. Maybe today I won't have to spend the better part of the day in bed.

I sit down to breakfast. Cereal. Milk. Strawberries. Herb tea with cinnamon. I start eating. Remind myself I have to stay alert so I can see what causes my asthma. A few minutes later, as I'm reading the *New York Times*, I start coughing, choking, drowning. I've already taken my medicine (two blasts of Ventolin, two of Atrovent, four of Vanceril), so I can't take any more for three or four hours. I forcibly exhale into my Peak Flow Meter. It reads "550." This means that my airways aren't dangerously constricted.

Still, I know that if I'm coughing this early in the morning, I'll probably have a bad day, and I'll have to go to bed.

I get my asthma diary, and think about the possible triggers for this asthma attack. Cereal, probably not. Milk, maybe. Strawberries, maybe. Cinnamon, maybe. Reading the *Times*, certainly.

So, what I'm supposed to do now is eliminate these things, one by one. Tomorrow, then, I decide I'll have the same breakfast, but I won't read the *Times*. See if I cough. See if I'm better.

By now it's nine o'clock. Time for me to start my writing day. But I'm already exhausted from coughing. Can't figure out how I can work under these circumstances. And I haven't learned anything, really, from this stupid exercise. I don't feel any more or less in control than I felt yesterday at this time; I feel overwhelmed. If this is what it's going to take to figure out what's causing my asthma attacks, I'll forget it. I don't have the time or the energy for this.

Day One. Afternoon.

I have a relatively good morning after all. Spend the morning in bed, scribbling a few sentences, sketching the work I'll do when I feel better. Have a slice of leftover pizza, a small salad, and an orange for lunch. And start coughing. Grab my asthma diary, make my entry.

After lunch, I take my second set of medicines for the day, which quiets my cough. Spend an hour at my computer, plugging in my few ragged sentences, printing them. Remember when I could work for eight hours straight, through lunch, with no ill effects.

A few minutes later, I'm coughing again. The kind of

coughing that's dangerous. I go back to bed. Pick up my asthma diary. "Computer," I write. "And printer." Wonderful. Here I am a writer, and my asthma might be triggered by working at my computer.

My friend Kate, my friend for thirty years, calls to see how I am. She's the only person who knows how desperate I have become. I've told her that I'm giving this six months, and if I'm still living like this, I might kill myself. She has listened without condemnation and said, instead, "It must be pretty bad if that's how you feel." I've promised her, though, that I'll tell her if my suicidal thoughts take a more serious turn. She checks in with me every day; tells me something that she knows will cheer me.

Today there's been a gigantic tie-up at the George Washington Bridge. There's also a new, very stupid, sign, she tells me. "Thank you for your patience," it reads. "The inconvenience is temporary. But the repairs are permanent." (A few years later, Kate calls to tell me that the sign guy is at it again. "Thank you for using the George Washington Bridge" has appeared in giant letters, just before the toll booths. "Instead of what?" Kate asks. "Rowing?")

Kate always makes me laugh. I start coughing. ("Laughing," I write.)

Day One. Evening. I realize that almost everything I've done is a potential trigger for my asthma. Eating. Drinking. Working. Laughing. If I do none of the above, lie flat on my back, and meditate, I figure I'll be fine.

Over the next few months, I learn that these are the things I have to avoid to not get an asthma attack. Pollution.

Exhaust fumes, particularly from diesel engines. Smoke. Perfume. Certain foods and herbs (shellfish, aged cheese, tomatoes, mushrooms, and thyme, for instance.) Nail polish remover. Hair spray. Sulfites. MSG. Preservatives. Aspirin. Paint fumes. Ink (newsprint; my printer). Cleaning fluid. Mold. Anything used by an exterminator. Rushing. Laughing. Fear.

I can't go anyplace that's polluted or where there's smoking or where someone might be wearing perfume. I can't get caught in a traffic jam. Sit in an airplane in a long queue waiting for takeoff. Wear nail polish. Have my hair cut in a place that gives manicures. Eat anything containing sulfites or MSG or preservatives or any of the other forbidden foods. Take any medicines containing preservatives or aspirin or MSG (including most painkillers; this means, for example, that I've had a root canal without one, and it wasn't bad at all—in fact, my dentist told me I did better than his heavily medicated patients. I had prepared myself by meditating for fifteen minutes and relaxed into the pain, instead of tensing to avoid it. Ernie was so proud of me after that he started calling me "macho woman"). Paint (I used to paint, in oils); have the bugs in my house exterminated; wear clothes cleaned at a drycleaner (unless my husband airs them for a long time). Read the *New York Times* (noxious ink fumes). Write in my journal using the Mont Blanc pen Ern bought me for a present—the ink makes me cough. Use my printer when I'm in the room. Drink beer. Walk without a mask in autumn. Roll around in a pile of leaves (this, I miss).

9 Sometimes I make myself crazy thinking about all the things I've lost, all the things I've had to give up since I've gotten sick. My spontaneity. My sense of invulnerability, of potency. Of trusting my body. Of not being constantly aware of it. A sense that I could, if I wanted, travel anywhere in the world. Now, I can't travel on an airplane where smoking is permitted. I can't go to a city where the air is bad, I'm just too scared, and so I know I'll never see Eastern Europe, or China, or Mexico City, and I'll probably never return to Los Angeles. I've lost friends, too, who can't stand to be around someone so preoccupied with her health, or who can't understand why I'm canceling yet another visit, or who think I'm making excuses when I call at the last minute to say I've had a really bad day, that I'm very congested, and that I think I should stay home.

I have to give up eating at most restaurants. I discover that I'm extremely sensitive to MSG and to preservatives, like sulfites.

This is what I have to do to eat out. I call the restaurant; ask if they permit smoking anywhere, including the bar or the restrooms; ask if the chef uses MSG, if they use a sulfite solution on the lettuce, if their lettuce mixes come packaged, or if the chef uses premixed sauces (which might contain MSG or preservatives). And has the exterminator been there recently? Have they had the place repainted, redecorated? The person you get on the phone usually doesn't know the answer to any of these questions. The person you get on the phone always thinks you're a nut, or extremely neurotic, or some kind of inspector. The person you get on the phone usually tells you they don't have a table.

Okay. Let's say I find a restaurant I can actually eat at. (And, to celebrate our anniversary in December, I think I have.) Ern and I jump into the car. I pack my trusty mask, in case we hit a traffic jam. We don't. Bliss. I let myself get excited.

We get to the restaurant. Settle in. The first course is exquisite. Freshly prepared ravioli stuffed with homemade ricotta and herbs in a vegetable broth. (No aged cheese, no mushrooms—I've asked.) At last, I'm going to have a good time. I'm in heaven; I'm not a freak; I'm getting better; I'm not going to have to stay home for the rest of my life.

But, as we await the main course (a simple roasted chicken with rosemary, roasted potatoes, and string beans with sun-dried tomatoes), as I sip a wine that doesn't contain sulfites, the maitre d' seats a very well-dressed woman next to us who, I swear, has taken a bath in very expensive perfume. Perfume that, to her, is an enhancement of her charm. Perfume that, to me, is a potentially lethal weapon. I tell myself to ignore it, that I'll be fine. But my eyes start tearing, my throat starts closing, I'm coughing, I'm suffocating, I'm drowning.

To Ern, I choke out that I'm going to the bathroom to take some medicine, I think I caught it in time, I'll only be a few minutes, I can quiet it down, I'll be all right, can he get us moved to another table? He's good at this, he's used to it. Still, I see the muscles in his jaw tighten. He doesn't like this any more than I do.

So, I go to the bathroom. But the place stinks of deodorizer. I walk out, I can't stay there, and I sink into a chair next to the door of the kitchen. Pull out my inhalators. Score. Wait. Score again. Wait. Score some more. The waiters look at me. No one asks what I'm doing or how I am. I snort and cough and spit into a handkerchief. I am not exactly the kind of client they had in mind when they planned this trendy, cream-colored, calla-lily-bedecked, up-scale, East-Side place. I put my head in my hands and look down, so I can concentrate on my breathing. Start counting my exhales to quiet things down. Then, start sobbing. This is too hard. This isn't worth it. And, I think, on top of it all, we're going to have to shell out a small fortune. Dinner at a place like this can cost the equivalent of a round-trip airplane ticket to Paris. We should have stayed the fuck home.

As you can see, I'm not exactly a fun date. As you can imagine, I almost never eat out.

At first, I miss eating out. Soon, though, I don't. And then a perfect, though often simply prepared, dinner in our home, accompanied by a glass of special wine, becomes the high point of our day. Perfectionist that I am and have always been about food, I must admit that eating out, even in the best places, usually disappoints me.

Though I have always been an avid cook, after I get sick, I develop an intense, ritualistic, contemplative relationship to the food I prepare, to the food I eat. If I eat the wrong food, I can get sick. But eating, now, if I pay careful attention, affords me the most intense pleasure I have, so I take my time with it. I appreciate, now, the look, the feel, the smell of ingredients.

Reading beautifully illustrated cookbooks (like Sally Schneider's *The Art of Low-Calorie Cooking, with photographs by Maria Robledo*), sunk to my shoulders in a hot bath, becomes one of my greatest sources of pleasure. Contriving weekly menus and shopping lists becomes a task I enjoy.

(Tuesday, risotto with sun-dried tomatoes, fresh asparagus with olive oil and balsamic vinegar, braised pears in red wine; Wednesday, orechiette with broccoli rabe and anchovies, fresh tomato salad with fresh orange vinaigrette, watermelon sorbet). Watching "Molto Mario" on the TV Food Network becomes as enriching as Masterpiece Theater used to be.

Shopping for special items of food becomes an almost daily outing for me, though Ernie continues his weekly ritual of stocking the larder. ("Come see the figs I bought," he shouts upon his return home, as proud as if he'd felled an antelope.) Our son Jason says it takes me as long to buy a bottle of balsamic vinegar as it takes Ern to shop for the whole week, and he's right. I seek out places that care about food, untainted food, the freshest heads of broccoli, mahogany-colored sun-dried tomatoes, unbruised garlic, snowy halibut.

Shopping Kings, Fairway, and Freshfields in New Jersey, and Dean and DeLuca, Grace's Marketplace, and Balducci's in New York become my favorite, most fulfilling, outings. I keep lists in my Dayrunner of the best places in New York to buy bread, scallops, olive oil. Saturdays, Ern and I can often be found standing in front of a vegetable display, debating whether we should buy the cherry tomatoes or the Japanese eggplant, which we can roast for a simple pasta sauce. I now enjoy shopping for food and preparing it the way I once enjoyed going to a museum, a Broadway play, or a concert at Lincoln Center. I tell Ernie that if a thief broke into our house and wanted to get out quickly, he should head for our pantry, not my jewelry box.

At six in the evening, Ern and I meet in the kitchen. I tell him our menu, tell him what, as sous-chef, he needs to do. We don't talk—don't need to—but concentrate instead on the food under our fingers. We have both come to realize that cooking, though we may initially resent having to do it, quickly gets us out of our work-a-day heads and connects us to our senses. Often preoccupied, even when not working, with a puzzle in an essay or book I have under way, I have found that paying attention to food can be deeply restorative. Cooking forces me to stop thinking about work, to put intellectual work into its proper perspective. Nothing, after all, can please the way a fabulous pasta can.

For the past few weeks, Ern and I have been cooking our way through *Rozanne Gold's Recipes 1-2-3*—gourmet recipes with just three ingredients. We have loved each of Gold's recipes that we have tried. Her preparations are simple, ingenious; the outcome, extraordinary, unexpected. Tonight we are making her Steamed Halibut with Bell Pepper Confetti. I am cutting perfect little squares of red and yellow peppers, which I will sauté in garlic oil, as Gold suggests. Ern is skinning a gorgeous, milky-white halibut filet, which we will steam, then cover with the pepper sauce. Our Rosemary Roasted Potatoes are cooking in the oven. Ern will make our green bean salad and dress it with a French walnut oil I have picked up recently.

As I take off my chef's apron and we sit down to the table that Ern has set with dishes we've carted back from Mexico, years ago, I know that we will have a perfect meal.

And, as I say often, life is too short to have even one bad meal.

Asthma has taken much from me—but asthma has given me this.

10 In the summer of 1993, I pick up Susan Sontag's *The Volcano Lover,* which I want to read because I love literate historical novels (this begins at the end of the eighteenth century) and because I share the Cavaliere's fascination with active volcanos (in his case, Vesuvius), though I am too timid (or too smart) to venture anywhere near one, even if it has remained temporarily inactive. Ernie says it's because I believe that if I go anywhere near even a dormant volcano, it will erupt on that very day, though, statistically, the chances are unlikely. He's right. To him, if something has a one in ten thousand chance of happening, he's safe. To me, if something has a one in ten thousand chance of happening, it means I'll be the one person that it will happen to.

On the second page of Sontag's novel, I encounter Catherine, the Cavaliere's asthmatic wife. She and her husband are traveling from London to Naples. The first stage of the journey will be made in a coach. "Catherine has already settled with her maid in the large post chaise, fortifying herself for the strenuous journey with a potion of laudanum and chalybeate water," Sontag writes. "The carriage with the Cavaliere's asthmatic wife was not to be jostled." Its windows were "closed against the coal-infested air."

I put down the book. I cannot, now, read on. Already, she reminds me of myself. I used to adore long car trips.

In my twenties, I drove, with Ernie, cross-country, and later, several times, through England and France. Now, though, the thought terrifies me.

Like Catherine, I ready myself with drugs—blasts of Atrovent and Vanceril. And arrange myself carefully in the passenger seat in front (before, I did most of the driving), with my emergency medicines (Ventolin, epinephrine injection) at the ready should I get in big trouble, a bottle of water to soothe my throat if I start coughing incessantly, a face mask I can don should we get into a serious traffic jam. I give Ernie instructions about driving carefully because I now am such a nervous wreck when traveling, so fearful of having a severe, potentially fatal, attack in a car. I make sure all the windows are closed; we drive with the air conditioner on, even in winter.

In a nightmare I have at least once a week, I am suffocating to death from an asthma attack in a car that is stranded in a monumental traffic jam. I can't get help. Help can't get to me. Living close to New York, I know how terrible traffic can be. I have been in tie-ups lasting as long as five hours, and commuters here share traffic jam horror stories the way folks in other parts of the world talk about dangerous bears they've spotted. There was the famous chicken tie-up on the George Washington Bridge, when a truck carrying live chickens got into an accident and the cages broke, and there were chickens running all around on the bridge. And the one where the tanker truck carrying a dangerous liquid spilled its cargo because of a faulty valve—I lived through that one.

Twice, I have had serious asthma attacks in a car. Once, when I was alone, stuck in a two-hour traffic jam on the

New Jersey Turnpike, unable to get help, unable to get out of the car, hunched over the steering wheel, gasping for air, trying to calm myself, sure that I would die. And once, with Ernie, before I knew I had asthma—stopped dead in traffic in a tunnel on the ring road on a sweltering day in Paris in a car without air conditioning. "I'm suffocating," I gasp to him, and he doesn't understand that I mean this literally. "What do you expect me to do?" he asks, irritated. "Nothing's moving."

Catherine is the first fictional asthmatic character I come upon after my own asthma is diagnosed. I recall that the hero of Marcel Proust's *A la recherche du temps perdu*, which I read in the seventies in graduate school, was asthmatic, and I remember our class concluding that, because the speaker was asthmatic, he must also be neurotic. We scoured *Du côté de chez Swann*, the first volume, for evidence, and found it, in what we believed to be his pathological need to have his mother close to him at bedtime (overlooking, of course, Proust's clear description of his parents' emotional abuse).

Six months later, I try to read *The Volcano Lover* again. And succeed. By now, I am reasonably certain that my treatment will prevent my getting a fatal attack, and that I know what to do if I have a severe one.

The character of Catherine makes me very, very sad, for I learn something of what an asthmatic's life was like, something of the disease's treatment, before modern medicine.

The Volcano Lover describes how winds from the northeast carried "a smoke cloud and the smell of coal" into the area of London where Catherine lived and how "dangerous to the asthmatic" was the "coal-infested air" of London that Catherine was forced to breathe and that she knew was harming her. (Different in degree, but not in kind, I think, from the air I am forced to breathe in New York City on a hot summer day.) Her medicines—laudanum (an opium derivative) and calybeate water (water fortified with iron) wouldn't have helped much. Laudanum is addictive, and Catherine has the "slightly staring eyes" of the addict. When I ask Ernie why laudanum was used, he tells me that it is an involuntary muscle relaxant and can sometimes help mild attacks, but, paradoxically, if an attack is severe, it has the potential to kill the patient by suppressing the drive to breathe. What Catherine was taking to help her could have harmed her. (Which of my medicines, I wonder, might harm me? I use meditation to calm myself, instead of drugs and sedatives. Once, though, when I was especially sick, I found myself drinking more wine than I should at dinner, and I once nearly took a glass of wine with lunch because I knew it would stop my cough. Instead, I called a friend. "Don't," she said. "If you start using booze in the middle of the day to stop your cough, you might not stop.")

"I pray I shall not be ill," Catherine says, as they begin their journey. "I will not be ill if I can help it," she corrects herself, veering from the contradictory crazy-making beliefs I know too well: The disease is unpredictable and I can't control it, though I can manage it; the disease is my doing, and if I can only get myself to have the right attitude, to do the right things, I can control it.

Catherine, though a superb musician, cannot use her talent except to please her listeners. In time, because her husband so often ignores her, Catherine develops an intense, asexual—though highly charged—friendship with a young man who eventually leaves her and who turns their experience into a book.

After this, her illness worsens. Her husband, somewhat jealous of the impact of this experience on her, begins to hate his sick, reclusive wife "for becoming old, for always remaining indoors, for looking as vulnerable as she was."

The symptoms of Catherine's final, fatal illness are "a difficulty in breathing, a hurt around the heart." The treatment: weekly bleeding with leeches. During her long, slow death, Catherine has a recurring nightmare of being buried alive.

Catherine dies at forty-four, filled with self-contempt, with longing for her lost love, and with unacknowledged rage at her husband (which Sontag links to her asthma). She dies, Sontag suggests, because she *has* been buried alive, because the life-force within her has been utterly constricted.

That Sontag uses *my* illness as her metaphor for Catherine's constrained life makes me angry.

Reading of Catherine in *The Volcano Lover* starts me on several quests. I want to find other fictional portrayals of asthmatic characters to contrast them with Sontag's and to see what I can learn from them. I want to learn, too, how doctors have conceptualized asthma, how they have treated it in the past. And I want to find out about the lives of asthmatic writers.

11   I begin my search for earlier treatments of asthma in the back issues of the *New York Times.*

Throughout the 1930s, doctors debated whether asthma should be called a disease or a functional disorder. Acquired asthma was thought by some to be a mental maladjustment, or a nervous disease, successfully treatable only by psychotherapy, family therapy, or hypnosis. By others, it was thought to have two contributing factors: an underlying physical susceptibility as well as a neurosis.

In 1935, doctors were using helium therapy experimentally with asthmatics when adrenaline didn't help them. During treatment, the patients continuously inhaled an atmosphere of 80 percent helium and 20 percent oxygen. This was, admittedly, no cure; rather, by supplying "thinner air," it provided relief for the "fatigue of the breathing muscles," making it more likely, doctors hoped, that the respiratory system might subsequently recover. By 1937, the Public Health Service was recommending helium therapy for more widespread use.

Also in 1935, a doctor from Connecticut, using an experimental treatment, announced that he had cured hundreds of asthma cases with an oral application of "dead progeny of avian turbercle bacillus."

In 1936, a new treatment, inhaling epinephrine hydrochloride vapor (an unsatisfactory precursor of medicines like Ventolin), was being recommended for childhood asthmatics.

In 1937, a doctor in Warsaw reported on his use of injecting just enough insulin into the bodies of asthma sufferers to send their bodies into shock. Doctors from the

American Neurological Association, though, warned against the potentially dire effects—sudden death or the destruction of brain tissue—of this rapidly growing treatment. By 1939, a doctor at Mount Sinai Hospital in New York was reporting on his use of insulin treatment with asthmatic children: he believed that injections of insulin stimulated the adrenal glands to manufacture more adrenaline, which helped the asthmatic seizure (but at very significant risk to the child's brain cells).

In 1942, X-ray treatments, administered twice or three times a week over the chest, were being used in New York in an attempt to cure severe cases of asthma. (Considering what is known now about the cumulative cellular damage caused by radiation, one wonders about the long-range negative effect of this treatment.)

In 1946, an aerosol of a stable form of hydrogen peroxide, combined with penicillin therapy, was being tried.

In 1948, an aerosol of isuprel (a beta-blocker, a direct precursor of Ventolin but with more cardiac stimulatory side effects) was being tried.

And in 1948, a professor of surgery at the George Washington University School of Medicine was operating on patients in "status asthmaticus" and reporting "brilliant success" with his procedure. During the operation, an incision was made from the back mid-chest area, and the pulmonary plexus of nerves was destroyed; then all branches of the vagus nerve to the lung were divided, and the sheaths of the pulmonary artery and veins were denuded. (In severing the nerve input to the bronchial tree, presumably some beneficial effect was achieved.)

This brief excursus into the history of asthma treatment

makes me glad I'm alive now. Since I'm getting better, I must conclude that my treatment is helping. Still, I have some doubts. Are contemporary doctors (certain that their conceptualizing of asthma as an inflammatory process is correct and certain of their treatment) as off-the-mark as most of these earlier physicians? Is there, I wonder, an asthma gene? Is anyone looking for one?

12 Asthma is a disease of exhalation. A person who has asthma traps stale air in her lungs. The first breath we take is an inhalation. The last breath, an exhalation. Maybe people with asthma don't exhale fully because they're trapping air. Maybe they're trapping air because they're afraid they'll die.

After I wonder about this, I ask a friend whether she thinks there might be a relationship between asthma and terror. She wonders, though, whether I'm trapping the air in my lungs because, symbolically, I'm afraid of letting go. Letting go of my sister, my mother, letting go of my fear, of my sorrow, of my rage. Is asthma, she asks, being unable to let go?

13 In the year that it takes for my asthma to begin to come under control, I pass through many emotional waystations. Some, I return to and revisit more than I would like to acknowledge: despair, rage, hopelessness, resentment (of the able), castigation (of the ill who do nothing to help themselves). And terror, yes, terror, my lifelong companion, whom I come to know intimately during this year, and whom I would banish if I could, but who, I realize, in time, is—like it or not—the warpstring of my existence.

Yet I find that I am becoming more real to myself, too, for I have been forced against my will into acknowledging that change is inevitable and that the working of my body, like everyone else's, is not completely within my control. I am being taught by what my favorite nun in grade school called "the most powerful teacher"—humility.

My progress—if one can call managing a lifelong ailment progress—comes so slowly that I have no emotional calipers for measuring it. I have never before realized how impatient I am, how unable to allow change to come in its own good time, how much I rush through life, how little room I give myself to breathe.

Often, it seems that in trying to manage my asthma, I'm playing a grown-up's version of that sadistic childhood game, "Take a Giant Step," in which players beg for permission to take giant steps, or baby steps, and are allowed to, or aren't, depending upon whim, and not upon reasonable, predictable rules. I return, in my reading, to the wisdom and the sacred books of the East, to the writings of mystics and Buddhists, and I find some solace there. Within that worldview there is the paradoxical lesson I must learn: to give up the expectation that one's actions will produce a desired result, to expect nothing and yet to continue to do everything I can to help myself. (This, I truly accept, I ruefully acknowledge, about once a month, maybe twice.)

I begin to learn, though, that I have a particular kind of

grit, a stick-to-it-iveness that I never realized I possessed—
what Winston Churchill called "mettle." I make promises
to myself—that I will do whatever I can to enable my body
to heal—and I keep those promises.

14 Asthma is interrupted breathing. I want to tell
you about the history of interrupted breathing in
my life.

My sister killed herself. She hanged herself. She interrupted her breathing. Permanently.

My son was born with his umbilicus over his shoulder.
When he was in the birth canal, each contraction cut off
his oxygen. During each contraction, he starved for air.
He almost died. He was born blue.

My mother, near the end of her life, struggled for air.
For weeks, I sat next to her as she lay dying, watching her
chest, hearing her breath. Inhale. Long pause. Exhale.
Inhale. Longer pause. Exhale. For weeks, I felt sure that
each of these breaths would be her last.

When I was a baby, my mother fed me on schedule.
Every four hours. When I got hungry between feedings, I
cried. But my mother didn't pick me up, didn't comfort me.
During the first seven months of my life, I cried so hard,
my mother told me, that I seemed to lose my breath.

When I was in grammar school, during air-raid drills,
I always fainted. I stopped my breath because my terror
was too overwhelming. I imagined low-flying planes strafing
our school. As a grown-up, I faint, too. When I'm terrified.
When I'm furious, and when I don't know that I'm furious.

When I was in high school, I drank too much—so much that I passed out and scared my friends. "We weren't sure," they told me when I came to, "that you would start breathing."

Throughout my life, I have had a recurring dream. I am waking from a sound sleep, struggling. Someone has put a pillow over my face. Someone is trying to smother me.

In the first months of my marriage, I am in an automobile accident. I am driving a car, the brakes fail, the car rolls backwards, down a very steep hill, and I jump out of the car, thinking it's the only chance I have to escape. I get hit by the car door and thrown to the ground, my head under the car, my face nearly touching a tire, and I'm dragged under the car, down the hill. I don't realize this, but my coat is caught in the car's axle. It holds me captive, for how long I do not know, until the car comes to a crashing stop against a telephone pole, and someone is lifting the car off my body, someone is slapping my face and telling me to breathe, goddamn it, start breathing.

When I was a child, I spent summers with relatives. I remember the bathtub where I was washed, and fondled, and I remember being nine or ten or six or five or four and being so afraid that I dared not move, so afraid that time stood still, so afraid that I was hardly breathing.

Does this history of interrupted breathing have anything to do with my asthma?

15 Late summer 1993. My plan, to give myself some breathing room, is beginning to work. My asthma, which has been disabling for close to a year and a half, is pretty much under control. I have times when I am congested and uncomfortable—mostly in the late afternoons on days when it is raining. Sometimes I have to go to bed. But I feel that my daily hard work to keep myself fit and relatively unstressed is paying off. I feel better than I have for years, though there are still problems. My chronic fears. My terror of losing consciousness, of fainting while I am in my car, stuck in a traffic jam, so that no one can get to me.

These are the questions I ask myself. Do I have asthma because I'm angry? Or am I angry because I have asthma? Do I have asthma because I'm anxious? Or am I anxious because I have asthma? Do I have asthma because of the grief I've had in my life? Or do I grieve because I have asthma? Do I have asthma because I'm always afraid? Or am I afraid (terrified, actually) because I have asthma?

16 While I am thinking about why I have asthma, Jean-Luc Godard's *Breathless*, starring Jean Seberg, comes to the Film Forum in New York City, and I go to see it again. My friend, Eunice Lipton, reminds me that the title of the film, in French, is *A Bout de Souffle*, literally, "At the End of Breath."

I have seen *Breathless* before, when I was young, in my late teens or early twenties. I remember how closely I identified with Patricia (played by Seberg)—not because she seemed so out-of-touch that she could hang out with a thug (who is a murderer) and not know it, not because of her existential dilemma ("Am I unhappy because I'm not free, or free because I'm not happy?"), not because she was having great sex with this guy. I identified with her because she wanted to be left alone, because she described herself as a coward, as someone who was always afraid. I chose *Breathless* as the title for this book because I trace the connection I make between breathlessness and fear to my seeing this film.

As usual, I arrive at the theater early. While waiting, to pass the time, I take a blank sheet of paper, and write the words "Breathless" and "asthma" in a circle in its center. Using a free association/clustering technique to inspire writing, which I've learned from Gabriele Lusser Rico's *Writing the Natural Way*, I will try to capture the unconscious associations that I have with these words.

I work quickly, spontaneously, writing words as they come to me, drawing circles round them, linking circle of meaning to circle of meaning.

When I see *Breathless* this time, there is a startling scene I have forgotten. Michel Poiccard, Patricia's lover, puts his hands around her throat and tells her that unless she smiles for him before he finishes counting to eight, he'll strangle her. She thinks he's playing a game—but we know this man can strangle her, stop her breath, kill her.

Before he counts to seven, though, she does smile for him, guilelessly. Her willingness to please him stands

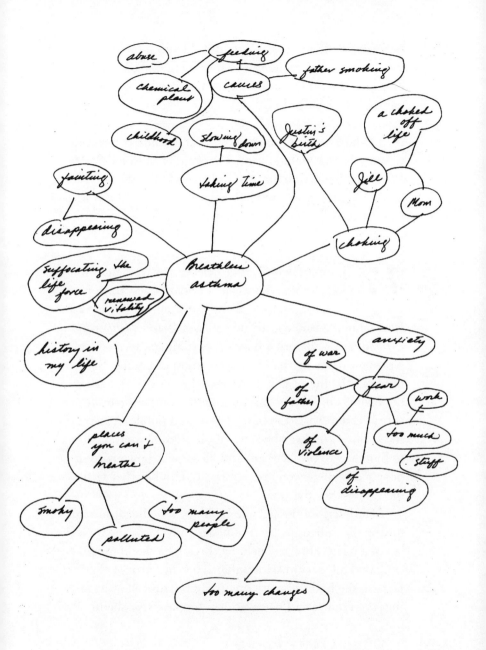

between her living and dying. But though the moment passes and she is no longer in imminent danger, we know he'd as soon kill her as fuck her. And Patricia is afraid because she senses this.

As a child I was afraid, always afraid, because I believed that my father could kill me. He came back from World War II a changed man, my mother had told me when I got older. He was easily enraged, volatile, violent. Once, when I was a teenager, he came at me with a knife.

17 I am at a conference celebrating women's literature, drama, and music in Southampton, Long Island, listening to the therapist and writer Renée Roth-Hano, author of the novel *Touch Wood: A Girlhood in Occupied France*, describe how she was hidden in a convent in Normandy during the Nazi occupation of France. She tells us about the life of Jews in France during the war. About her feelings of sorrow and humiliation on the first day she was forced to wear the Star of David in public. About how she survived the war because of the steps her parents took to hide her, to protect her. And also about how eighty-nine people she knew were exterminated, and how her father died soon after the war.

She describes the terrible bombings she lived through during the Allied invasion of Normandy. How she took shelter in a barn. How she held her breath as the bombs exploded all around. How, after the war, during her life in France, she had difficulty breathing because she was angry that the French had betrayed her people. How she finally emigrated to New York and likes it there, because she feels you can breathe without anybody bothering you. And that it has taken her forty years to begin to breathe more easily.

breathless, adjective. 1. with the breath held, as in suspense, astonishment, or fear. 2. causing loss of breath, as from excitement, anticipation, or tension.

18 These are the reasons I might have gotten asthma.

When I was an infant, I wasn't taught to control my hyperarousal. My mother, following the doctor's orders, had put me on a rigid schedule. For the first several months of my life, I wailed for hours at a time.

When I was a child, I was afraid of my father's temper.

My father was a heavy smoker. (I was a heavy smoker.)

We lived downwind from a chemical plant. On damp, windy days, you could taste the sick sweet fumes as you inhaled.

We lived downwind from a coal-burning electric plant. The smell of burning coal was always in the air.

I have lived two houses away from a six-lane highway for twenty-three years. In my backyard on a fresh spring day, all you can smell is exhaust.

I work in a sealed building at Hunter College. To me, the air inside is bad. For several years, I had an office next to a professor who chain-smoked cigars. Those years, I got sick often. Bronchitis, I thought it was. Those years, my friend Kate told me I was getting sickly. I had no idea why.

When I was younger, I took birth-control pills; now, I

take estrogen. (A study I read about in a recent issue of *Weight Watchers Magazine* has linked taking estrogens with a higher incidence of asthma in the study's participants.)

Sexual abuse.

None of the above. Some of the above. All of the above.

19 I have discovered that driving, cleaning the house, and walking outside when it's cold are much less of a problem for me if I wear a face mask. I shop for face masks now the way I used to shop for shoes.

I have a bandit-type mask that you wear over your nose and mouth and tie at the back of your neck. It comes in three colors (red, purple, and black) and I order it from Canada. It's worn by the Canadian mounted police. I always remember to take it off before I enter my bank so I won't be mistaken for a robber. "In purdah," and "Go back to your own country," I've heard from largish blond men on the streets of New York City when I wear it.

I have the kind of mask that bicycle messengers wear if they're smart—one with replaceable charcoal filters that straps around your face. I wear this when I take airplanes. Otherwise, the exhaust fumes that are sucked into the plane while it's waiting to take off would send me into dangerous paroxysms of coughing. Before I don it, I warn the stewardesses and my seatmates because I don't want to be mistaken for a terrorist. When my kids see me wearing it, they call me "Darth Mother."

And I also have several varieties of your standard drugstore face mask (it comes in white or blue) that makes you look like you're impersonating a surgeon. This I carry with me always. Once, I'm wearing a blue one as I pay the toll at the George Washington Bridge. I have been in an hour-long traffic jam; wearing the mask lessens the risk of a bad attack. Having a bad attack in traffic is my worst fantasy.

"Wait a second," the tolltaker tells me. I think he's holding up traffic, the way they sometimes do at the bridge, to let someone cross. But no, he's calling a pal over to gape at me.

"Get a load of this," he says, loud enough for me to hear. "I ain't ever seen this before." They laugh, roll their eyes. I pause, consider taking my mask off, spitting at them, telling them I have the new, virulent form of T. B. and they have just been infected. But I don't.

"Just wait, you bastard," I think, "just wait till something like this happens to you, and it surely will, because all day, taking tolls, you're inhaling exhaust fumes, and you don't even know how dangerous your work is." I know that in time, he, too, will have his turn, for, as Nancy Mairs has observed, "Disability is the one minority group we will all belong to."

20 It is now two years since I've gotten sick, two years since I've spoken in public, two years since I've gone far away from home by myself. Before I got asthma, I was intrepid, though I was often afraid. When my kids were babies, I thought nothing of putting them in the back seat of my sassy orange Volkswagen hatchback, and driving for hours to take them to a lake, a zoo, the Jersey shore. Older, I traveled by myself, even after marriage (which stopped solo travel for many of my friends), to England, France, California, Texas, Illinois. I trusted that, no matter what happened, everything would turn out fine—or, if it didn't, I could take care of myself.

But after I get asthma, I'm suddenly afraid of going anywhere alone. I have nightmares of having an asthma attack when I'm alone in my car, in a movie theater, in New York City, even when I'm walking the streets of my neighborhood. I am so frightened that, for my birthday, I ask for, and get, a portable telephone so I can dial home or "911" and get help wherever I am. Though my husband thinks I'm overdoing it, I tuck my phone into a fanny pack when I take my morning walk. "Answer the phone if it rings," I command. "It might be me, I might need help."

Whenever I summon up courage and decide to treat myself to a day alone, roaming the streets of New York City (my favorite pastime before I get sick), I imagine myself in Times Square, or Greenwich Village, inhaling diesel fumes, gasping for air, losing consciousness, falling to the sidewalk. I imagine people (lots of them) stepping over my prone body, ignoring me, as they rush rush rush to wherever they're going. I am in grave danger. Unless I get to a hospital fast, I'll surely die, but getting help in the middle of a crowd in this city isn't easy.

So usually I decide it would be more prudent to stay home.

My imaginings are not all that paranoid. One of my students, Cynthia Ward, a writer, who has breast cancer, collapsed in wintertime on a New York City sidewalk two blocks from her home.

"Then it registers in me," Cynthia Ward writes, in an

award-winning essay about her experience, "that no one is stopping. I am lying here and very well could all day. I am embarrassed, but mostly stunned, disoriented. Don't they see me? It is confusing to be so conspicuous, and at the same time invisible, isolated, alone."

Luckily, this happened outside a greengrocer where Cynthia often shopped. The shopkeeper recognized her, cared for her, then called the doorman from her building to take her home.

"My rubbery legs are walking me home in a daze and I notice I have no shoes on. And no hat either. . . . I ask no questions, and no one offers any explanation. . . . This is beyond looking homeless."

While she was unconscious, someone had stolen Cynthia's hat and shoes. "My purse, I can understand," Cynthia tells our class, after she reads her piece. "But how low do you have to be to steal a hat and shoes from an unconscious woman when it's twenty degrees outside?"

In time, I believe that my asthma is under sufficient control so I can travel by myself. And, for the first time since I've gotten sick, I accept an invitation to speak in public at a bookstore in Washington, D. C. Unless I want to drive four hours or more, and run the risk of sitting in the inevitable traffic jams that occur on the New Jersey Turnpike, I will have to take an airplane and have someone pick me up at the airport when I arrive. This worries me. I worry now, always, when I move into an environment I can't control.

I'm anxious, but I decide that if I plan, I can minimize the risk of having a serious attack. As I imagine and prepare for everything that might go wrong, I realize that

I must call my host with many questions and requests to ensure that I'll be well enough to speak. This is the part I hate, though I must do it, for it singles me out as different, and, depending upon a person's capacity for empathy, it brands me as someone who is sick/fragile/needy/a rip-roaring pain in the ass.

I have to make sure that her car has air-conditioning (so we can ride through traffic with the windows closed, protected from exhaust fumes), that she won't smoke, or wear perfume, or have one of those foul-smelling deodorizers that dangle from the rear-view mirror hanging in her car. (A few months earlier, I treat myself to a complete car wash. As a "bonus," the carwash attendant hangs a pine-scented, tree-shaped deodorizer in my car. One whiff, and I start choking. I can't drive the car home, can't go near it for a week.)

I stop for a moment to prepare for the call I will make. Practice what I will say and how I will say it. Not the kind of thing I did before I got asthma. Not the kind of thing I needed to do. Making demands like this is new to me since I've had asthma. Before, I tended to roll with the punches, take things as they came.

"Hello," I imagine myself saying, when I get her on the telephone. "This is Louise DeSalvo. I have a few things to ask of you when you come to pick me up at the airport because I . . ."

I stop, and pause to consider what I should say next. This is going to be even harder than I thought. I run through the possibilities.

"I have a few things to ask of you when you come to pick me up because I have asthma."

I see myself, stepping from the gangway, carrying a copy of my book in one hand, so she'll recognize me, and a little parcel labeled "asthma" in the other.

No, this won't do, I think. I can't tell her I have asthma. That sounds like I hold/possess/own/contain a thing, separate from myself, called "asthma." That my asthma is something I can take up or put down, whenever I choose. I haven't chosen asthma—far from it—though asthma has surely chosen me.

I stop. And write down the various ways I can tell someone about myself and my asthma. I haven't given what I call "myself" much thought until now. I was too sick, before, too focused on trying to get better, to consider the ontological implications of how I will now refer to myself and my condition.

I understand, though, that this is something important, this is something I have to figure out. I can tell people:

I have asthma.
I am asthmatic.
I am an asthmatic.
I am a person with asthma.
I suffer from asthma.
I get asthma attacks.
I have asthma attacks.
I have asthmatic episodes.

Whichever I choose, though, has different connotations, different and far-reaching implications about how I see myself and how others see me. Do I have asthma? Or am I an asthmatic? Good ex-Catholic school girl that I am, I figure it will be easier to choose what I'll say if I diagram these sentences. Diagramming will make the relationship between the parts of the sentences clearer; diagramming will make the hidden meaning in them apparent.

I	have	asthma
(subject)	*(transitive verb)*	*(object)*

Here, "asthma" is the object of the verb "have." I like the way the line that marks the direct object looks like a little barrier. Still, it won't do—and for the reasons I described before.

I	am	asthmatic
(subject)	*(linking verb)*	*(predicate adjective)*

This is especially troublesome. The angled line that indicates the predicate adjective marks too close a connection between me and asthma. It's like a little slingshot, flinging the word "asthmatic" back at me.

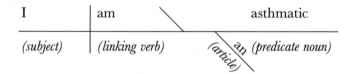

This is even worse. Using asthmatic as a predicate noun creates the impression that the only thing I am is asthmatic.

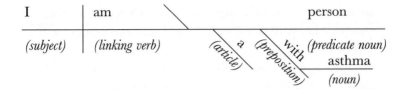

I	am				person
(subject)	*(linking verb)*	*(article)* a	*(preposition)* with		*(predicate noun)* asthma *(noun)*

   This seems as if I have to assert that, despite my asthma, I am still human.

   I stop. I see that this is getting me nowhere. I call my husband at work to ask him if these sentences mean different things to him as they mean different things to me. But he's no help. To him, they all mean the same thing.

   I know this is getting out of hand when I reach for a copy of the *Oxford English Dictionary*. I do this anytime I'm having a hard time thinking about something or writing about something, or anytime I don't want to be thinking about something or writing about something. Sometimes doing this helps. Often it doesn't. When I was writing my book on Virginia Woolf as an incest survivor, I would stare at the word "incest" and its meanings in the OED for hours, as if somewhere within the history of the word's usage or its etymology I might discover precisely what I needed to know, to say.

   Today, the OED is getting me practically nowhere, though I like learning that, in the sixteenth century, asthma was called "asthmasy." "Asthmasy" is wonderfully onomatopoeic; it sounds like the sounds people with asthma/who have asthma/who suffer from asthma make when they're having an asthma attack and when they're in *status asthmaticus* (a very frightening term I decide I will never use because it sounds as dangerous as a nuclear attack, and, though I know that asthma can kill, just saying *status asthmaticus* scares me).

I learn, too, that another possibility is that I can tell someone that I am asthmatical. I've never heard this word before, but, apparently, it's still a common usage.

I am asthmatical.

This, I like. It makes having asthma sound like having an attribute, like being musical, or practical, or mathematical. Asthmatical. "I am asthmatical" sounds like I have a quality, not a condition, not a life sentence, something that distinguishes me, something that marks me as special.

For a couple of days, I start saying "I am asthmatical," when I have to explain what or who I am (but not to the woman in Washington, D.C., though, to whom I say, after all this, "I have asthma.") Soon, I stop, because everyone I say it to keeps asking "What?" and my husband tells me it's an affectation, it's driving him crazy. To him, "asthmatical" conjures an image of Marcel Proust, wrapped in scarves and shawls, in a cork-lined room, coughing into a lace handkerchief ("How do you know it was a lace handkerchief?" I taunt him), pen in hand, writing.

21 How long can we sit and listen to a sick person's testimony about their bodily ills? A few seconds? A few minutes? An hour, maybe?

When I was at my worst, and could only talk about how sick I was (for my illness had become my only reality), I once calculated that the most that any listener—husband, child, relative, close friend, distant acquaintance—could endure without changing the subject, was about thirty-five seconds. Which is one reason I went back into therapy—to pay someone to listen to me since I needed to talk about what it was like to have asthma.

I once had a student of writing whom I believed to be especially talented. I called him into my office to say that I wanted to work with him on an independent study project and that I thought he had a great career ahead of him. If we worked hard, I predicted he would publish before finishing his undergraduate degree.

My words, which I thought would cheer him, made him weep.

He took a few minutes to compose himself, then said, "Let's start right away. Now. This afternoon."

"Not now," I countered. "Take the summer off. Rest. Relax. In the autumn, we'll have all the time we need."

"We won't, and I don't have a great career ahead of me, though I want to write more than I can say. But whatever work we do," he told me, "will have to be done quickly. I have AIDS."

That summer, I learned through Geoffrey that it was important for his work that he tell me how afraid he was that he'd die before writing anything significant, how worried he was that every cough or sniffle was a signal that he was near death.

I couldn't listen to Geoff for very long. Though I wanted to hear what he was telling me, I felt myself resisting, watched my mind wandering.

Once, when Geoffrey sensed this, he said, "Goddamn it, you've stopped listening to me," and I had to acknowledge that it was true.

Geoff was angry with me, and with good reason. "Look," he said, "this is a waste of our time. Just let me go home and write down what I want to tell you. I'll turn it into a story, then you can read it, and after you read it, maybe you can listen to me. And to others like me. And besides," he said, "if you're reading it, you can put it down whenever you want, and I won't know that you're not paying attention."

I felt I had betrayed Geoff, but I knew that what he said was true. At first, the only way I could listen to him, to act as witness to his pain, would be to experience his testimony through an art that I could take in at my own pace.

When I next saw Geoff, he said he really didn't want to meet, but that he was working on something, and though he wouldn't yet tell me what it was about, it was something he had been wanting to write for a while.

I told him I was sorry about what had happened at our last meeting, but he brushed off my apology. He said he realized that he had to teach me about AIDS, not by talking about it in the privacy of my office, but by writing a story I could read, and that would, in time, be published. In this way, he would show many more people what it felt like to have his disease. Geoff's art became, for both of us, and for his readers, "a place of safety," as the critic Joshua Fausty has put it, where we could explore Geoff's world—one in which there was no safety. Geoff taught me something I needed to learn. That works of art make the act of listening to the testimony of human suffering possible. That even though listening is difficult, it is also, as Arthur W. Frank puts it in *The Wounded Storyteller*, fundamentally a "moral act." This act, Geoff was enabling me to perform.

Geoff's first piece about AIDS was an award-winning elegy called "Passing Time." To me, the power of the narrative in this story came from the dreadful position of the central character, nicknamed "Angel" by his lover, who acts as witness to his lover's torturous death from AIDS—the same kind of death that, Angel suspects, he, too, will experience.

I remember taking up Geoff's story, "Passing Time," in the heat of a beautiful summer day, some eight years ago, and reading the images, moments Geoff had conjured to describe Angel's experience, so exquisite and powerful, that I can recall them still. How Angel and his lover dance cheek-to-cheek to Mable Mercer records. How, near the end, Angel hopes that if he becomes "as still as the rolling hills and silent river" he sees in the French countryside, where the pair spend a few final days together, "time, too, would pass us by." How Angel listens to the "stainless steel words" of the doctor rendering his diagnosis. How alarm runs through Angel's body "like a freight train." How "a brand new mountain of question marks" had been delivered into his life. How, in one moment, Angel had been propelled into a different universe, one where "the soundtrack of everyday existence had ground to a silent halt." How the flesh of his lover's dead body reminds Angel of the color of "faded white lilies."

Yes, I said to myself as I read, I can now see something of the way that it is for Geoff.

But the following morning, as I awakened from a sleep

that had been peopled with the characters in Geoff's story, I understood that, in writing "Passing Time," Geoff had described the way it is for us all. As Geoff had reminded me one day (when he told me to lighten up because I was becoming way too lugubrious about him), "Look, you may not realize this yet, Louise, but you're going to die, too, we're all going to die; you think I'm going to die before you, but you can never be sure."

Before he died, Geoff taught me—and all who read his work—that works of art make the overwhelming experience of trauma, suffering, bodily pain, and the inevitability of death bearable, and so, render them partially comprehensible.

22 My worst asthma attacks now come at 1:00 A.M. When I awaken, heart pounding, chest tightening, throat tingling, mucus clogging, I don't even need to look at the clock to know what time it is.

This happens five or six times a month, when I haven't taken a high enough dose of my medicines, when I've not been extremely careful about what I've eaten, when I've found myself in a place where there is smoking, or if the air's been very bad (as it invariably is in summer), when I've wandered too long on the streets of New York, or if I've gotten stuck in traffic behind a foul-smelling diesel engine on the highway, or when I've found myself on line at the supermarket behind a woman wearing a strong perfume. These days, an unbroken night's sleep is something I treasure.

By now, though, I know what to do, and these attacks don't terrify me as they once did. And I'm usually confident that, because my asthma is under control, because I have trained myself to relax at the first sign of an attack, I'll soon be fine.

By reflex, I swing out of bed, take a blast of my medicine, wait, take another, then lean back into my pillow. I pull on the earphones of my Walkman, and turn on my relaxation tape. If I'm lucky, I can quiet the attack and get back to sleep in half an hour, an hour at most.

Some nights, though, when fear or rage kick in, or when it takes longer than usual for my breathing to soften, I know that I am in for a bout of insomnia.

Insomnia. Another of asthma's curses.

And, on one such recent insomniac night, I get out of bed, not wanting to awaken Ernie, and collapse, to regulate my breathing, on the sofa in my study. I decide that while I wait to calm this attack, while I wait for sleep to come, I might as well read a book. But what book?

On the coffee table, and on the floor surrounding it, are the piles of books that I want to read as I write *Breathless*. These will help me learn how other writers have interpreted the experience of having asthma.

There are the novels that I've been buying or pulling off my bookshelves and the list of novels I have scribbled that I will buy—more novels with asthmatic characters than I ever imagined existed. Virginia Woolf once said that we must think back through our mothers (both symbolic and actual) if we are women, meaning that women are inspirited by the experience of reading the works of other women writers, in a way they're not by reading the works of men. And an important part of Woolf's life's project was discovering, rediscovering, and popularizing the works of women writers, well-known and little-known—Jane Austen, George Eliot, Aphra Behn, The Duchess of Newcastle, Ella Wheeler Wilcox, Eliza Haywood, Olive Schreiner. Similarly, I now believe that reading about the lives of asthmatic writers and reading the portraits of asthmatic characters in fiction, which has recently taken on a compelling urgency for me, will provide the models and inspiration I need to do my work. Or, to paraphrase Woolf, we must think back through our asthmatic mothers and fathers if we are asthmatics.

I want to read, to reread them all. Erika Duncan's *Those Giants Let Them Rise!* (whose asthmatic heroine, Melanie, struggles to break a too-strong bond with her psychoanalyst mother). Carole Maso's *Ghost Dance* (the narrator, Vanessa Turin, has trouble breathing when her mother, a gifted and disturbed poet, is about to leave her). Isabel Allende's *House of the Spirits* (her asthmatic heroine is comforted when she's in distress by her grandmother's embrace). Anne Finger's *Bone Truth* (whose artist heroine, Elizabeth Etters, has asthma and a host of other physical complaints, some of which are the consequences of her father's vicious beatings in childhood). A. S. Byatt's *The Virgin in the Garden* (the asthmatic Marcus Potter is disconnected from reality and has frightening hallucinations; his father is a bully and has terrified his son, damaging him emotionally). Salman Rushdie's *The Moor's Last Sigh* (the narrator of this tumultuous family saga, Moraes Zogoiby of Bombay, is asthmatic). Garcia Marquez's *Of Love and Other Demons* (whose elderly asthmatic Bishop, a believer in demonic possession and exorcism, causes the torment of the novel's heroine). Pat Barker's trilogy: *Regeneration*, *The Eye in the Door*, and *The Ghost Road* (its bisexual, working-class, traumatized, asthmatic character, Billy Prior, serves four rounds of duty at the front during World War I. Prior's asthma is better when he is away—even in the trenches—than it is at home). Jessica Auerbach's *Catch Your Breath* (I'm drawn to this novel because it investigates the link between asthma and abuse in the life of its two-year-old character Jason).

There is also John Updike's memoir, *Self-Consciousness*, which describes the onset of his asthma in adulthood after a visit to his mother. I highlight Updike's description of an attack.

> An asthma attack feels like two walls drawn closer and closer, until they are pressed together. Your back begins to hurt, between the shoulder blades, and you hunch. I could not stand up straight and looked down at the flourishing grass between the sandstones. I thought, *This is the last thing I'll see. This is death.* The breathless blackness within me was overlaying the visual world. . . . My children and parents had come out on the back porch to watch me, and a rictus twitched my face as I thought how comic this performance must look, this wrestle with invisible demons. . . . I felt immensely angry at my own body and at everybody. Like a child blind in his tantrum I thought, *Serve them right,* and waited to die, standing bent over and gasping, of suffocation.

But it is Updike's story, "His Mother Inside Him," in *The Afterlife and Other Stories,* that compels me, for in the character of Allen Dow, Updike creates a fictional character whose asthma is related to his terror.

Allen Dow had been fearful, in childhood, of his mother's unhappiness, which would vent itself in sudden storms of temper that flattened the other occupants of the house into corners and far rooms. Once he saw his father cowering under the dining table while his mother, red-faced with fury, tried to get at him to slap him again. . . . Allen never forgave her for that—for her doing it, for his seeing it. . . . [H]e remained wary of the rage inside her that he had been permitted to glimpse. She made him nervous, and nervousness became his mode. All the complaints of nervousness—skin rashes, stammering, asthma, insomnia—were his. It took him decades of living hundreds of miles beyond her reach to begin to breathe.

I have listed books I am hunting down but don't yet have: Tahar Ben Jelloun's *Corruption*; Jilly Cooper's *Appassionata*; Martha Grimes's *The Horse You Came In On*; Allan Hollinghurst's *The Folding Star*; Angela Huth's *Land Girls*; Ferdinand Mount's *Of Love and Asthma*.

But on this insomniac night, for some reason, it is only Proust I want to read. I am beginning to read about Proust for this book, and Painter's biography, a volume of Proust's letters, and my three-volume set of *Remembrance of Things Past* teeter in an unsteady tower on my coffee table.

In graduate school, for an independent project, I have read all of *Swann's Way*, *Within a Budding Grove*, *The Guermantes Way*, *Cities of the Plain*, but stopped halfway through *The Captive*. Of the life goals I scribbled for myself many, many years ago (write; marry well; stay well-married; stay sane; raise happy, well-adjusted, cherished children; keep physically fit; walk the Southwest Coast Path in England; walk the Coast-to-Coast Path in England; read *Remembrance of Things Past*), I have never completed the last two, and, with age, I have realized that the others could never really be *accomplished*, only continually worked at.

It is now time, I tell myself, to begin to read all of *Remembrance of Things Past*. In the past, such a task seemed daunting. But I quickly calculate that, if read slowly, at the rate of ten pages a night, I can read it in a year—in nine years' less time than it took Proust to write in. (How inequitable, the relationship between writer and reader, I have always thought. Virginia Woolf spends seven years struggling with *The Voyage Out*, a novel that can be read in a few evenings.)

On my last reading of Proust, I was in the thick of graduate school, of raising children. I hardly had the time to do my schoolwork, and so, regrettably, I abandoned reading *Remembrance of Things Past*. Now, I am older, a grandmother, my children are in their own homes, and my house, at one in the morning, is quiet and still—as still, I imagine, as the room in which Proust wrote—and I am trying to calm my breath.

I pick up *Swann's Way*, and begin: "For a long time I used to go to bed early." And before I am finished reading my self-imposed ten-page quota for this night, I must close the book, for I find that I am weeping. For it is in *Remembrance of Things Past* that I think I will find the ultimate expression of the asthmatic life—what the asthmatic's relationship is to time. Since I've gotten asthma, my own relationship to time has changed completely. There is nothing that makes you as conscious of time present, and time future, as not being able to breathe. Moment by moment by moment, the asthmatic is aware of the breath. Moment by moment by moment, the asthmatic waits for the breath to ease, knowing that one day, perhaps this day, it might not. Asthma is a perverse form of meditation.

It is only now that I have asthma that I understand the enormity of what Proust has accomplished, in spite of his asthma, and perhaps, too, because of his asthma—because, in having asthma, he was acutely aware of time. I imagine him, insomniac, too, asthmatic, too, tugging for air, writing these lines in the middle of the night, as I read them in the middle of the night. And, I can feel Proust breathing through his prose, I can see him writing the experience of his body into his work—the rapid gasping burst of phrase after phrase, the long slow draw of a sentence, the dizzying spiral of a page-long paragraph.

If you want to read Proust, truly read him, read him in those hours of darkness when he wrote his work, when there are no distractions, when our relation to time becomes different, becomes more like Proust's relationship to time. Read him in those luminous dark hours of deep night when the act of making memory reigns.

A friend who knows I've been reading fiction depicting asthmatic characters asks me which character is my favorite, which, the most complex. Besides Marcel, of course.

She is tired of hearing about Proust, and I think she's trying to urge me onto a new topic of literary conversation. Every few days, when we talk, I tell her about how excited I am about Proust's description of a church steeple, or a hawthorn bush, or about what Aunt Leonie, who spends most of her life in bed, is doing (or, more properly, isn't doing), or about how the kitchen maid has gotten pregnant, or about how Swann is far more important than Marcel's family understands, and how fantastic and subtle is his first love scene with Odette.

"This is worse than if you were watching the soaps," she moans. "If you were watching the soaps, you'd be too ashamed of watching them to carry on like this."

I know what she means. Each day, I look forward to the next installment of *Remembrance of Things Past* as avidly as someone else might look forward to watching *One Life to Live* on television. And I *have* started to talk about Proust's characters as if they are real people. Maybe it's my age. Or maybe, as my students would say, it's time for me to "get a life."

It's true that asthma, as a subject of study, has completely taken over my world in the same way that incest, or adultery, or creativity has taken over my world in the past. In almost every letter I receive, a correspondent is replying to my request that they tell me anything they know about asthma. My friend Jane Marcus writes me from Europe, telling me that her husband Michael wants me to know that Olive Shreiner was friends with Cecil Rhodes, and that he died a horrible death in South Africa from asthma. "Is this going to be a gruesome book?" she asks me. How can I express to her that learning about asthma, writing about it, has been exhilarating?

"What are you doing these days?" an acquaintance asks.

"Having a fantastic time," I reply.

"Doing what?" she persists.

"Writing about asthma," I answer.

"Oh. . . ."

From the tone of her voice, I know that she thinks I'm demented. I don't know her well enough to tell her what I mean. What I mean is that I have become thoroughly inspirited by the *connection* I am feeling between myself and Proust, and between myself and all the other asthmatic writers and characters about whom I am reading.

For the first time since I've gotten sick, in reading the records writers have made of the experience of being asthmatic, and in writing about asthma, I am less terrified than I once was. I find myself wanting to recreate one of Elizabeth Bishop's trips to Newfoundland; and I have sent away for walking trip brochures. Now that I can fly to Europe on a smoke-free plane, who knows, I might fulfill a dream, to hike the Coast-to-Coast Path. Most important, working on this book has shown me that I am not in this struggle alone.

I tell my friend that, without a doubt, the most complex portrait of an asthmatic character I have found in fiction is Isabel Allende's Clara in *The House of the Spirits*. I like that Allende links Clara's asthma to her terror (Updike, too, makes this connection in "His Mother Inside Him") because she is witness to, and victim of, the emotional and physical brutality of members of her family, and of a political reign of terror. Yet, it is because of the record of her own life that Clara has kept in her notebooks that her granddaughter Alba can heal from the ordeal she has suffered as a political prisoner by writing about it.

"My grandmother wrote in her notebooks that bore witness to life for fifty years. . . . I have them here at my feet, bound with colored ribbons. . . . Clara wrote them so they would help me now to reclaim the past and overcome terrors of my own."

"Does Allende have asthma?" my friend asks.

"I don't know," I tell her. None of the scores of interviews with her I have read mention asthma. But I do know, from reading them, and from her memoir, *Paula*, that Allende was sexually abused as a child, and that she was, of course, no stranger to personal and political terror.

23 Since I was a girl, reading novels, biographies of writers and their diaries, memoirs, and letters has illuminated subjects I wanted to learn about. Through reading about others, I could learn what I needed to know at a safe distance. Writers are such careful and accurate observers of themselves and their surroundings, and such consistent and eloquent recorders of their experiences and their times, that I have always learned more, say, about the Nazi bombing of London during World War II and the dispiriting effect the fear of invasion had upon the British by reading Virginia Woolf's diary than by reading other forms of nonfiction. (I learned that Woolf lost her home in the bombing, yet miraculously her diaries were not destroyed, although her treasured library had become a waterlogged, sodden mess; that her husband Leonard saved enough petrol so that they could asphyxiate themselves in their garage when the Nazis invaded, that each successive week in early 1941 was thought to be the one earmarked for invasion, and that Woolf herself became unhinged because of this chronic stress).

Before I had asthma, I looked to the lives of writers for examples of how to live a writer's life. Born of working-class parents, and the first person in my extended family to go to college, I never had a model for what a writer's life was like until, in 1975, I started reading the diaries of Virginia Woolf. I wanted to be a writer and I thought that if I learned about Woolf's work habits and copied them, then I, too, might write. And so, sure enough, in time, I wrote my first book.

Woolf wrote three uninterrupted hours a day, from ten to one. Sometimes she stole a few minutes from whatever creative project she was writing to pen an entry into her writer's diary, where she described what was happening in her life and also assessed her feelings about her work, monitored her progress, made schedules to ensure the completion of her books, dreamed new books, and worried about the reception of her publications. Sometimes she saw friends for lunch; often she didn't.

Afternoons, she did what she called the "donkey work" of a writer's life—typing what she had composed in the mornings, correcting proof, writing letters, reading for reviews. Whether in London or in her country house in Sussex, in the late afternoons she took very long walks, both to clear her head from the pressure of creative work, but also to think through puzzles or stumbling blocks in the work. (These walks, I believe, kept Woolf emotionally stable and depression-free for long periods of time. At the end of her life, Woolf was deprived of her walks. The South Downs were littered with unexploded bombs; a lone walker was an easy target. Partly because of the wearing effects of the war and deprived of the walks that stabilized her spirits, Woolf eventually became seriously depressed and killed herself.)

Evenings, Woolf saw friends or went to a concert or a play (when in London), or read, or played bowls with Leonard (when in Sussex), or, later in life, listened to recordings on the gramophone.

But always, always, her creative work came first. And always, always, she assessed the impact of the way she was living her life on her productivity. If her writing was not going well enough because of too many social engagements, she cut back on her attendance at dinner parties.

And so, in imitation of Woolf, but with some adjustments, I instituted my own version of her schedule: awakening, 6:30; breakfast, made by Ernie (in imitation of Leonard Woolf's bringing Woolf her breakfast in bed), 6:30–7:30; straightening the house (which Woolf, with servants, didn't have to contend with), 7:30–8:00; walking, showering, and dressing, 8:00–9:00; uninterrupted writing, 9:00–12:00; lunch, 12:00–1:00; donkey work, 1:00–4:00; meditation, 4:00–4:30; errands, calls, collapsing on the sofa, cooking (with Ernie as sous-chef), 4:30–7:00; dinner, 7:00–8:00; reading, relaxation, or movie, 8:00 to whenever. Unlike Woolf, I am not all that social. I see friends a few times a week, but sometimes not for a few weeks at a time. Family, though, I see often, mostly for meals. What our family shares is a passion for cooking. (Once, a student, eager to hear the details of my life, told me she imagined that Ernie and I often engaged in intellectual discourse. "About what?" I asked. "Oh, philosophy," she answered, "or books." "Oh, no," I replied, needing to be honest, "but we talk a lot." "About what?" she asked. ("About what we're going to have for dinner," I replied.)

It is my schedule, modified from Woolf's, that has kept me writing, that has kept me sane.

When I get sick and find out I have asthma and can't keep to this schedule, I feel as if I'm coming unhinged. I believe that I need guidance in managing this difficult transition in my life, so I find myself doing what I've always done—looking to the lives of writers for information, but now, about how to be a writer who has asthma. Or, in the words of Arthur W. Frank, author of *The Wounded Storyteller: Body, Illness, and Ethics*: What does it mean to be a writer with a wounded body? I want to place my singular experience as an asthmatic into an historical context.

I want to learn about writers who were asthmatic. I want to know what they suffered, how they described their illness in their letters and diaries, how they interpreted it, how their families and friends interpreted it, and whether the descriptions of pain and psychic trauma I suspected I would find were understood or even heard by their associates. I want to learn how they were treated by their doctors, and whether their asthma was used as a subject in their art. I want to know whether their having asthma affected their work, and if it did, how it did. Now only did I want to compare their experiences with mine to better assess what I live with and to learn from their example what to emulate or avoid (although this is certainly a prime motive), I also want to act as a witness to their testimony about what it was like to live with asthma, and to share what I learn with my students, with my readers.

I decide to start with the writers I know—Djuna

Barnes, Marcel Proust. But when people learn about my project, they tell me about other writers whose lives I should study. Beth Houchin, a student in one of my classes, asks me whether I know that the Pulitzer-Prize-winning poet Elizabeth Bishop was an asthmatic. I don't. Beth refers me to an article she has read recently, "The Closet of Breath: Elizabeth Bishop, Her Body and Her Art" by Marilyn May Lombardi. My friend, critic and scholar, Jane Marcus, tells me about Olive Schreiner and John Updike. Another friend, Frank McLaughlin, my first editor, and himself a writer, tells me about Dylan Thomas.

I am in the earliest stages of a project that I know will continue for years. I begin, as always, unsystematically, reading a biography of Bishop, some Proust letters, some Bishop letters, some Bishop poems and autobiographical pieces, and Schreiner's famous novel *The Story of an African Farm*.

I quickly learn that what I suspect is true. Asthmatic writers have left detailed descriptions of their asthma history, of their symptoms and suffering, and of their doctors' treatment protocols. Because they so often describe their work habits and what prevents them from working, the diaries (Elizabeth Bishop's "Key West" diary, for example) and letters (Proust's, to his mother; Bishop's, to her doctor) of asthmatic writers are a treasure trove for studying the way the disease has been interpreted and treated and the impact of various treatments on writers' work and lives. It is important and inspirational to see these writers grapple with precisely the same issues I have: Why am I sick? Can I make myself better?

.   .   .

Above my desk, I start to pin pictures of asthmatic writers as I learn about them. I buy postcards when I see them, or cut pictures from editions of books I own or buy. "The Asthmatic Hall of Fame," I call it.

These pictures look down on me as I do my work. I look to them for guidance and inspiration to assure myself that I, too, can work through my worst days. I also look to them for warning: to remember what I must avoid. In time, there are many pictures that surround me: Djuna Barnes, Edith Wharton, Dylan Thomas, Marcel Proust, Elizabeth Bishop, Olive Schreiner, John Updike.

As I'm nearing the end of this project, I add the pictures of Olympic athletes who also have asthma: Jackie Joyner-Kersee, Amy Van Dyken, and Tom Dolan.

Djuna Barnes

I learn that Djuna Barnes's important modernist novel *Nightwood* was begun in the wake of a terrifying early-morning asthma attack that prompted her to move from Paris, where she had been living since 1921, to England.

In August 1932, Barnes left Paris for Hayford Hall, bordering on Dartmoor, after Peggy Guggenheim (who was renting the place) persuaded her that the country air would be better for her and, under the circumstances, it would be wiser for her not to live alone. Barnes had told Natalie Barney the attack was so severe it made her heart pound and her hair stand straight up on her head.

And it was at Hayford Hall that Barnes began *Nightwood*, the most important work of her career. An asthma attack had precipitated a move she never would have made otherwise, and at Hayford Hall she found the circumstances favorable for writing, although her life was in turmoil—what with the sadness of the aftermath of her long love affair with Thelma Wood and a briefer affair with Charles Henri Ford, both still lingering. "God knows," she wrote to her friend Emily Coleman, "who could have written as much about their blood while it was still running. I wrote [*Nightwood*] you must remember . . . when I still did not know whether Thelma would come back to me or not . . . whether I could live with her again or not; in that turmoil of Charles [Ford] . . . sickness, Hayford Hall— everything."

At Hayford Hall, though ill and in despair, Barnes also could walk in the rose garden, swim, engage in stimulating conversation, or get advice about her novel if she chose, though it became necessary for her to guard her manuscript from Emily Coleman, who threatened to burn it if Barnes, who was loose-lipped, gave any of her secrets away.

Barnes was left alone to work for hours at a time, and she was unimpeded by the distractions of Paris and what had been her nightly cruises of nightspots like the Dome or Le Train Bleu, although at Hayford Hall ("Hangover Hall," they called it), she was hardly a teetotaler—she was drinking a bottle of whiskey a day. (Years later Barnes stopped drinking because, as she put it, she was tired of waking up in strange places with some of her clothing missing.)

Guggenheim gave Barnes a rococo bedroom in which to work, because she believed it suited Barnes's style. During the summers of 1932 and 1933, when she awakened, Barnes put on her make-up, stayed in her nightgown, and crawled into bed to write. Although one could take magnificent walks from Hayford Hall onto the moor, initially

Barnes stayed mostly inside. Its bleak landscape and the "dead ones"—animal skeletons that one stumbled upon —terrified her at first.

In writing *Nightwood*, Barnes recalled and described the desperate masochistic unhappiness of her love affair with Thelma Wood (who became the character Robin Vote in the novel). She learned that her affair with Thelma was rooted in the misery she had experienced as a girl, in her grandmother's sexual abuse of her, and in her father's violence. "For Robin," Barnes wrote, "is incest too."

Barnes described her grandmother's too-ardent love for her, and how she loved her grandmother "more than anyone," and how her father had arranged to have her raped.

> I had gone down on the floor and hugged my grandmother by her knees, dropping my head down, saying "Don't let it happen!" and she said, "It had to happen." And I was in bed that first night, and he said, "Christ! You don't bleed much." And I said, "It is all the blood it has." . . . So I took the carving knife and leaned across the table, strong and blind with something coming up in me out of what my father had in his head for women and love. . . . And I came back home and I wasn't crying. And then I got thin, and fell when I walked. . . . And that too was my childhood.

When Djuna Barnes's mother read her daughter's *Nightwood*, she told her, "You have condensed your agony until it is pure platinum."

.   .   .

In rifling through a biography of Elizabeth Bishop written by Brett C. Millier, I learned that Bishop, too, wrote a breakthrough work because of an asthma attack.

Alone on New Year's Eve 1935, sick, with asthma, treating herself with "adrenalin and cough syrup," Bishop spent the night looking at a glass-encased map of the North Atlantic, depicting the Canadian Maritime Provinces where she was born, and then writing a poem, "The Map." Like Barnes's *Nightwood*, it was a breakthrough work that questioned her origins—Millier calls it the first of her mature poems. "We can stroke these lovely bays," she wrote, "under a glass as if they were expected to blossom, / or as if to provide a clean cage for invisible fish." The image of the cage is prophetic, for, throughout Bishop's career, she used images of entrapment to describe her childhood and her asthma.

I move to Marilyn May Lombardi's "The Closet of Breath: Elizabeth Bishop, Her Body and Her Art," a brilliant article based upon the careful, archival research I admire, but with a respectful sensitivity to the artistic process and to the effects of a lifelong incurable illness—which is extremely rare in biographers.

Here, I learn about diaries Bishop kept when she lived in Key West, recording her "almost nightly attacks of debilitating asthma" and "her dreams and anxieties."

Bishop, Lombardi tells us, wanted to write works about Job, Jonah, St. Teresa (whose *Way of Perfection* Bishop had in her library), and St. Anthony—others who had suffered bodily afflictions as severe as hers. She was fascinated with the figure of St. Sebastian, with whom she compared herself, because she was so often forced to inject herself with cortisone or with adrenaline (often hourly). "I finally got sick of being stuck with so many things like St. Sebastian," she wrote on January 8, 1952, in a letter to her doctor from Brazil, where she suffered a serious allergic reaction to the fruit of the cashew.

Bishop's illness, Lombardi states, contributed to her sense of homelessness for, as soon as Bishop found a place she wanted to live, her asthma started to bother her again. Often, she moved. She began to feel that no place was safe and that, in consequence, no place was home.

Although Bishop did not often write directly about her illness in her creative work, Lombardi observes that Bishop transformed her bodily ills "into a rich cache of metaphors that help enact her sense of the world"—images of caging, entrapment, smothering, suffocation, and constriction that define how Bishop viewed human interaction and that she developed, for example, in her well-known poem "The Fish." Bishop also used the image of the dying mermaid "washed ashore and gasping for breath" to explore "the yearnings, imprisonings," and anxieties of "the eroticized female body." For Lombardi, this image encapsulated Bishop's sense of "estrangement as an artist and a lesbian." Lombardi believes that Bishop relied upon her "physical ailments," primarily her personal battle against suffocation, to develop a "poetic of healing" that confronts the myriad ways in which culture stifles "personal and erotic expression."

In "The Closet of Breath," I learned about Bishop's correspondence with her friend and medical advisor, Doctor

Anny Baumann, which describes in detail what Bishop suffered, the treatment she received, and her attempt to locate the cause of her illness in her early childhood experiences, primarily those of maternal deprivation. After her father's untimely death, when Bishop was five years old, her mother was institutionalized, and Bishop never saw her again.

After a brief time, Bishop was removed, "unconsulted and against my wishes," from her maternal grandparents' home in Nova Scotia to the repressive, gloomy household of her paternal grandparents in Worcester, Massachusetts. There, she developed severe asthma, eczema, symptoms of St. Vitus's dance, and almost died. In the late 1940s and early 1950s, Bishop read newspaper and magazine articles defining asthma as a psychosomatic illness. "Everyone," she wrote Baumann in 1951, "now thinks it is almost entirely, if not entirely mental." Bishop, who also suffered from eczema, linked the painful, inflamed swellings of her body with the "morbid swellings of the conscience," a deep sadness rooted in all the losses and pain she experienced in childhood that were not permitted expression.

Based upon Bishop's "The Country Mouse," Lombardi links the onset of Bishop's asthma, and her being "trapped forever within her 'scabby body and wheezing lungs,'" with the repressive nature of her paternal grandparents' household, and its stifling of the female spirit, and also with her mother's unpredictability—"emotionally numb one moment, she would spill over in rivulets of fiery, hysterical emotion the next."

(In "The Country Mouse," Bishop recalls that her

grandfather "smoked thirteen or fourteen cigars a day" and that the house reeked of them. Couldn't this, too, I wonder, have contributed to Bishop's asthma?)

Elizabeth Bishop's poem "O Breath," Lombardi tells us, uses "asthma to describe the stifling pressures that impinge on her life as a poet" and as a lesbian.

> Beneath that loved   and celebrated breast,
> silent, bored really   blindly veined,
> grieves, maybe   lives and lets
> live, passes   bets,
> something moving   but invisibly,
> and with what clamor   why restrained
> I cannot fathom   even a ripple.
> (See the thin flying   of nine black hairs
> four around one   five the other nipple,
> flying almost intolerably   on your own breath.)
>
> Equivocal, but what we have in common's   bound to
>   be there,
> whatever we must own   equivalents for,
> something that maybe I   could bargain with
> and make a separate peace   beneath
> within   if never with.

What is only hinted, Lombardi argues, is "a faint image of erotic coupling, or its aftermath." What we see clearly is the "broken contours" of the poem, and how its "gasping, halting rhythms and labored caesuras mimic the wheezing lungs of a restless asthmatic trying to expel the suffocating air." "O Breath," then, gives "the agonies of asthma visible shape," and how envious the asthmatic is of those who breathe freely, easily, unthinkingly.

Next, I carefully reread Brett C. Millier's biography, *Elizabeth Bishop: Life and the Memory of It*, and read *Elizabeth Bishop: One Art*, a collection of her letters, selected and edited by Robert Giroux. In these volumes, I discover the extent to which Bishop's life was impeded by the quantity of medicines she took to enable her to breathe and the major role that alcoholism, too, played in Bishop's life.

According to Millier,

[S]he was treated with multiple doses of injected adrenaline, sometimes three or four cubic centimeters two or three times a night. Later she experimented with nearly every other possible treatment for asthma, including large does of oral cortisone. The condition dominated her life between 1934 and 1951. It fed her sense of homelessness and sent her away from places she would rather have stayed. A self-proclaimed poet of geography, she often traveled specifically in search of air she could breathe. . . .

Asthma is depressing. Not getting enough oxygen in the bloodstream is chemically depressing, and the fear of an attack, anxiety about breathing, and the limitations the disease can place on the asthmatic's activities and destinations, the sleep lost to nighttime ambushes from unseen enemies, the sense of weakness and betrayal by one's body, the manipulation of one's moods by drugs—all conspire to keep the sufferer from rising above her illness.

. . . The major breakthrough in the management of

chronic asthma—the introduction of corticosteroids into
her therapy in 1952—gave her unprecedented relief
from prolonged attacks. . . . Between 1952 and 1954, she
took oral and injected cortisone over four extended periods. She was subject to most of the drug's major side
effects, including weight gain and extreme nervousness
and sleeplessness, but for a time these seemed a reasonable price to pay to breathe freely. Whatever else the cortisone might have done to her, it always cleared her
lungs. But taking cortisone over a long period in the
spring of 1954, Elizabeth found herself unable to tolerate
. . . the "jag" of sleeplessness and nervousness . . . and
she began to medicate that nervousness with alcohol.
Because she was an alcoholic, she could not control this
drinking on her own. . . . [S]he began a program of aversion therapy using Antabuse, which she maintained,
with a few lapses, until 1964.

Alcoholism. I wonder, as I read Millier, whether Bishop's
alcoholism, which, Lombardi tells us, afflicted her father,
grandfather, and three of her uncles, was, nevertheless,
related to her asthma. I wonder whether she used alcohol to
self-medicate, to stop her coughing, and to blunt the rage
she felt at her disability.

In the edition of her letters, I am pained as I read Bishop's
letters to Dr. Anny Baumann, asking for advice. One, written in 1947, from Nova Scotia, reports that Bishop had
been having severe asthma attacks steadily for weeks.

I was taking about 2cc of adrenaline every night. I guess the two nights on the train didn't help much, and it's been getting worse ever since—I have to take about 2cc during the course of the day and 3 or 4 during the night. I stayed in bed yesterday, thinking if I didn't move it might help, but last night was as bad as ever. There is absolutely nothing here that I can think of that might cause it—the boardinghouse is very clean, it's on the ocean, the animals aren't near, etc. . . .

Maybe this will wear off after a while. The only thing I can think of is that maybe you could suggest a change of medicine or something drastic to break it up.

This is one of the most beautiful places I have ever seen. . . . We want to take a lot of trips and long walks, etc., that's what makes the asthma so discouraging. . . .

I haven't had anything to drink.

Bishop tells us what life was like for a severe asthmatic before contemporary treatment—one that enables someone like myself, who carefully follows my doctor's treatment protocol, to lead a relatively normal, though carefully controlled, life. But despite Bishop's descriptions, I can't even imagine what it felt like to live with asthma, when the only way to breathe freely or to secure temporary relief was through the constant injection of medicines with terrible side effects.

In an interview with Elizabeth Bishop that I read in *The Paris Review*, I learn that Bishop composed her autobiographical "In the Village" as she was being treated with cortisone for a severe asthma attack.

After having made notes for the story, she was "given too much cortisone—I have very bad asthma from time to time—and you don't need any sleep. You feel wonderful while it's going on but to get off it is awful. So I couldn't sleep much and I sat up all night in the tropical heat. The story came from a combination of cortisone, I think, and the gin and tonic I drank in the middle of the night. I wrote it in two nights."

"In the Village" describes how Bishop was routinely abandoned by her mother, how unsafe her home felt, how terrified she was by her mother's unpredictability and her violence, how unwilling her other relatives were to explain what was happening to the young child and why her mother was institutionalized, and how ashamed she was at being required to bring packages addressed to the sanitorium to the post office.

In this autobiographical work, I learn that Bishop explores *why* she got asthma *when* she is having an asthmatic attack. She describes how confused and terrified she was. She tells us how, in response to the events in her life, she began to have trouble breathing. Everything, she wrote, "except the river [that ran close to her home, and that separated where she lived from the sanitorium housing her mother] holds its breath."

What would I have done had I been forced to live like Bishop? Would I have been as intrepid as she was? Lived in Brazil, journeyed to Nova Scotia, Newfoundland, Europe, down the Amazon? Would I have become alcoholic? Could I have published more than the ninety-five poems that Lombardi tells us she published in her lifetime?

I don't travel much. Surely won't go to places now where I can't get good emergency medical treatment. I suspect that I wouldn't have chosen to continue to live had I been forced to live as Bishop did; I don't think I would have had the stamina or the courage. I can't imagine doing productive work under Bishop's circumstances. I feel certain, though, that Lombardi is right when she calls Bishop's poetry "healing."

Reading her life humbles me, makes me grateful that I'm living now, not then. I consider her struggle heroic, her achievement of monumental importance.

According to Bishop's biographer, the poet David Wagoner (who knew Bishop at Yaddo, where she was composing "O Breath") memorialized the poet and her composition of "O Breath" in his own "Poem about Breath (*a memory of Elizabeth Bishop, 1950*)." It reads, in part:

> She was at work on a poem about breath.
> She asked what punctuation might be strongest
> For catching her breath, for breath catching
> Halfway in her throat, between her straining breastbone
> And her tongue, the bubbly catching of asthma. . . .
>
> people with trouble breathing
> Think about it, and breathe, and think about it.
> They think too many times of clearing the air
> They have to breathe, about the air already
> Down there in their lungs, not going out
> On time, in time, and when it's finally gone,
> Not coming back to the place longing to keep it.

Each breath turns into a problem like a breath
In a poem that won't quite fit, giving the wrong
Emphasis to a feeling or breaking the rhythm
In a clumsy way, where something much more moving
Could happen to keep that poem moving and breathing.

When I am still reading about Elizabeth Bishop, I turn to
Marcel Proust. I begin with George D. Painter's two-
volume biography, which provides much important, detailed
information about the onset of Proust's asthma and how
Proust himself interpreted it. But then, exasperated by Painter's attitude—that Proust "used" his asthma to secure the
affection of his mother—I move on to Proust's writings, to
his letters, and I begin *A la recherche du temps perdu*. Then I
read a brilliant article, "Proust's Asthma," by Michael
Wood, illuminating not only Proust's relationship to his illness, but also the puzzling nature of the experience of
asthma itself and how it has been interpreted in medical
textbooks. The major question asthma poses, says Wood, "is
what to do about the unknown; or rather . . . what to do
about the partially, inadequately known, about a condition
which is violent, unmistakable, treatable (some of the time),
intermittent, unpredictable, and (however we read the relation between body and psyche) intimately connected with
the mind and the feelings. . . . [Asthma] does happen, and
when it does happen, it seems to be causeless." Wood
argues that, for Proust, asthma is a kind of language that is
"hidden, strangled, missing"; asthma is "what can't be
said."

     ·   ·   ·

From Painter, I learn that when Marcel Proust's mother was pregnant with him in 1870, the city of Paris was cut off from the outside world by the German army, and Mme Proust, like other Parisians, went hungry. After the Germans entered Paris, there were the terrors of the Commune to be endured. During this period, Mme Proust was terribly fearful for herself and her unborn child. After Proust's father's near death—"he was narrowly missed by a stray bullet," Painter reports—Mme Proust was overcome with shock, and she was moved to a relative's house in the suburb of Auteuil, where Marcel was born. As an infant, he was judged too weak to survive.

Proust believed that "his lifelong ill-health" resulted from his mother's privations when he was *in utero*. And we now have scientific evidence for what Proust understood intuitively: that maternal nutritional deprivation can adversely affect the developing organ systems of the fetus. Proust's mother also believed this: she "felt responsible for history's injury to her unborn child" and "she tried to redeem her guilt with exaggerated care." Proust thought that "she loved him best when he was ill and he tried to win her love by being ill." Painter calls Proust's relationship with his mother "incest." And though Proust seemed devoted to his mother, Painter says that he was surely also deeply enraged at her.

Two events in Proust's life hint at his deep and perhaps not completely acknowledged rage at his mother and suggest that perhaps he unconsciously associated her with an over-ardent affection. After her death, he gave her furniture to a brothel that he frequented, aware that this gift was a profound desecration of her memory. And he often publicly profaned his mother's photo by showing it to friends and asking, "And who the hell's this little tart?" Proust's habit of bringing himself to orgasm by watching young men pierce the bodies of rats with hatpins and beat them to death with sticks also suggests that there was, in his psyche, a deep link between eroticism, helplessness, rage, and bodily affliction.

In Painter's rendering of Proust's life, Marcel gave himself asthma to ensure himself of his mother's continuing care—even though, throughout his life, he battled against her ceaseless vigilance. The key moment in Proust's life (which Proust transformed in his *magnum opus*) occurred when, as a child, his mother neglected to give him his accustomed good-night kiss. This caused Proust such trauma (according to Painter) that he unconsciously chose the life of an invalid to repay her for this single slight.

Proust's father maintained the view that Proust's asthma was neurotically caused. He believed that there was nothing wrong with his sickly, disappointing son that "will-power" wouldn't cure. Dr. Merklen, who treated Proust, also believed that Proust "wanted" to have asthma: Merklen challenged Proust to "unlearn" it.

Painter sees Proust's asthma as self-willed and as evidence of his inherently evil nature. Proust, he tells us, "had sinned through his lungs when in childhood he used his asthma to compel his mother's love, and to punish her fancied refusal of love." Ultimately, in dying from pneumonia, "he was to perish by his lungs."

Proust's friend, the writer André Gide, until nearly the end of Proust's life, believed that Proust exaggerated "his ill-health to protect his work." (This view is also taken in

Diana Festa-McCormick's article, "Proust's Asthma: A Malady Begets a Melody," in *Medicine and Literature*. She argues that "Proust sought not merely refuge, but also identity, in malady," that his asthma was "a weapon" for him, and that he used it as "a valid explanation for a phobia of the outside as the writer became enmeshed in the tentacular world of *Time Past* and the need to shape it." In Festa-McCormick's view it isn't merely that Proust adjusts his life so that he can write a book because he has limited physical and emotional resources due to his illness. Instead, he wants to write a book that requires tremendous effort and so uses asthma to keep himself free enough to pursue his goal. Nevertheless, I find it interesting that McCormick sees Proust's asthma as a way for him to keep himself home so that he wouldn't continually dissipate his energies by living the life he described in *Sodome et Gomorrhe*. In this sense, McCormick sees Proust's asthma as protection against something worse.)

Proust came to believe that he had caused his affliction. He obsessively read works like Ribot's *Diseases of the Will* and Dubois's *The Psychoneuroses*, which claimed that diseases were caused by the unconscious. So, besides suffering from asthma, Proust also believed that his ailment was his own doing.

But as I read Proust's life, I have no doubt that his asthma was related to his severe allergies—he seems to have been allergic to just about everything—and that his condition worsened in emotional crises. When grief-stricken, like after the death of his lover Agnostinelli, or intensely excited, like after he was awarded the Goncourt Prize, he often became extremely ill. His illness was also surely exacerbated by some of the treatments his doctors prescribed for his symptoms. In *A la recherche*, for example, he relates that his doctor prescribed not only caffeine, but also beer, champagne, or brandy—his attacks would subside, he was told, in the "euphoria" induced by the alcohol. Other treatments surely had negative side effects—smoking Espic asthma cigarettes, fumigating with Legras anti-asthma powders, and drugging himself with amyl, valerian, morphine, opium, veronal, trional, and even perhaps mercury enemas (a colleague of Proust's father, Dr. Eduourd Brissaud, author of *Hygiene for Asthmatics*, believed that asthma was caused by worms and should be treated with mercury enemas).

His early childhood, then, became emblematic of everything that he lost in becoming ill. (I immediately think of the loving attention paid to the flowering hawthorn bush in *A la recherche*.) When Proust was deprived of flowers, it was, to him, "torture." Later in life, if his friends wore perfume, he would have an "appalling attack."

As a little boy, Proust's favorite places were the flowerbeds, the giant trees, and the fountains of the gardens of Auteuil and Illiers that he visited on holidays (which he immortalized as the gardens of Combray in *A la recherche*). After he became allergic and had his first asthma attack in 1881, though, when he was almost ten years old, there wasn't a flower—except pansies—that he could have near him without paroxysms of coughing. When he became asthmatic, he was no longer allowed to visit these places and they became for him symbols of everything—the places and the experiences—that his illness denied him. In later life, knowing that he longed for the flowers he loved but could not have around him, a friend, Mlle Nordlinger, gave him presents of flowers worked into enamels or watercolors of trees—objects of beauty to substitute for the pleasure of the living things he could no longer enjoy.

In Proust's letters, I found analogies to my constant search for the causes of my illness. Here is one example.

Saturday [evening 31 August 1901]

My dear little Mama,

"Misery of miseries or mystery of mysteries?" That's the title of a chapter in Dumas, which could apply to me at the present time. After writing to you yesterday, I was taken with uninterrupted asthma and flux, obliging me to walk doubled over, to stop in at every tobacconist's and light [anti-asthma] cigarettes, etc. And the worst of it is, I went to bed at midnight after long fumigations, and three or four hours later came the real summer attack, something quite unprecedented. That had never happened before, outside of my regular attacks. . . . my asthma has been much better today, I've had just a little this evening (it's half-past seven now), but nothing to speak of, I haven't even had to smoke. If it recurs in the next few nights, I shall have to give up my schedule for a while, because my attacks come in the middle of the night, when there's no one to light my candle or to make me something hot when it's over. . . . I think I shall have good nights again. Obviously I don't attribute these incomprehensible attacks to my new life. They must have a definite cause, but I don't know what it is. It's not the Bois, because I'd given it up. . . . Marie thought it might be the saffron she uses . . . but I doubt it. And I wondered while reading a page of Brissaud [*L'Hygiène des asthmatiques*] if I didn't have helminths [worms]. . . . Actually, I'm fine this evening. . . . My slight oppression has passed completely in the course of this talk with you, my dear little Mama, because of the affectionate need I felt for you. I shall have a good night.

With many kisses,

Marcel

In his letters, Proust is always trying to figure out what triggered an asthma attack. Was it the smell of perfume a friend wore? The damp air? That he forgot to shut his window tightly before retiring? Because asthma is such a quixotic disease, Proust seemed as baffled and mystified by what caused his bouts of illness as I have been. Nevertheless, his relentless search for understanding, like mine, continued.

I saw, in reading Proust's life, a parallel to my feelings about how dangerous a place the world is for the severely asthmatic. If flowers trigger asthma, then I'll have to avoid flowers. If mist triggers asthma, then avoid mist. If dampness, then damp. If the smoke from candles, then candles. If dust, then dust. If being in the outside air, then being in the outside air. And so forth and so on until you are avoiding everyplace and everything and spending your life almost entirely in bed, sleeping, resting, and working, as Proust did—once for two years straight and, toward the end of his life, for six and a half days a week. What Proust did, in trying to avoid "triggers," he did not because he was neurotic, as Painter and Festa-McCormick believe, but because he was trying to exert control in a world that had become unfathomable and dangerous. (An alternative to Proust's way was Elizabeth Bishop's: she seems to have concluded that since there was no place she could be sure of being free of asthma, she might as well go exactly where she chose and take her chances. In this sense, Bishop's life, I think, can act as an example for me.)

Proust's addiction to caffeine—he once consumed seventeen cups on a day's journey—was self-medication: theophylline, found in coffee, is used to treat asthma. His chronic sleeplessness, too, and his complaining of heart palpitations was not neurotic but, rather, the aftereffects of the immense quantities of caffeine and other drugs he consumed for relief of his symptoms. (A friend with asthma once suggested that if I ever ran out of medicine and got an attack, drinking several cups of strong coffee would bring it under control.) His overuse of drugs, too, was an attempt on his part to lessen the severity of his attacks. (In overmedicating himself, though, he was often following current medical advice.)

It is a testimony to Proust's strength-of-will and endurance that he could work as intensely as he did and create such a monumental work (of a million and a quarter words) while suffering through disabling bouts of spasmodic coughing. (I think here of Elizabeth Bishop's ninety-five published poems.)

Proust's illness didn't give him the time he needed to write, as Painter maintains; Proust wrote despite his illness and in heroic defiance of its threat to deny him his ability to work.

Proust worked throughout the night and slept through the day. And although Painter interprets this as evidence of his subject's neurosis, I understand why. The night air was probably far easier for Proust to breathe—there was less traffic on the streets, less dust stirred up. Sleeping during the day, according to Proust's own admission, took the edge off his inability to lead a normal life. If he were awake with the sun out but unable to go out, he believed it would have been too easy to succumb to despair.

What Proust suffered from such a severe a case of asthma, I cannot even begin to imagine. When he was too breathless or weak from an attack to speak, he wrote his servant Celeste notes. One reads, "I've just coughed more than three thousand times, my back and stomach are done for, everything. It's madness. I need very hot sheets and woolen pullovers. Remember, all your sheets have a smell that starts my useless coughing. I hope you'll take strict account of my order, otherwise I shall be more than angry."

Often, I'm sure, when so incapacitated, Proust contemplated, as I had, the sweetness of being delivered from his suffering through death. Once, near the end of his life, he "accidentally" poisoned himself by taking an enormous overdose of veronal and opium. Another time, he took an overdose of adrenaline to counteract an overdose of the veronal that he took routinely to induce sleep (for his cough was often so severe that he couldn't sleep unless drugged). And when, at the end of his life, he refused treatment for the pneumonia that killed him, he probably knew he was hastening his demise.

(I ask Ernie if Proust's dying of pneumonia had anything to do with asthma. He tells me that asthmatics are especially prone to pulmonary infection—particularly if the underlying inflammation of the disease is poorly treated or not treated at all, as it was not in Proust's time. If the epithelial lining of the airways is inflamed or denuded, it can become more easily infected. Also, if the asthmatic uses sedation to suppress the cough, then the secretions that are normally cleared from the lungs through coughing pool there, providing a perfect culture medium for bacteria. This is why, he tells me, it is imperative to treat the underlying inflammation with inhaled steroids and not merely suppress the symptoms. This is why all the asthmatics I have spoken to who don't use inhaled steroids are putting themselves at risk.)

Proust had managed to keep himself alive, though, long enough to become famous, long enough to finish *A la recherche*—which is, I believe, the most important literary work ever created describing the consciousness and sensibility of an asthmatic writer.

In Proust's dying moments, he drew the pages of the manuscript littering his bed toward him—he was correcting a typed copy of *La prisonnière*—called out the single word "Mother," and died. When his friends were called in to see Proust's body (with the flowers that he so loved, prohibited in life but now ranged round him in death), one of them, Jean Cocteau, noticed the twenty manuscript volumes of *A la recherche* piled on the mantelpiece, "continuing to live, like the ticking watch on the wrist of a dead soldier."

In reading Proust's life, I learned of the enormity of the losses that Proust—and many asthmatics—are forced to endure because of their disease. Because of his illness, Proust's emotional life was one of continual loss, mourning, longing, and nostalgia. And, in his famous cork-walled room, confined to his bed, surrounded by pillows and bol-

sters, dressed in sweaters, with his dictionaries, works by
Ruskin, notebooks, pens, and pen holders ranged round
him, writing on a piece of paper held high in the air and
dropped on the floor when finished, Proust became the
world's foremost interpreter of the interminable losses that
are a consequence of being human, which we all suffer, but
which he suffered in far greater measure.

The only way that Proust could get back the life that he
had lost in actuality was to imagine it and to write about
it, so that what he had lost, he could give back to himself
through his imagination and through his art. What he lost,
then, could become eternally present to him. Is it too much
to say that the profound sense of loss of time past, the loss
of the places and people that one has loved, which suffuses
Proust's work, and the triumph of time regained, has much
to do with Proust's awareness of the losses he suffered
because of asthma and his awareness, too, of the power of
the imagination in recovering what ill health and time and
circumstance has taken from us? Is it too much to say that
Proust's attempt to recover what he lost through the work of
memory and imagination and writing was, at least in part,
the result of his trying to give himself something of the
many, many things that asthma had wrested from him?

Olive Schreiner

Before I learn that she had severe asthma, all I know about
the late-Victorian South African writer Olive Schreiner is
what I learn about her feminist politics from my friend Jane
Marcus—that she was the too-little-known foremother of
the women's emancipation movement in England—and

what I read about her in a review of her collected letters written by Virginia Woolf.

Woolf noted that Schreiner was well-known for her one remarkable and famous novel, *The Story of an African Farm.* After that, further achievement eluded her, and she was unable to complete another major work, although she labored for years at what Woolf believed was a potentially "stupendous work upon woman." At her death, all that she left behind were incomplete fragments. "The only feeling I have about my life," Schreiner wrote, "is that I have thrown it all away, done nothing with it."

Woolf believed that Schreiner's life exemplified the "discrepancy between what she desired and what she achieved." The major question, for Woolf and for other students of Schreiner's work, has been why Schreiner never fulfilled her early promise.

To Woolf, it was because Schreiner dissipated her energy and wasted her artistic talent in the service of politics, in her commitment to dealing with "sex questions." Schreiner, Woolf believed, was a martyr who sacrificed herself to a political cause. Paradoxically, Woolf observed, Schreiner was too interested in men: "Nothing matters in life but love," Schreiner wrote, a year before she died. And it is true that Schreiner was, in her lifetime, involved with many men, among them Havelock Ellis and Cecil Rhodes.

Schreiner believed that "for a successful sexual union it is absolutely necessary the woman should be materially independent of the man, and have her own work life, otherwise *he* is not free." Her feminist classic, *Women and Labour*, published in 1911, attacked the economic "parasitism" of women. She was a socialist and a staunch anti-imperialist. And she was an advocate for a multiracial, decentralized South Africa, for which, she believed, there were only two substantial political questions: "the native question and the question Shall the whole land fall into the hands of a knot of Capitalists?" She was the first feminist to link sexual and racial oppression.

Woolf acknowledged, though, that Schreiner's asthma might have contributed to her inability to finish another major novel in her lifetime. Schreiner was "driven by asthma," Woolf wrote, "to travel perpetually," and so her life, Woolf concluded, was one of "unrest, dissatisfaction, and, in the end, a profound loneliness." As Schreiner herself once said, "I am only a broken and untried possibility."

After rereading Woolf's essay, I read some of Schreiner's letters. Schreiner was born in 1855, before all the asthmatic writers whose lives I've started looking at (Proust was born in 1871; Elizabeth Bishop, in 1911), and so I am curious about what her letters and accounts of her life will reveal about her attitude toward her illness, and how it was treated, and whether it was similar to or different from Proust's. I am curious, too, about whether Schreiner stopped writing because of her illness.

In a letter to her platonic lover, Havelock Ellis, Schreiner speculated on why she suffered from asthma, and she linked it to the extreme neglect and brutality of her parents in forcing her from her home to earn her living as a governess when she was fifteen years old.

"Did I ever tell you how my chest got bad?" she asked Ellis. "I was four days quite without food, and travelling all the time; I had nothing but a little cold water all that time. I had no money to buy food. . . . I got this horrible agony in my chest, and had to rush out, and for weeks I never lay down, night or day. I suffocated if I even leaned back. Ever since that, if I get to a place that is close, and damp, and *hot*, it comes back. . . . They all say they have never seen a case just like it, and I don't like to tell them how it began. Somehow one can't go back into the past without blaming those that are dearest to one, and it is better to let the past bury its dead, eh?"

Schreiner came to this conclusion about the psychogenic causes of her asthma in 1884.

Elsewhere, Schreiner described herself as homeless, not only because she moved about, but also because she had never known the safety of a nurturing family. "Oh, I've been so desolate all my life. . . . I've never had a home. I've never had anyone to take care of me." As a child, she was the victim of her mother's brutal beatings. "My mother has never been a mother to me," she wrote, "I have no mother." She believed that for abused children like herself, "it would have been far better if they had died as little babies."

Next, I read *The Story of an African Farm* in search of images of breathlessness, and I find them, in abundance. What I find, too, is that Schreiner has transformed her family's household, the neglectful and brutal one that had harmed her irreparably, then cast her out to fend for herself, into a terrifying household where no child is safe, where every child is in grave danger.

The novel was published in 1883 in London under the pseudonym "Ralph Iron." It was written in the middle of the night, when Schreiner was in her early twenties, working ten-hour days to support herself as a governess to a family in the isolated countryside of the South African Karroo. During this extremely difficult period, suffering from asthma, Schreiner lived "in my books"—the works of Herbert Spencer and John Stuart Mill—"and in my scribbling."

The Story of an African Farm was a sensational bestseller and widely discussed because of its bold feminist stance. Lyndall, Schreiner's central character, chooses to live with a man without marrying him. To her childhood friend Waldo, she speaks of the inequity women of her generation faced: "It is not what is done to us, but what is made of us that wrongs us. . . . The world tells us what we are to be. . . . To you it says—*Work!* and to us it says—*Seem!* To you it says . . . as your arm is strong and your knowledge great, and the power to labour is with you, so you shall gain all that human heart desires. To us it says—Strength shall not help you, nor knowledge, nor labour."

To many critics and readers, *The Story of an African Farm* is important because of its outspoken support of the rights of women. To me, the novel is important because it depicts a dangerous household in which the well-being of the children who must live there is continually threatened. To me, Schreiner's socialist/feminist politics originate in the brutality she experienced as a child. As one of her fictional mistreated children says: "I will hate everything that has power, and help everything that is weak."

In *The Story of an African Farm*, Schreiner transformed the household she knew as a child, the one that had harmed her irrevocably, into a chillingly realistic depiction of a chaotic and potentially lethal household where children are offered no protection, only abuse, and where they are expected to work without respite or reward.

Here, as in Schreiner's household, there is no protective mother- or father-figure. Rather, children have been abandoned or neglected. Lyndall says she was created "to feed like a dog from stranger hands." Here, children are caged or beaten brutally for imagined transgressions or for no reason at all by one of the most sadistic characters I've encountered in fiction, the aptly named Bonaparte Blenkins. This is a household where children dare not show their pain—for if they do, they become even more vulnerable—and where they are continually holding their breath, waiting for the next blow to fall, or trying to catch their breath after they've been mistreated.

In the novel, Schreiner recreates the physical abuse she suffered as a child in the sadistic sixteen-lash, blood-letting horsewhipping that Bonaparte Blenkins gives the idealistic young boy Waldo on his naked back. Growing up in this atmosphere, it is no mystery why Schreiner's heroine, Lyndall—witness to this brutality and a fellow sufferer, too—has such difficulty breathing after she leaves the farm (like Schreiner herself) that she feels she is suffocating.

Lyndall compares the restrictions placed upon women with the difficulty she has in breathing in the company of women leading traditional house-bound lives. "It is suffocation only," she remarks, "to breathe the air [traditional women] breathe."

Like Schreiner, Lyndall, though she has done some writing, dies before she fulfills her potential. And her death seems caused by her inability to breathe. To me, Lyndall's death is a fictional representation of what has been reported in the medical literature as suicide by asthma.

"Why am I alone?" Lyndall asks, near death. "I am so weary of myself! It is eating my soul to its core—self, self, self! I cannot bear this life! I cannot breathe, I cannot live! Will nothing free me from myself? . . . I cannot bear it any more! . . . will no one help me?" No one can; no one does.

After *The Story of an African Farm*, Schreiner continued to publish—short stories and essays about the need for racial understanding (*Closer Union, Thoughts on South Africa*), the novella "Trooper Peter Halket of Mashonaland," all fragmentary, and she worked on *From Man to Man* (the monumental novel to which Woolf referred) for more than thirty years throughout her life, without ever finishing it.

When I ask Jane Marcus whether she thinks Schreiner hadn't realized her potential because she was debilitated from asthma, she tells me that Yaffa Draznin, who worked on Schreiner's papers at the Humanities Research Center at the University of Texas, Austin, had done important work on Schreiner's asthma.

Draznin's award-winning article, "Did Victorian Medicine Crush Olive Schreiner's Creativity?" is a classic example of how a careful historian can challenge commonly held misconceptions about a person's life. In its methods and conclusions, it reminded me of Stephen Trombley's *"All That Summer She Was Mad": Virginia Woolf and Her Doctors*. Trombley, like Draznin, questioned "conventional wisdom" about Virginia Woolf—that Woolf was "mad." Instead, Trombley concluded, Woolf's apparent madness was caused by the side effects of the drugs her doctors gave her. Trombley's archival detective work included his combing Woolf's manuscripts and letters for descriptions of her so-called illnesses, and publications like *The Lancet*, for evidence about Woolf's medical treatment. In one issue of *The Lancet*, for example, Trombley found a letter accusing one of Woolf's doctors, Sir George Henry Savage, of "imprudent and excessive use of drugs [with side effects including the symptoms used by earlier critics to prove Woolf 'mad'] as a means of enforcing quiet among patients."

Draznin, too, questioned the accepted analyses of Schreiner's life—that she produced little of value beyond her one famous novel because she was blocked as a writer because she was extremely neurotic, or that she wrote little because she suffered from asthma because she was neurotic. Draznin instead concludes that Schreiner didn't produce as much as she could have in her lifetime or complete what she started because she was severely disabled by the aftereffects of the many varieties and massive doses of drugs prescribed by doctors to relieve the severe distress she suffered because of her asthma (which Schreiner herself believed to be the result of her childhood mistreatment.)

At first, Schreiner adopted the treatment protocol of Dr. Henry Hyde Salter, who wrote *On Asthma: Its Pathology and Treatment* (1864), the definitive nineteenth-century text on asthma. Salter's "treatment" stressed prevention. It involved identifying substances that triggered asthmatic attacks and avoiding them, and avoiding, too, tiredness, stress, and "violent mental emotions." If this didn't work, "the asthmatic was urged to move to some place where the attacks diminished in frequency and severity." (Many critics of Schreiner, even sympathetic ones, it must be noted, have seen her peripatetic existence as clear evidence of her neurosis. But, Draznin says, Schreiner moved so often in order to find a place where she could breathe freely.) Only if this failed, did Salter resort to other measures—drinking hot, strong coffee, smoking strong cigars, the use of chloroform, ether, Indian hemp, and iodine of potassium.

Draznin reports that during Victorian times, doctors were not paid for diagnosis; rather, they were paid for "the drugs they compounded and sold to their patients." An 1888 textbook of pharmaceuticals, Draznin discovered, listed forty-three medicines for asthma.

Until 1884, according to Draznin's research, Schreiner moved from one locale to another to try to ease her asthma. Although she complained about what she suffered in her chest and her lungs, she could still write—she wrote and revised *African Farm*, drafted a second novel, *Undine*, started a third, and wrote some stories and a novella despite her illness.

But in 1884, in London, after Schreiner met Havelock Ellis (then a medical student) and H. Bryan Donkin (a physician), she began to use medication for her asthma. And she started to complain, in her letters, about "violent headaches, pain and weakness in her legs, neuralgia contractions, and gastrointestinal disturbances," about "unexpected outbursts, excessive crying jags, hallucinations, suicidal urges, feelings of dejection or despair . . . weakness." All prevented her from writing or killed her desire to write.

The drugs Schreiner took, Draznin concluded, *caused* Schreiner's disability. They were: high doses of *quinine* (which could produce headache, palpitations, and visual disturbances); *nux vomica* (containing strychnine, which could produce gastrointestinal disturbances and motor impairment); *chloral* (which could cause gastrointestinal disturbance, heart palpitations, pain in the limbs and joints, mental disturbance and memory impairment, exaggerated nervousness, restlessness, morbid states of melancholy, anorexia, and suicidal ideations); *potassium bromide* (causing tremors, weakness, excitement and depression, delusions and hallucinations, lethargy, sleepiness, and violent headaches); and the highly addictive *morphia* (which induced lethargy and sleepiness).

By the middle of 1886, Draznin tells us, Schreiner was "a virtual recluse," her "personal and emotional life was chaotic," and she had what was thought to be a "nervous breakdown."

For Draznin, the drugs Schreiner took did not merely contribute to her lifelong inability to work; they caused it. "As a result of the drug therapy used to relieve her asthma and subsequent drug-related illnesses," Draznin concludes, "Schreiner suffered physical disorders and mental disorientation. . . . Victorian medicine, inadvertently but undeniably, conspired to deprive Olive Schreiner, and the world, of the fruits of her creative genius."

After I reread R.W. B. Lewis's biography of Edith Wharton, articles about Dylan Thomas, and John Updike's autobiography, I stop to list what I have learned so far from reading about the lives and works of writers with asthma.

I've learned that most writers with asthma are, considering how disabling the disease can be, amazingly productive and long-lived.

I've learned that the productivity of writers with uncontrolled asthma is sometimes compromised (Elizabeth Bishop), though, it seems, sometimes not (Marcel Proust).

I've learned that writers with asthma write about their condition often (Updike, Schreiner), and sometimes incessantly (Proust, Bishop), in their letters, journals, and works of art. In their writing, they try to understand and gain some control over this mysterious ailment that has transformed their life.

Writers often overtly link their condition to their parents' abusive behavior and to the overwhelming feelings of uncontrollable terror and vulnerability they felt as children—Schreiner, to her parents' neglectful abuse; Updike, to the terror invoked in him by his mother's rage; Bishop, to her mother's unpredictable, terrifying, insane behavior and to her homelessness after her mother was institutionalized.

Some writers—Elizabeth Bishop, Djuna Barnes, and Marcel Proust—even wrote works while they were in the midst of severe, uncontrolled asthma attacks that linked their asthma with what had happened to them in childhood. It's as if being sick prompted them to speculate, in their works of art, on the reasons why they were sick.

I've learned that the severe aftereffects of the medicines Olive Schreiner took for her asthma so disabled her, both mentally and physically, that she was unable to complete a second major work of fiction in her lifetime. (I suspect, too, that the breakdowns in Edith Wharton's life might be similarly explained.)

I've learned that writers with asthma often self-medicate, sometimes with alcohol, to relieve the distress of their disease or because of their abusive pasts, and that asthmatic writers often abuse drugs and/or alcohol. This adversely affects their life and their work. (I think here of Djuna Barnes, Elizabeth Bishop, Dylan Thomas, Marcel Proust.)

But I've also learned that, without writing, these asthmatic writers would have lived severely impoverished lives. That writing helped to center them, to give them something of import in their lives besides their illness (which could easily overtake their lives), to counteract their feelings of helplessness and vulnerability, and to understand their suffering. Although writing surely has not cured them, surely writing has—though perhaps only temporarily—helped them.

24 "After a traumatic experience, the human system of self-preservation seems to go onto permanent alert, as if the danger might return at any moment. Physiological arousal continues unabated. . . . Traumatic events appear to recondition the human nervous system." This is post-traumatic stress disorder, as described by Judith Herman in *Trauma and Recovery*.

A recent study done at Harvard of patients with post-traumatic stress disorder have demonstrated, by using positron emission tomography, that subjects exposed to traumatic scripts manifested increases in normalized blood flow in right-sided limbic, paralimbic, and visual areas; but showed decreases in the left inferior frontal and middle temporal cortex. Which means that emotions associated with post-traumatic stress disorders activate the body's more primitive nervous system, unmediated by higher cognitive processes, and that the "reexperiencing" aspect of the disorder also includes visualizing (or revisualizing) a traumatic event.

Asthma is but one of many possible manifestations of post-traumatic stress.

An article, "Childhood Sexual Abuse in Patients with Paradoxical Vocal Cord Dysfunction," by Michael R. Freedman, Ph.D., Samuel J. Rosenberg, Ph.D., and Karen B. Schmaling, Ph.D., in *The Journal of Nervous and Mental Disease* (1991, 179:5) reports on the recently recognized psychosomatic disorder, paradoxical vocal chord dysfunction (adduction of the vocal chords on inspiration; abduction on expiration) "typically misidentified as bronchial asthma," though it might coexist with genuine cases of asthma, in patients reporting "a history of childhood sexual abuse."

One thirty-eight-year-old woman, diagnosed with asthma at five, reported a severe reemergence of her symptoms after a fight with her father "when he called her a 'slut'" for planning a vacation with a male friend. She reported that, between the ages of ten and fourteen, she had vaginal and oral intercourse with her drunk father and, afraid that she would be beaten, she had "remained silent." A thirty-one-year-old woman diagnosed with unmanageable asthma (and a history of substance abuse, depression, and suicidal behavior) had been abused by her father, probably while her mother knew, yet she maintained close contact with her parents.

The authors hypothesize that "the symbolic meanings associated with the function of opening or closing bodily orifices and passages" and a "history of oral sexual abuse" might contribute to the "specificity" of the dysfunction of this particular organ system, and that this physical symptom may have developed to express psychological difficulties. "Does this symptom," they ask, "effectively, albeit unconsciously, recapitulate an abuse relationship?"

After I published my book on the sexual abuse that Virginia Woolf suffered in her girlhood and young adulthood, and its effect on her life and work, I received letters from scores of incest survivors (both women and men), and talked to many, many more as I traveled through the United States and Canada to speak about my work. I was at first surprised that my book elicited such an outpouring of personal testimony from common readers— I believed it would interest only scholars. But one reader told me it was because realizing that someone as famous as Woolf could lead a productive life, while grappling with the aftershock of her personal history, was inspiriting. Often, too, in these letters, I was told of what my correspondent had endured— chronic depression, suicide attempts, alcoholism, drug abuse, morbid obesity, panic attacks, agoraphobia, anorexia, bulimia, gastrointestinal problems—that they now believed were related to their early, traumatic experiences.

Once, in an overheated auditorium in New York City before my talk, a woman introduced herself as a survivor, then asked if I would mind if she lay down on the floor to listen to me because she had had serious and disabling back pain since her teens. Another time, in a bookstore in Washington, D.C., a young woman told me that although she had driven from Virginia and wanted to stay, she might have to leave because she suffered from migraines and feared one was coming on. In New Haven, Connecticut, a woman showed me the disfiguring eczema on her arms and legs: "I have come to regard this," she said, "as a badge I wear for courage under fire"; her father had forced her and her sister to have sex with his bowling buddies; he kept a Polaroid handy to make a weekly record of his daughters' degradation. In Boston, a woman told me she used to "cut" herself. And in Toronto, a woman told me she had nearly died, twice, from severe asthma attacks: "While it was going on," she said, "I held my breath and looked at the mirror and told myself it wasn't me I was seeing."

The body remembers. The body communicates.

In Dusseldorf, Germany, early in 1988, a seventeen-year-old woman called Melanie, who has become increasingly withdrawn and uncommunicative in school, suddenly develops a serious breathing disorder: she feels she is suffocating, and fears that she will die.

In April 1988, Melanie visits her sister and tells her that, for the last several years, her father has been coming into her bed against her will, and stroking, kissing, and licking her breasts and vagina. He tried to sleep with her, too, but stopped "because it hurt her so much." Instead, she has "to gratify him with her hand." The sister replies that he has done "the same to her for years"; this is why she's left home.

After, each sister tells their mother, who becomes extremely upset, and promises to confront their father, but, instead, does nothing.

Melanie's breathing difficulties worsen, and she seeks

and receives medical care. Her doctor diagnoses "bronchial irritations" and treats her.

In September, a teacher speaks to Melanie about why she seems so depressed, why her academic performance has slumped. Melanie tells her teacher about the incest and makes her promise not to tell; the teacher keeps her word.

A few days later, Melanie tells a neighbor, who informs the youth welfare office. Melanie is admitted into a home and the police press charges against her father. Melanie continues attending school; no one talks to her about what she's endured; she receives no psychotherapy; and she is returned to her parents' home at Christmas.

In January 1989, Melanie becomes completely withdrawn. Her breathing difficulties now become acute and dangerous. The doctor who treats her notes her "marked respiratory distress" and diagnoses "bronchial asthma" triggered by dog and cat hair. On her fourth visit to the hospital in 1989, Melanie reports the incest and, finally, psychotherapeutic treatment is offered to Melanie and her parents.

Melanie's story—typical of the thirty-two youngsters he studied—is reported by Eugen E. Jungjohann in "Symptom as a Message: Psychosomatic Reactions as Signals in Sexual Exploitation of the Child," *Acta Paedopsychiatrica* (1990, 53:1). Jungjohann believes that incestuous households "do not allow the child to inform the outside world about its experiences of violence" and that, following futile attempts to get the help they need from neighbors, teachers, and healthcare and government workers, "the children . . . give up further reports of their experiences of violence and . . . incest" and begin to communicate instead "in a semeiotic way, by means of body language," by becoming "physically ill" in a way that requires treatment. In Melanie's case, it was only after fifteen more months of further sexual exploitation that "the asthmatic state" finally acquired Melanie "an audience." Melanie had at first tried assertive verbal communication; when it failed, her body resorted to telling her story through physical signs that indicated Melanie's helplessness. When violence or abuse begins early (before language is acquired) or is unstoppable by using language, Jungjohann believes, physical signs—hysterical conversion symptoms— inevitably substitute for spoken communication.

Many studies of deaths in young people from asthma (summarized in Margaret S. Friedman, Psy.D., "Psychological Factors Associated with Pediatric Asthma Death: A Review," *Journal of Asthma*, 1984, 21:2) report the puzzling observations that, before dying, the youngsters exhibited "preterminal anxiety, emotional lability, and panicked behavior, . . . wild thrashing, aggressive outbursts, crying, screaming, hysteria, and psychological decompensation," even regression "to infantile levels (rocking and sucking objects) for hours or even days during attacks." It has also been observed that "the dying asthmatic seems to give up the struggle to breathe," and that the "death was preceded by loss of confidence, feelings of helplessness, [and a state resembling] depressive psychosis." Can it be that these physical signs, which puzzle the doctors who observe them, indicate a kind of conversion hysteria—outward physical manifestations of an abuse that, as Jungjohann argues, cannot be otherwise communicated?

An article, "When the Body Remembers," in the
March/April 1994 issue of *Psychology Today*, reports on a
study about the prevalence of asthma and breathing difficulties in adults with multiple personality disorder, a condition linked with abuse. In therapy, six of the subjects
"recalled having been choked as a child into unconscious-
ness by their abusers." Bennett Braun, M.D., a psychiatrist,
concludes: "It's possible that strong emotions, like anxiety,
trigger somatic memories of this experience and the person
starts to constrict his or her larynx, unconsciously reliving
the abuse."

While I am writing *Breathless*, I begin reading Michael
Ryan's extraordinary autobiography, *Secret Life*. I am drawn
to it because it is about how Ryan was sexually abused as a
boy of five and how he connects this experience with his
compulsive sexuality. Sexual abuse is a subject I continue to
study.

In *Secret Life*, Ryan tells how a neighbor's handsome son,
Bob Stoller, just back from Korea, started taking pictures of
him—as an angel and as a devil—with his mother's consent, in his photography studio (which also housed his gun
collection). Ryan's detailed, minute-by-minute account
shows how an innocent, trusting child can be turned into
the victim of a sexual abuser.

Soon, Stoller asked Ryan to undress himself before don-
ning a costume, and, incrementally, Stoller's words of praise
and hugs (which, of course, made Ryan feel special) and
seemingly accidental touching of Ryan's genitals escalated
into a request for Ryan to take a bath and, while bathing,

show Stoller how he masturbated. "Did I ever make it stiff so it stood out straight?" Stoller asked. "I said I did, looking down shyly. . . . Then he asked if I would touch myself and show him how I did it."

Stoller promised Ryan this would be their special secret. He toweled Ryan off and "now it felt dreamy and warm . . . and he told me to put my arms around his neck to steady myself while he did it and I did, in a swoon, the classic gesture of surrender and embrace."

After, Stoller began caressing Ryan, told him there was an even better secret they could share, and taught him to suck his penis. "Sometimes," Ryan says, "I still remember how it felt and tasted: hot—hotter than the temperature in my mouth—and it pushed my mouth open as wide as it could, too wide, it was too much in my mouth."

Stoller told Ryan that if he ever told anyone about what they did, Stoller would be sent to jail. "Because no one else could understand our secret, just like my playing with myself in the bathtub."

Stoller abused Ryan for a year. Ryan kept his promise to Stoller until he wrote *Secret Life*. But the consequences of Stoller's abuse have been long-lasting.

As a child, Ryan believed he was guilty for what Stoller had done to him. When the nuns in the Catholic school he attended told him about the Last Judgment, about being reunited with loved ones, Ryan said "I knew I wouldn't be."

And then the asthma attacks started and, to Ryan, they were punishment for what he had experienced.

I started having asthma attacks. They came in the middle of the night, and I would wake up choking, unable to breathe, still the most terrifying sensation I've ever had. It's like drowning, but if you inhale hard enough, with all your strength, you can get a teeny, teeny breath of air, enough to keep you alive. Then you have to do it again, and again, and very soon your lungs and chest muscles are excruciatingly sore, so that getting that teeny breath hurts more every time. The more afraid you are, the worse it gets, and the worse it gets, the more afraid you are. I'd wake up knowing I was dying—the punishment I deserved. . . .

[T]he asthma attacks continued. Nothing helped. . . . The attacks came only at night, and I began to be afraid to go to sleep.

Inhale. Exhale. Inhale. Exhale.

25 When I first get asthma, I sneak off to the bathroom to take my medicine. Soon, though, I start taking my drugs in public when I need them, at dinner tables, in restaurants, at concerts, during my office hours at Hunter College, in the classes I teach, at the podium when I'm lecturing. Someone tells me that this is a radical act. I hadn't thought of it that way, but it's true that although there are millions of asthmatics, I've never seen anyone (except, recently, the Olympic gold medalist Tom Dolan) do their asthma drugs in public.

I've never taken illicit drugs (except one inhale of a marijuana cigarette in the seventies when everyone was smoking—it made me sick), yet, sometimes I adopt the persona of a junkie as I pull out my medicines, and announce, with a pseudo-hip air, "Drugs." Some of my students, former bona fide hipsters, who know how straight I am, think this is very funny. I do it to amuse them, also to turn my dependence on these drugs into an act that suggests I'm doing this to be cool.

I carry around a plastic bag with the meds I take every day—Atrovent, Vanceril—and Ventolin and an Epi-pen (an injection) for emergencies, and a water bottle so I can rinse after I take Vanceril.

When people see me take my drugs, they often tell me that they, too, have asthma. Or they tell me about their uncle who died of it. They share stories of breathing difficulties, of near tragedies, of strategies for survival, of remedies that worked.

There is, I have learned in writing this book, an asthma underground. Once I start paying attention, I find stories about asthma, about labored breathing, about breathlessness, everywhere.

A student of mine at Hunter College comes to class late. She has been writing eloquently about her lifelong struggle with asthma, about how, as a girl, she had been unable to join into games of jump rope, or of hide-and-seek, and how she was taunted by her classmates.

She apologizes, settles into her seat. I hear her labored breathing, and ask her if she's all right. She says she hopes so. She tells the class that her baby was wheezing so badly, she had to take her to the hospital. A neighbor she trusts will stay there with her daughter until her classes are over for the day; she doesn't want to miss any more, she's been out too much this term.

She tells us that every child who lives in her apartment house in Harlem has asthma.

I ask her why. She tells me she can't figure it out, but there was a gunfight in her neighborhood last night, and the kids always seem much worse after. What she wants, she tells us, is a peaceful life for herself and her daughter. She has a feeling that if she could live calmly, they would both be much healthier.

I tell her I think she's right. I know that in Britain, the asthma mortality rate rose significantly during 1940, the year in which the Germans began their heavy bombing raids.

breathless, adjective. 1. with the breath held, as in suspense, astonishment, or fear. 2. causing loss of breath, as from excitement, anticipation, or tension.

On May 23, 1996, the program *All Things Considered* on National Public Radio reported that the South Bronx in New York City, the poorest congressional district in the country, has "one of the highest asthma rates" in the United States—up to ten times that of the national average. The community's economy depends largely upon waste recycling. And it is the pollutants released by this industry, residents believe, that are primarily responsible for the severe breathing difficulties of the people who live in this neighborhood.

The Hunt's Point peninsula of the South Bronx is home to dozens of waste transfer stations, garbage dumps, junk yards, recycling centers, and a sewage treatment facility. A fertilizer plant produces two hundred twenty tons of dried fertilizer pellets each day from sludge (or human excrement) that used to be dumped at sea; the sludge is trucked in daily from the city's sewage treatment plants.

Hunt's Point is also home to fifteen thousand people. The air here, because of these industries, is especially tainted. Often, it is so foul that people can't go outside. And it is the children who are most affected.

Melissa Block, a reporter for NPR, visited P. S. 48 in Hunt's Point, where at least half the school district's eleven hundred children have asthma. She visited school nurse Barbara Loyadis's office, and learned that, over the past three years, the incidence of asthma has soared among these children.

Loyadis herself suffers from asthma. In the three years since she's worked at P. S. 48, her three annual asthma attacks have escalated to three or four every day. Loyadis has decided that, despite her loyalty to these children, for the sake of her health, she must retire. She can leave, and, perhaps, her asthma will improve. But the children can't.

Though more children in Hunt's Point are getting sick, the community has no medical facility to treat asthmatic children in crisis. The closest medical facility is Lincoln Hospital in the Bronx, several miles away, where the rooms for treating asthma are often full.

When NPR reporter Block visited Lincoln Hospital, she observed a doctor treating Hazel, a six-month-old baby, back in the emergency room, soon after she left the hospital after a weeklong stay. Hazel has had asthma since she was three months old.

Lincoln Hospital reports fifteen thousand emergency room admissions and more than two thousand yearly admissions for asthma. And twenty-two deaths. (The Centers for Disease Control and Prevention in Atlanta have reported that blacks, from birth to twenty-four years old, are four to six times more likely to die of asthma than whites. Blacks who are poor, on Medicaid, and who live in urban areas— particularly in New York City and in Cook County, Illinois—are especially affected.)

Doctor Harold Osborne, director of emergency medicine at Lincoln, says that indoor pollution—from cigarette smoke, dust mites, cockroaches, and rodents and the insecticides used to treat them—besides air pollution, plays a significant role in what Osborne refers to as an "asthma epidemic" that is raging in the South Bronx.

A kindergarten teacher, Ina Nager, says that the kids bring their asthma "pumps to school the way children used to bring G.I. Joe." Stop and talk to the kids in the school yard at P. S. 48 (if the wind direction that day makes it possible for them to go outside), and they'll tell you how they, or their mother, or their cousin or best friend has asthma. Several schoolchildren at P. S. 48 spend half an hour of each school day hooked up to nebulizers, plastic masks strapped onto their faces, inhaling medicated steam to open their airways.

To Nager, a five-year-old child "shouldn't have to worry about breathing. That seems to be a God-given right, and it seems to be taken away from them, and that is the shame of our country. When children can't breathe, how can they possibly learn?"

The teachers, too, have gotten sick. They complain of "asthma, headaches, dizziness, nausea, and nosebleeds."

As a lesson in community action, a fourth-grade teacher

at P. S. 48 helped pupils write letters to President Clinton asking for his aid. In reply, the children received a boiler-plate letter thanking them for writing to him about their concern for the environment. He encouraged them to recy-cle, use mass transit, and think about making a career in environmental technology.

The children wrote back.

"Dear Mr. Clinton. Thank you for the letter, but you didn't do anything about the pollution. We told you once and you didn't do anything. We're getting sick because of the pollution."

Antoinette Mildenberger, a school aide who lives in the neighborhood, calls what is happening in Hunt's Point "environmental racism." Almost all the students in Hunt's Point are African-American or Latino. And all are poor. Mildenberger asks, "Why is the Bronx targeted for gar-bage? . . . Is that all they think we're good for?"

Friday, May 24, 1996, Rachel L. Swarns of *The New York Times* reported that nearly eight hundred children were evacuated from Bronx elementary school P. S. 4, after a chemical plant, Clay-Park Labs at 1700 Bathgate Avenue, directly across the street from the school, "spewed throat-burning, eye-watering fumes into the school's open win-dows, leaving some children vomiting and struggling for breath."

Fifty-three children and nineteen adults were treated for nasal burns and sore throats. A photograph accompanying the article showed seven-year-old Milagra Briggs, in tears, as she watched her teacher, Sheila Morris, being given oxygen. Another showed first-grader Charles Robinson, his face strapped to an oxygen mask, being carried into an E.M.S. vehicle after being overcome by chemical fumes.

It was reported that Clay-Park Labs would be cited by New York City's Department of Environmental Protection for "unlawful emission of air contaminants." Bernard Ettinger, the president of Clay-Park Labs, denied that his company was responsible for the calamity. The amount of the chemical released, he argued, was too small to cause such an extreme reaction. He suggested that the chlorine from the school's pool was the more likely caustic agent.

A study appearing in the March 26, 1992, *New England Journal of Medicine* reported that the cost of asthma-related illness (including hospital care, physicians' services, medications, and work loss) in the United States in 1990 was estimated to be $6.2 billion, with the cost of medicines approaching $1 billion.

But what is considered a "cost" to one person is considered an "earning" to another. Put another way, hospitals, doctors, and pharmaceutical corporations earned roughly $3.6 billion dollars treating asthmatics. The treatment of asthmatics is a very nice-sized business. The increase in asthma rates, I remark to myself, after reading this study, though very bad for people, is very good for the health care and pharmaceutical industries.

Recently, a mailman delivered a registered letter to our home about the proposed expansion of the elementary school, the one my children attended, just a block away from where we live. The letter invited us to respond to the Environmental Protection Agency. Would the new building, it inquired, potentially impact upon any wetlands that we knew about?

Although I am surely against the degradation of New Jersey's few remaining wetlands, none of which is near the elementary school, this letter seemed ludicrous.

The elementary school is next to Route Four, a six-lane highway. Eastbound, it is a major commuter route from the bedroom communities of Bergen County to the George Washington Bridge and into New York City. Westbound, it provides a direct link from New York to the malls located in Hackensack and Paramus. In the mornings and evenings, when traffic is at its peak, the stench of exhaust fumes fills the air.

I have watched for years as the trees that line the Route Four corridor have weakened and died. I am watching, now, as a stalwart old tree on the school's front lawn, one that has shaded many class picnics, many springtime commencements, begins to sicken. What, I often wonder, will be the long-term effect on the health of these children (and on my family's) from breathing the neighborhood's carbon-monoxide-ridden air?

I am caring for my grandson Steven, and, to pass the time, I pick up the March 1996 issue of *Natural History*. I read "The Tenacious Scientist and the Elusive Fish Killer Phantom," an article about the work of scientists who discovered the organism *Pfiesteria piscicida*, which is responsible for fish kills along the North Carolina and other coasts.

Although the organism (a dinoflagellate) has been around for millions of years, its existence has only been discovered recently. It can kill fish anywhere, but it is deadliest in polluted water.

In laboratories, infected fish, exhibiting sores and signs of neurological impairment, often die near aerators, as though they are starving for oxygen.

In 1993, Howard B. Glasgow, Jr. and JoAnn Burkholder, two researchers working with the organism, came into contact with neurotoxic aerosols that escaped from the "hot zone" of their laboratory through a faulty ventilating system. Both became extremely ill. Their symptoms, like those of the infected fish, included extreme respiratory distress. (They also suffered from severe stomach cramps, eye irritation, blurred vision, erratic heart beat, short-term memory loss, and cognitive impairment.) For eight days Burkholder couldn't form a sentence; now, every time she tries to exercise, she winds up with bronchitis or pneumonia. Burkholder maintains that, as her experience indicates, contact with this organism can affect humans. She maintains, too, that water pollution from human and animal sewage has stimulated the most deadly effects of this organism.

(As I am finishing *Breathless*, an article on the subject appears in the August 27, 1996 *Science Times*. It reports that Burkholder's contention is a touchy subject in North Carolina, which has recently grown to become a top hog producer, because swine excrement has been implicated in the fish kills. Burkholder has received anonymous phone calls threatening her, saying that "if I knew what was good for me, I would drop the research—only more bluntly than that.")

breath, noun. 1. the air inhaled and exhaled in respiration. 2. respiration, esp. as necessary to life.

On Tuesday, May 7, 1996, an article appearing in the *New York Times* reporting on an article appearing in *Nature*, related that a group of scientists, working in mountain forests of the Adirondacks in northern New York and the Green Mountains in Vermont had, for the first time, linked "patterns of heavy-metal pollution directly to a physical response in the trees."

The Adirondacks and Green Mountains are "routinely bathed in clouds laden with a stew of acids and other pollutants that travel hundreds of miles from power plants, refineries, ore smelters, and vehicles in the industrial Midwest."

Red spruce in these forests are especially susceptible; many, many trees have died. The growth rate of surviving trees has declined severely.

Dr. Andrew J. Friedland, co-author of the report, said that studying this species might provide a window into the effect of pollutants on other species of trees "in the same way that we can learn the most about the health effects of air pollution by studying the most susceptible people, like asthmatics."

On Thursday, May 9, 1996, an article appearing in the *New York Times* summarized the findings of an environmental group, the Natural Resources Defense Council. It estimates that more than five thousand deaths in the Los Angeles area, more than four thousand in New York, and more than fifty-six thousand deaths nationwide each year are caused by fine particles in air pollution (caused by coal-fired power plants and gas- and diesel-burning engines), which are not now regulated by air pollution controls because these now only supervise large particle pollution. The deaths associated with small particle pollution "are mostly among people who already have breathing problems, including asthmatic children and some elderly people." They cluster mostly in metropolitan areas, such as Chicago, Philadelphia, Detroit, Pittsburgh, St. Louis, and Cleveland.

A spokesperson for the electric utilities industry said that cutting down on particle pollution raises electric bills and "costs billions of dollars a year"; a representative of the American Automobile Manufacturers' Association said that "the case against small particles had not been proved" and he urged further study before tightening current Federal standards; and a spokesperson for the American Mining Association said that the research was "junk science" and that the report would "needlessly alarm Americans."

On Friday, June 14, 1996, an article appearing in the *Boston Globe* summarized the proceedings of a worldwide conference on asthma being held in London under the headline "Studies Appear to Rule Out Pollution as Raising Asthma Rate."

The findings of two studies, which, "doctors said . . . cleared air pollution as a cause of a worldwide increase in asthma cases," concluded that because air pollution had "dropped dramatically since the 1950s" throughout the world, and there had nevertheless been a significant worldwide surge in asthma, it was illogical to conclude that air pollution was a major factor in its increase.

Instead, researchers reported that asthma is best understood as "an abnormal reaction of the immune system," and that it was imperative that researchers discover "what caused changes in the immune system" because, "once there, [they] seemed to be permanent."

The condition, researchers now believe, "might start in infancy or before birth." Risk factors, such as smoking, diet, and living in houses "sealed off from the outside world were all important factors that needed to be studied more."

On Friday, June 21, 1996, Reuters Ltd. summarized a Harvard Public School of Health report done for the American Lung Association, based upon a survey of thirteen U.S. cities. It "found that exposure to ground-level ozone, or smog, was linked to up to 50,000 emergency room visits" a year and to "the prevalence and severity of asthma, and respiratory ailments involving coughing, shortness of breath, and chest pain."

The Association urged Congress not to retreat from the nation's commitment to cleaner, healthier air. "Any member of Congress needing more evidence," Fran Du Melle, an official of the association, remarked, "should talk with patients and staff in a hospital emergency room."

What do I make of this?

I believe that asthma is a breathing disorder that is caused by abuse and that it is probably a manifestation of post-traumatic stress. I believe that asthma tells us that the person who has it is, or once was, so terrified that s/he feared s/he would die.

I believe that asthma is caused by terror, by trauma, by abuse (of a child, of the environment), by deprivation.

I believe that in the life history of a person who has asthma, there has been a (perhaps abusive) crisis or crises— emotional, physical, sexual, environmental—during which the infant's or child's natural ability to breathe freely has been severely compromised.

I believe that asthma is difficult to treat because it is necessary to "retrain" the now-automatic responses to stress and stimuli, to the organism's state of near-permanent alert. And I believe that there can be no "cure" for asthma, nor any diminution in the numbers of people afflicted, unless the link between terror and asthma and abuse and asthma is recognized.

What I believe we need to do to stop the alarming increase in the number of asthma cases:

1. Stop abusing the planet. Clean up the air.
2. Stop abusing our children, stop terrorizing them, stop sexually abusing them.
3. Stop trauma. (This includes stopping war.)

How optimistic am I about our doing this?

Not very.

My student Leota Lone Dog, a Lakota Indian living in New York, tells me about "Trail of the Otter," a contemporary Native dance performed by Muriel Miguel, a Kuna-

Rappahannock Indian, and Floyd Flavel, a Cree Indian. In "Trail of the Otter," which draws from contemporary Native American legends about an otter named "Lola," a cough, followed by heavy breathing—a signal that the oxygen in the Earth's atmosphere is being depleted—is the first sign Lola recognizes of what will be an impending environmental disaster. In the dance, Lola brings the message of her witnessing the breathlessness, sickening, and death of members of her species and its eventual extinction. The dance is both testimony and warning: If one species inhabiting the Earth becomes extinct because its environment has become ravaged, eventually, all species inhabiting the Earth (including human beings) will become extinct.

In today's mail comes the latest *Self-Care Catalog*. It advertises a new product, "a hat that's a portable, wearable air filter." The hat comes with a face screen, a filter, a tiny electric blower, and a battery pack that you wear on your belt.

Anyone who suffers from sensitivity to airborne contaminants "knows the routine during EPA alerts: Stay inside, avoid activity," the ad reads. "Well, what if gardening sounds like more fun?" Wearing this new breakthrough product, though, allows you to go outside "even during . . . pollution alerts."

This ad scares me. Everyone I know drinks bottled water or has a water purifier. Those of us who have it spend money on consumer products to assure ourselves that the water we drink is uncontaminated. We have, it seems, given up our right to pure water without much of a struggle.

How long will it be until those of us who can afford

it will hook ourselves up to portable air purifiers to go
outside?

I sometimes wonder who is the more highly evolved. The
person who responds adversely to chemical fumes, exhaust
fumes, cigarette smoke, noxious odors, trauma, or the person who doesn't. Maybe, I tell myself, I'm like the canary in
the mineshaft. Maybe my gasping for air is information
that other, less sensitive people should heed. Maybe the fate
of the planet depends upon people like me whose responsive bodies are telling us all that there's something very
wrong going on around here. As John Updike put it in *Self-
Consciousness*, "We move and have our being within a very
narrow band of chemical conditions, on a blue-skinned
island of a planet from which there is no escape, save for
the legendary few who have enjoyed space travel or bodily
ascension."

26 I'm grabbing a slice of pizza for lunch, near
Hunter, and I bump into an acquaintance I haven't
seen for a couple of years. She tells me I look wonderful. Asks me if I'm still sick. I tell her I'm much better,
but that it takes a lot to keep me well. I sketch what my life
is like. Briefly.

"It's wonderful that you've recovered," she beams, "and
that you've taken responsibility for your illness."

Suddenly, I'm furious, and I excuse myself as graciously
as I can, pleading an appointment.

I storm down the street. Recovered? I haven't recovered.

I'm dealing with asthma daily. She wants to think that, though I was broken, I am now fixed, and that I have fixed myself. I want her to understand that I am what I am, whatever that may be.

Today, on my drive into New York, I stop paying attention for a couple of seconds, forget to hit the recirculate button in my car as I pass the sewerage treatment plant on the Hudson, and, suddenly, I'm coughing so hard I think I'll have to stop the car on the highway because I'm afraid I'll faint. But stopping on the side of the West Side Highway is dangerous, and if I stop the car, I might find myself in trouble. So, I begin to count my exhales, search my bag for my Atrovent, pump myself full of drugs, pray that they'll kick in quickly, that I'll be fine, that I can get off the highway safely.

Inhale. Drown. Cough. Cough. Splutter. Cough. Force the exhale. Better.

Why should I have to take responsibility for my asthma? I ask myself. How can I personally take responsibility for assuring the purity of the air I breathe?

I see the perniciousness of the word "recovery," for it suggests that the illness or the condition (asthma, whatever) is over, though it isn't. It suggests, too, that people are personally responsible for curing their illnesses. I realize that I am against the neatness and the lie of what I suddenly recognize as the comforting arc of the recovery narrative. The narrative that says, in essence, I was sick, I suffered, I did this and that and the other thing, I figured it out, I made changes, I'm now much better, don't worry, there's nothing urgent we really need to do as a people to help prevent

asthma—every asthmatic can take personal responsibility
for their recovery.

In the true American tradition of Benjamin Franklin, I,
the imperfect asthmatic, try to improve myself, and, lo and
behold, I succeed. I make myself over. I cure myself. And
I am a much, much better person for it. Because of my
ordeal, I have discovered inner peace/my own strength/
things I never knew before/a community of likewise
afflicted people. Because of my ordeal, I have entered the
morally superior realm of people who are "in recovery"
and I can look down my nose at all of those morally inferior poor slobs out there, still suffering from this or from
that, who haven't had the will/strength/grit/gumption/
desire to accomplish what I have accomplished. In fact, if I
didn't have asthma, I would go out and find a way to *get*
asthma, because having asthma and recovering from it was
such an amazingly important learning experience.

Still, the next time someone asks me how I am, I
find myself unable to fracture the form of this by-now-
comfortable narrative and tell my story in the most subver-
sive, hostile, irritating way I can. For I realize that the story
people want to hear from me about my illness is a story
that will make them feel better. I only hope that the story
I tell here, at least in part, isn't that story. I must admit,
though, that during the months I am writing *Breathless*,
I have been taking less medicine. I have been breathing
more easily.

Before I got asthma, my sentences were as long as Virginia Woolf's; they went on for the better part of a para-

graph; they contained lots of dependent clauses, lots of semicolons.

After I get asthma, I start writing very short sentences. Then I start fracturing my sentences. Like this. A friend tells me that my new way of writing is driving her so crazy, she can't read my stuff anymore. I sound like a moron. A sixth-grader. Can't I, please, go back to writing the way I used to?

For a couple of days, I try. I pull some sentences together; try semicolons, my by-now-unfamiliar friend. But it's impossible. My body, my breathing, are different. So my writing is different. I'm not the same self I once was. Not the self who can take in enough air to exhale long, deep, complex sentences. These sentences that chop and sputter their way through space are the only ones I can now write.

It is 11 P.M. I am lying awake in bed, alone. I think that I am going to die. I can't catch my breath. I feel like I'm suffocating, like I am trying to draw in air through the tiniest of straws, as if I am trying to breathe through a roomful of sodden feathers. I feel that I am drowning, drowning. I have the telephone number of the police plugged into my portable phone so that I can get help by hitting the "Send" button.

I try not to panic. Panic will only make it worse. I put on the earphones to my Walkman. Listen to a relaxation tape.

"Lie down now, and make yourself very, very comfortable.

"Relax your face. Relax your neck. Relax your shoulders.

"Concentrate on your breathing."

I listen to the tape three times. By the third go-round, I'm relaxed enough to drift off to sleep. Tonight, I'm lucky, I tell myself. Tonight, it worked. But what about tomorrow?

breathless, adjective. 1. without breath or breathing with difficulty; gasping; panting. 2. with the breath held, as in suspense, astonishment, or fear. 3. causing loss of breath, as from excitement, anticipation, or tension. 4. dead, lifeless.

breath, noun. 1. the air inhaled and exhaled in respiration. 2. respiration, esp. as necessary to life. 3. life, vitality.

Library of Congress Cataloging-in-Publication Data

DeSalvo, Louise A., 1942–
    Breathless: an asthma journal / Louise DeSalvo.
        p.   cm.
    ISBN 0-8070-7096-3
    1. DeSalvo, Louise A., 1942—Health.   2. Asthma—Patients—United
States—Biography.   I. Title.
    RC591.D47   1997
    362.1'96238'00092
    [B]—DC21   96-46405

The Land and People of Holland

The LAND and
PEOPLE of
HOLLAND

BY ADRIAAN J. BARNOUW

Portraits of the Nations Series

J. B. Lippincott Company
Philadelphia · New York

Contents

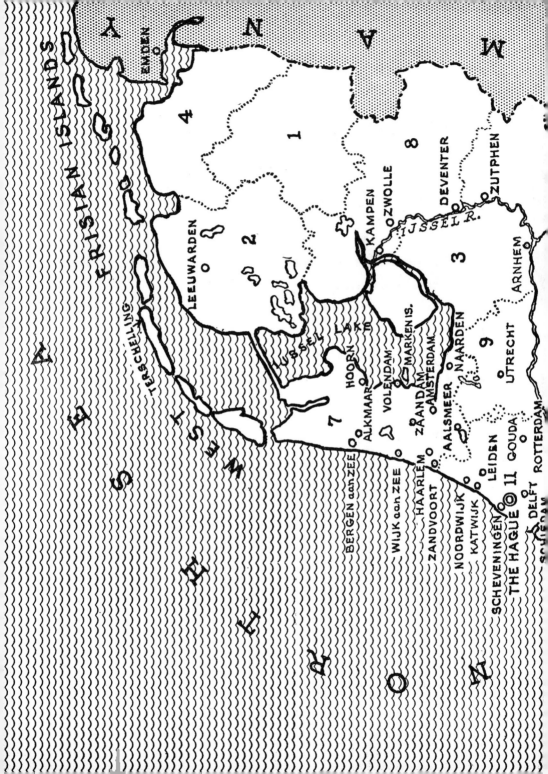

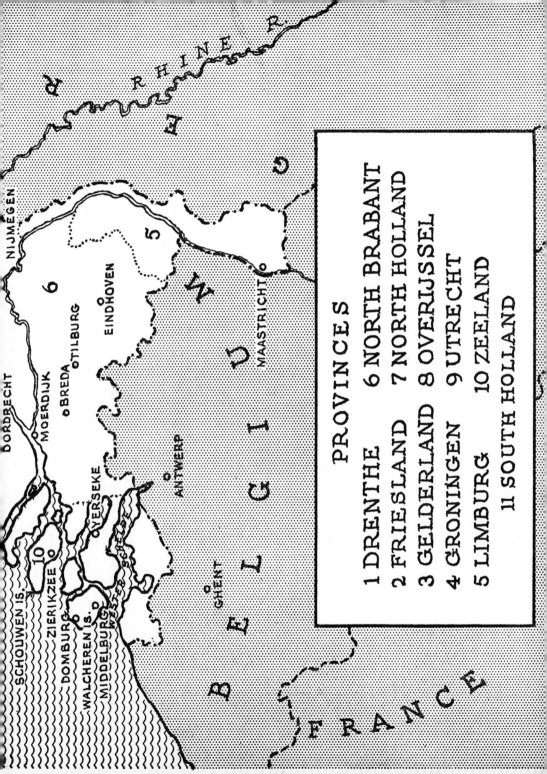

RHINE R.

NIJMEGEN

DORDRECHT

MOERDIJK

BREDA

TILBURG

EINDHOVEN

6

5

ANTWERP

GHENT

BELGIUM

FRANCE

SCHOUWEN IS.

ZIERIKZEE

DOMBURG

WALCHEREN IS.

MIDDELBURG

WESTER SCHELDE

OVERSEKE

MAASTRICHT

10

PROVINCES

1 DRENTHE   6 NORTH BRABANT
2 FRIESLAND 7 NORTH HOLLAND
3 GELDERLAND 8 OVERIJSSEL
4 GRONINGEN 9 UTRECHT
5 LIMBURG   10 ZEELAND
         11 SOUTH HOLLAND

The Land and People of Holland

CHAPTER ONE

A Bird's-Eye View of Land and People

Holland is a flat, low-lying country. The Dutch people are so accustomed to an unimpeded view across their land that the slightest elevation interfering with it receives the name of *berg*, which means mountain. The only height that deserves the name is the Saint Pietersberg, in the southernmost part of the province of Limburg, which rises over a thousand feet above the surrounding region, but there are many other "mountains" that are actually mere hills. The Dutch language has a word for hill, but *heuvel* is less common in place names than *berg*. The people's preference for the latter word must compensate them for the lack of variety in altitude that is typical of the Netherlands. In vacation time they go to Switzerland and revel among the Alps in scenic beauties that nature has denied to their fatherland. But they never stay long. They feel cooped up among those high mountaintops and long again for the flatlands stretching away towards the dim horizon.

The imaginative among them know that Holland is no less beautiful and romantic than Switzerland. She too has a kind of mountain scenery, the ever shifting cloudscapes that often assume a startling grandeur. Dutch artists have reproduced it on their can-

13

vases, Jacob van Ruisdael in the seventeenth century, in the nineteenth Jacob Maris, Weissenbruch, and Voerman. The clouds
create fantastic shapes and the sun, playing hide-and-seek among
those masses, produces an illusion of snow-capped summits and
dark crevasses.

It is an illusion that does not happen every day. Sunless days
are not the exception in Holland, but the rule. The atmosphere is
humid and the vapors that rise from the rain-soaked grasslands
weave a curtain of mist that the sun cannot always pierce. The
Dutch call their country a *kikkerland,* a land good only for frogs,
because of its wet climate. They would not want to live anywhere else, but their affection for it does not prevent them from
running it down on occasion. One of them told me a story about
Dr. Coué, a Frenchman who half a century ago acquired international fame by his propaganda for autosuggestion as the best cure
for all our ills. One day he gave a lecture in Amsterdam, and
after the lecture a man from the audience accosted him and asked
him for advice. He suffered from deep melancholia, caused, he
said, by his never seeing the sun. It rained nearly every day, and
even on rainless days the sky was overcast. "My business keeps
me in Amsterdam, but I am dying here for lack of sunshine," he
concluded. "Well, my friend," said Dr. Coué, "I would advise you
to tell yourself every morning before breakfast, 'the sun is shining, the sun is shining,' and repeat it twenty times, and do that
again every day before lunch and again before supper and see
what happens." A year later Dr. Coué was back in Amsterdam for
another lecture, and he called up the house of Mr. Willemse, being
anxious to hear how he had fared. A lady answered his call and
said, "I am sorry, sir, Mr. Willemse is dead." "Dead? I am sorry
to hear it. What did he die of?" "Of sunstroke, sir."

The story serves as a good illustration of the Dutch climate and
of the wry humor that is typical of the Dutch. They like to poke
fun at themselves and the country they love. A century ago a

poet, Petrus Augustus de Génestet, inveighed against its climate in this whimsical outburst:

> O land of mud and mist, where man is wet and shivers,
> Soaked with humidity, with damp and chilly dew,
> O land of unplumbed bogs, of roads resembling rivers,
> Land of umbrellas, gout, colds, agues, toothache, flu.
> O spongy porridge-swamp, O homeland of galoshes,
> Of cobblers, toads, and frogs, peat diggers, mildew, mold,
> Of ducks and every bird that slobbers, splutters, splashes,
> Hear the autumnal plaint of a poet with a cold.
> Thanks to your clammy clime my arteries are clotted
> With blood turned mud. No song, no joy, no peace for me.
> You're fit for clogs alone, O land our forebears plotted
> And, not at my request, extorted from the sea.

Clogs were an indispensable footwear of the countryfolk in former days. When the roads, in the rainy season, became impassable, everyone, man, woman, and child, wore *klompen*, as they are called in Dutch. Modern means of transportation have turned them into an old-fashioned oddity. Cyclists and motorists insisted on more efficient surfacing of country roads and lanes, and now the farmer and his wife, the farmhands and the dairymaids travel smoothly on wheels where their grandparents used to plod through the slush. But after a heavy downpour or a snowfall the wooden shoes regain their favor. They are brought down from the attic and assist the wearers across ruts and puddles where wheels would skid and throw the riders. No one coming home through the mud is allowed to walk into the house in his dirty clogs. He leaves them outside by the front door and, when the entire family has assembled for supper, one can tell by the number of pairs around the stoop how many there are in the household. Broek in Waterland, a thriving village north of Amsterdam, is a typical example of a rural community of clog wearers. As its name indicates, it is a watery region where every farmstead is an island, separated from its immediate neighbors by ditches. You have to cross a bridge to reach the farmer's home, and he is able to make access to it less easy by pulling up the bridge or pulling it in. A Dutch polderman's home is his castle indeed.

These countryfolk are not bumpkins. They receive good schooling and are acquainted with city ways and manners. No rural district is very far from a town. Great distances do not exist in little Holland, hence each urban center radiates its light of culture on its environs. As a result there is little that distinguishes the townsman from the countryman. They wear similar clothes and furnish their homes with unimaginative similarity.

There are, however, exceptional spots that are remarkable for the uniqueness of the local costume. In Friesland, on the erstwhile Zuider Zee islands, in the fishing villages along the coast of that inland sea, and on the islands of Zeeland and South Holland quaint garbs are still worn by men, women, and children. These vary in design and color from place to place. Marken and Volendam are the most famous among such places in which a more picturesque past survives. It is often said that the villagers dress up for the benefit of American tourists, but that is not so. The tourists flock to these places because the people, loving tradition better than change, are so picturesquely dressed.

These archconservatives live chiefly along the coasts of the country and draw their livelihood from the sea. Their dangerous life is a constant gamble with death. When they return from the herring catch, they like to find everything at home as it always was, an unchangeable anchorage as firmly fixed as the sea is inconstant and unstable. Their wandering, often storm-tossed life creates in them a craving for immutable permanence on land. Even the fisher-folk of Scheveningen, the fashionable seaside resort close to The Hague, are impervious to the urge so natural in most people to imitate the manners and copy the attire of the visitors they see crowding to the pier and the beach. The boys and their sweethearts walk among them in their peculiar garb, not arm in arm but, according to local custom, with their little fingers linked together. They do not fancy bright colors, as do the people of Marken and Volendam. Black is the predominant tone of the Scheveningen costume, which is relieved only by large silver buttons. The men walk with a peculiar swinging gait, as if their bodies, adjusted to the dancing motion of their pink, their fishing smack, could not drop it on land.

Nor do they care to join the bathers along the beach. They go to sea for a living, not for pleasure. They would be ashamed to be seen in a bathing suit; that's the sort of thing only townspeople wear. The fisherfolk all along the North Sea coast and the shores of the Zuider Zee think alike in this matter: they do not care for either sea or sun bathing. The beaches are good for their pinks and smacks to lie on in vacation time; you never see these seafarers relaxing on the sand themselves.

Another popular seaside resort is Domburg, on the isle of Walcheren in Zeeland, a quaint old village at the back of the dunes from the top of which one overlooks a summertime bathing beach. It has the advantage over the one in Scheveningen that it is harder to reach and consequently not overrun day after day by trippers from the cities. There is only one large town on the island, Middelburg, the capital of the province of Zeeland, and the Domburg beach is spacious enough to accommodate any urban invasion in addition to the resident summer guests.

An even quieter and equally pleasant resort is the one near Haamstede on the island of Schouwen, north of Walcheren. The only town here is Zierikzee. In former days it took a long trip by steam tram or boat to reach it, but since the KLM opened a daily air service to the island it has become easy of access and Haamstede beach has gained in popularity.

North of Scheveningen are two very popular resorts near the fisher villages of Katwijk and Noordwijk, west of Leiden. Noordwijk has a magnificent beach and an excellent hotel and restaurant which attract visitors not only from among the Dutch people but also from foreign countries, especially Germany and England.

Zandvoort, farther north, west of Haarlem, is the chief summer playground of the people of Amsterdam. Its nearness to the city has its disadvantages. On hot summer days trains and trolley cars and motor buses and autos and bicycles carry hordes of towns-people to Zandvoort for a day of relaxation and turn its beach into a Dutch Coney Island. The fastidious who prefer the sea without a fringe of sprawling humanity will find more elbow room and less vociferation in Wijk aan Zee, a small resort a little farther north, or, better still, at Bergen aan Zee, west of Alkmaar.

The region north of Haarlem immediately east of the dunes is called Kennemerland. Wealthy merchants of seventeenth-century Amsterdam were attracted by its lovely woods and built their summer homes amidst their foliage, and now that Kennemerland is but a short motoring distance from the metropolis, commuters have their villas there summer and winter. Traveling from Haarlem to Alkmaar along the road that winds through this lovely scenery, you can catch glimpses on your right of the polderland, whose flat pastures, dotted with grazing cattle, offer a stark contrast to the wooded sand hills on the other side of the road.

Five centuries ago this polderland was mostly water, and Kennemerland, between the North Sea on the west and the Zuider Zee on the east, was known by the name of *Holland op zijn smalst*, meaning Holland at its narrowest. It is all land now, and very fertile land that yields an abundant crop to the farmer and provides good grazing for his livestock. Here most of the Dutch cheese is produced, and carried from the farms to the cheese market in Alkmaar. Friday is market day there. The barges are moored along the quay in front of the weighhouse, where porters, wearing headgear of many colors, await their arrival. The round cheeses are tossed by a man on the barge to a porter on the quay, always two at a time, and the catcher never misses. No cheese is ever dropped into the canal; the tossing and catching have become mechanical motions that are errorproof. The porters pile the cheeses on stretchers and run them to the weighhouse in a swinging gait that never fails to arouse the wonder and admiration of the tourists who flock to Alkmaar on market day. When the weights have been determined and the sales been made, the cheeses are carried back to the quay and rolled along chutes into the hold, where the tossers, now acting as catchers, deposit them neatly in well-ordered rows. By noon all this activity is over. The sightseer who wants to witness this colorful market scene has to go to Alkmaar early in the morning.

Alkmaar has its cattle market, too, but dairy farmers preponderate in North Holland. Leeuwarden is the principal live-stock-trading center. The Frisian farmers take great pride in the magnificent specimens they breed. Compared to these, Potter's famous bull is but a scrawny creature. The latter is on view in the Royal Museum in the Mauritshuis at The Hague. This painting is one of those institutions that seem to have been devised for the special delectation of tourists. Potter has painted better pictures, but his bull is the one to which he owes his international fame.

The narrow strip of land east of the dunes that bears the name of Kennemerland north of Haarlem runs southward as far as The Hague. Here is the heart of Holland's horticulture. Close to Haarlem lies the village of Aalsmeer on the edge of the *Groote Poel*, the Big Lake, which has not been turned into a polder. The Aalsmeer gardeners are grateful for that, for their lilacs thrive on the mud which is dredged from its bottom. These lilacs are the chief pride of the nurserymen. They go by planeloads to the United States and reach florist shops of New York two days after they are cut by the growers.

The Aalsmeer flower market is an even more exciting spectacle than the cheese market at Alkmaar. As seen from the air, its gardens look like square little islands dotting the mirror of the *Groote Poel* along its frame. As each nursery is surrounded by water, the cut flowers are carried to the auction house by boat. The barges slip quietly into the center of the building, where the bunches and sheafs of blooms are wheeled on movable counters into the auction room. There is no quieter auction room in all the world. No voice is heard there except the one of the auctioneer. The bidding is done by the pressure of the finger on a button. The auctioneer stands on his platform underneath a huge dial which is studded with little electrical bulbs, as many as there are seats on the amphitheater that faces the dial. There is no outbidding, the procedure being what in English is called a Dutch auction. The auctioneer offers the flowers at gradually decreasing prices. He starts by demanding a high price, and when nobody bids, he lowers it until some one on the amphitheater presses the button in front of him and the corresponding bulb on the huge dial lights up and clinches the deal. At the same time the hand of the dial indicates the price at which the item has been sold. The first bid is a purchase; there is no outbidding. Thus with little noise and little loss of time thousands of sheafs of flowers are sold in a couple of hours.

The close proximity of Schiphol, the airport of Amsterdam, makes it possible for the nurserymen to ship their sales with small delay to all parts of the world. The flowers are taken there by trucks, transferred into the planes with little loss of time, and reach their various destinations almost as fresh as when they left the nursery. They are scattered to the four winds, to Hamburg, Bremen, Copenhagen, Malmö, Hannover, Berlin, Frankfurt, Basel, Brussels, Paris, London, New York—not only lilacs, but also roses of many kinds and names, dahlias of many colors, begonias and, in the fall, chrysanthemums.

The nurserymen have an open-air show place in a famous old estate called *De Keukenhof*, not far from the village of Sassenheim. Here, in beautifully landscaped grounds, visitors can see the effect of the blooms in garden surroundings. In spring and summer the Dutch come from all parts of the country to see the display, and foreign tourists often swell their numbers. The flowers show up here to better advantage than in the hothouses of the nurseries.

The Keukenhof lies in the very center of the bulb-growing district. April and May are the months in which the crocuses and hyacinths and tulips are in bloom, and cyclists crowd the roads that lead to their festival of colors. The flowers are not picked for sale in the florists' stores. The nurserymen's profit is in the sale of the bulbs. The blooms are thrown away or sold to the cyclists, who pay with a mere tip to the pickers. They are strung together into garlands, with which the pedaling sightseers decorate their bikes and themselves. The bulb fields are a sight worth seeing. They look like parade grounds where regiments in uniforms of various colors stand arrayed in serried ranks. The crocuses are early risers. Then follow the hyacinths, which show up best in masses on the field, blue ones and white and purple blooms. The most gorgeous colors are those of the tulips, which are the tardiest to appear. A bunch of hyacinths makes a stiff, choked-up bouquet, as if their own fragrance suffocated them; tulips are born aristocrats and carry themselves gracefully in a drawing room. They also make a spectacular showing in brilliant squares on the vast checkerboard of the parade ground.

Florists' stores are numerous and flowers are cheap in Holland; pushcart peddlers hawk them from house to house. It is perhaps the grayness of Holland's misty days that makes the Dutch so fond of bright-colored blooms. They grow them in window boxes on the sill, and those who are lucky enough to have a garden use it as a painter uses a palette, arranging the colors in a carefully planned sequence.

South of The Hague lies a fertile market-gardening district that is known by the name of the Westland, and the street that leads toward it out of The Hague is called Westeinde (West End). Early mapmakers placed the map of the Netherlands with the coast line facing north, but their modern successors make it face west; in other words the projection on the page in modern atlases has been turned round to the left a full quarter of the dial. As a result the Dutch nowadays call west and east what were south and north to their forebears, and many topographical names are intelligible only in the light of the early mapmakers' practice. The sea west of Holland is called North Sea; the Zuider Zee did lie south of Holland on the old maps, and hence the region south of The Hague retains its ancient name of Westland.

It supplies The Hague and Rotterdam and other parts of the country with a rich assortment of vegetables and fruit, mostly grown under glass so that the vagaries of the Dutch weather cannot damage the crop. Westland asparagus is considered a delicacy by gourmets in Holland and abroad. And the hothouses in which the farmers grow their grapes are show places that no tourist should fail to visit. The grapes are grown for eating only, not for wine making. Their huge dark-blue bunches, suspended from the glass roof, dim the light that filters through the panes.

In the nineteenth century agriculture, market gardening, dairy farming, and livestock breeding were the country's chief sources of revenue. But gradually industrial production began to outstrip the production of the farm lands. Today a much larger percentage of the population is employed in the country's factories and work-shops. The late war and the loss of valuable colonies in the East Indies impelled the Dutch to recoup themselves by increased industrial production and export.

They have been successful in this beyond the most optimistic expectations. The leader in Holland's industrial development is the Philips concern. Starting from a cottage in a country town with an attached workshop where lamps were made in the early 1890's, this enterprise has grown into one of the largest industrial concerns of the world, employing nearly two hundred thousand men and women in various parts of the globe. Its birthplace was the then unimportant town of Eindhoven in the province of North Brabant. Its headquarters are still there, but they now cover an area of nearly three hundred acres and control a plant whose activities are spread over some two hundred buildings. Its rapid growth, however, has spread beyond the narrow bounds of its native town in Brabant. Two thirds of its nearly two hundred thousand employees live and work in countries other than the

Netherlands. The company has become an international federation of industries, though it is still controlled from its nerve center at Eindhoven. It still makes lamps, but also electric-light bulbs and radios and television sets and anything in the field of electronics, from the simplest to the most intricate and most sensitive devices.

Holland's textile industry is centered in Twente, which is the southeast corner of the province of Overijssel; the manufacture of ceramics in Delft; in Amsterdam diamond cutters and dealers are at work; in Schiedam, between Delft and Rotterdam, the distillers of Dutch gin. The name of the town has in some cases become the name of its product, delft meaning glazed earthenware and schiedam meaning gin. Yet glazed earthenware is being made in other towns of Holland—in Gouda, in Maastricht, and in Amsterdam—and distilleries are not the monopoly of Schiedam. One of the most popular gins now on the market is called Bokma, for the firm that makes it, and this is located in Leeuwarden, the capital of the province of Friesland. Another famous and well-established firm is that of Lucas Bols in Amsterdam. Equally old is the one of Wynandts Fockink, whose liqueur shop in the Pijlsteeg at Amsterdam is a show place that no gourmet and connoisseur should fail to visit. The Pijlsteeg is a narrow and inconspicuous alley, and a stranger in Amsterdam would have difficulty in finding the shop but for an arched passage cut into the block that separates it from the much wider Damstraat. Through it one gets a glimpse of the picturesque façade of Wynandts Fockink while on a shopping expedition in the Damstraat.

When you enter the liqueur shop you are suddenly transported back into the seventeenth century. The place has not changed from what it was three hundred years ago. The old dark-green bottles with pictures painted on their bellies are still standing on the shelves along the walls. Here connoisseurs order a drink called "half-and-half," a specialty of the house. The bartender places a little glass shaped like a chalice or flower cup upon the counter and fills it to the brim. But one doesn't lift it—that would be a breach of etiquette, the bar man will tell you. One must bend down and take the first sip, like a kitten lapping up his milk from the saucer. After that it may be brought to the lips, as the danger of spilling a drop is past. The liqueur is too precious to let any be wasted.

The glazed tiles that were made chiefly in Delft were not merely a decorative means of covering walls; they also served an educational purpose. Little children learned from them at home a lot of useful knowledge that modern children have to acquire in the schoolroom. Picture tiles were the washable, untearable, and thumb-proof picture books from which Dutch youngsters learned their first Bible lessons and the rudiments of history and geography. The Delft potteries turned out educational sets of tiles on various subjects: tiles of Bible stories, of natural history showing native and exotic birds and animals, of landscapes in Holland and in foreign countries, of costumes worn by people in the Far East of whom the Dutch sailors told strange stories. In short the tiled walls in a Dutch home were a household book of multifarious information. The tiles have since become collectors' items, having been removed from the walls and passed into the possession of dealers and art connoisseurs. There are not many homes left in Holland that preserve these lovely old tiles intact. But excellent tile and ceramic wares are still produced in Delft today, carrying on the tradition.

To judge from the paintings of Pieter de Hoogh and Jan Vermeer and Jan Steen, the Dutch homes of the seventeenth century were much more beautiful than those of modern Holland. In recent years individual taste has had to yield in this overcrowded country to wholesale production. Most Dutch town houses nowadays are built on the same plan. If you know your way inside one, you know it in most of the others. After passing through the front door, you enter a hallway at whose farther end is the door to the kitchen. The hallway is more spacious near the front than in the rear, for in the middle its width is partly taken up by the staircase. Adjoining the hall, either on the right or the left, is a suite of rooms of which one faces the street, the other the garden at the back. The latter, being next to the kitchen, is the dining room, the other the drawing room, which in some families is used exclusively for the reception of visitors.

The householder who has rented a newly built house of this description will not find it habitable on taking possession. It lacks the fixtures that make life in it possible: the bathtub, the stoves, the lamps must be put in at his own cost, and in choosing these he can lend an individual touch to the place. The walls and floors also need covering, and after he has chosen the wallpapers and the carpets or linoleums that suit his taste, he has to wait until the upholsterer has finished his job before he can move in.

The Dutch housewife does not have to do much marketing. Most purveyors deliver their wares at the door. There is constant bell ringing: the milkman, the grocer's and butcher's boys, the baker, the garbage collector come around every morning. The orders for the butcher are traditionally written into a little order book enclosed in a tin case so that it does not get stained by the delivery boy's greasy hands, but it does get stained in the long run; the *slagersboekje*, the butcher's booklet, is a proverbial object of loathing. In addition to these indispensable callers many an unwanted bell ringer disturbs the peace of the household: hawkers who have pencils and paper for sale, the Dutch equivalent of America's Fuller Brush man, organ grinders who beg for alms after playing a few tunes in the street, mendicants who request the return of the printed material they have dropped into the letter box, etc. On many doors you find a notice: "We do not buy at the door," "Printed matter will not be returned," "Between twelve and one we don't answer the bell," and similar warnings intended to save the lady of the house and her servant from annoyance.

The hall of every home is cluttered up with an array of bicycles, for everyone cycles in Holland, from five-year-olds to octogenarians. The members of the family speed off on wheels to school and their various occupations as soon as breakfast is over. That is a very simple meal, much less elaborate than the English breakfast. No fried eggs and bacon, merely bread and butter with cheese or *rookvlees* or honey or jam on top. *Rookvlees* is a typically Dutch meat from the delicatessen that I have never tasted else-where, very thinly sliced smoked beef that is used only for sand-wiches. The drink at breakfast is tea or milk, or buttermilk for those who like it. The Dutch are great tea drinkers. They imbibe it again at about five, and a third time after dinner. The tea hour at night is quite a ceremony. The lady of the house presides behind her tray and pours the tea, and the family sit round the table, talk-ing or reading a book or the evening paper. Coffee is drunk only at lunch, and this is such an old, established custom that coffee is the Hollander's name for lunch. *Kom morgen bij ons koffie drinken,* one Hollander may say to another, and the invitation is no guarantee that his wife won't serve chocolate instead.

The children go to school from nine till noon and from two till four on week days and on Saturdays only in the morning. There are few special holidays, but in winter when it freezes hard school children have a half holiday once a week for skating, and on Saint Nicholas Eve, which is the fifth of December, they get the after-noon off. And of course the Queen's birthday, which falls on the last day of April, is a holiday. But the Dutch do not have any days that are sacred to the memory of the nation's heroes such as Wil-liam the Silent and Rembrandt and Hugo de Groot. They are not given to hero worship, though they will honor, when occasion offers, eminent men of the past at commemorative exercises and unveilings of monuments. Parades are rare and flag waving is not popular. Patriotism is as strong a passion in the Dutch as it is in other peoples, but they keep it under control from a self-conscious feeling that to give vent to it vociferously is undignified.

CHAPTER TWO

The Menace of the Sea

A few years ago Dutch archaeologists discovered, at a depth of more than two yards, an ancient boat in a peat bog near Pesse, a hamlet in the province of Drente. An analysis (by the carbon technique developed by Professor Libby of Nobel prize fame) of the wood and of the peat in which it was embedded proved that the vessel was about 8300 years old. Drente that long ago was a coastal region. When the northern icecap melted, the level of the sea rose and flooded all the land that is now the maritime part of the Low Countries. The men who sailed that boat left no other record of their existence. Two hundred generations of human beings were to follow them and pass into oblivion before the land they had occupied began to attract the attention of the rest of Europe.

In 57 B.C. Julius Caesar started his conquest of the Low Countries south of the Rhine, and in 12 B.C. Drusus subjugated the tribes then living north of that river to Roman rule. Their conquests marked the beginning of Netherlands history. We have no written record of what happened there previously. The stress should be laid on *written*, for the people who inhabited that swampy, wind-swept, and sea-menaced region in prehistoric times unwittingly recorded the story of their lives. Modern archaeology has opened up the book of Netherlands prehistory. For some twelve thousand years parts, at least, of the Low Countries were never without inhabitants. Race upon race swept over the land from its dark, arctic past until the dawn of history. We do not know their names, but we know the shape of their skulls, the tools and weapons that they wielded, the utensils they fashioned and decorated, the kind of game they hunted, the manner of their burials.

The archaeologists have given them names, or rather have given names to the cultures that marked the differences between them. The earliest inhabitants belonged to the Hamburgian culture. The Hamburgians were followed in succeeding millenniums by other invaders from the east, who brought new customs, new skills, new burial rites, such as the so-called funnel-beaker men (c. 2500–1000 B.C.), who were the builders of the *hunebeds*, megalithic mass graves that are still a conspicuous feature of the landscape of Drente.

Among the eleven provinces of the kingdom of the Netherlands Drente is the one least favored by nature. It is a region of mostly sand and gravel from which the peasant by hard labor can wrest only a scanty livelihood. Modern science has developed means of making this arid land more productive, but in prehistoric times the builders of the *hunebeds* cannot have extracted more than a bare subsistence from that barren soil. They had good reason, though, to prefer that part of the country to the region west of it, for that was a marshy lagoon feebly protected against the inroads of the sea by an ever shifting wall of sand dunes. Even in present-day Holland tens of thousands of hands are at work day and night to keep the threatening water under control. It has been said that if the entire population should emigrate, Holland would soon disappear from the face of the earth. It is kept from drowning only by the constant watchfulness and labor of its inhabitants. Large parts lie below sea level, and if the pumping stations should stop working, the land would soon turn back into the kind of brackish swamp that it was before the dawn of the Christian era.

The disastrous effects of the sea's inroads can be seen at a glance on the map. South of Holland proper lies a group of islands that once were part of the mainland. The sea tore them loose and still holds them in its embrace. They form a separate province that bears the telling name of Zeeland, meaning Sea Land. Its coat of arms is a lion, half submerged by the waves but struggling to keep head and shoulders above water. The device makes the lion say in Latin: *Luctor et Emergo*, I struggle and emerge. That is indeed what these islands are doing; they are forever waging war against the water.

Incidentally, Hollanders have nothing but ridicule and contempt for what they call the silly story of the little Haarlem boy who stopped a leak in the dike with his finger. Unwieldy bags of sand, each much heavier than that little fellow, are the only protection on which the Dutch farmers rely for stopping a breach in the dike. Dutch schoolbooks ignore the little hero, but not a certain class of grownups who should know better. They do know better, yet being commercially-minded, they exploit this absurd legend to please foreign sightseers. Visitors must be treated to what they like to see. And of course they will like to see the little boy whose story they have read in "Hans Brinker or the Silver Skates." So they had a sculptor model a statue of the tiny water tamer, and now he stands on top of the dike he is supposed to have saved, for tourists to see and wonder at.

Windmills were in former days the most striking feature of North Holland scenery. Some nine hundred could be seen there in the eighteenth century, revolving their crosses above the low-lying land. They served all sorts of industrial purposes. They sawed wood for the shipbuilders, ground flour for the bakers, peeled rice, and pounded rags for the paper mills. Their beauty is now gone because they have lost their usefulness. The wind was not always at the miller's beck and call, and when electricity created an ever available power, the winged giants were felled to make room for brick-built factories that are devoid of beauty and visible mobility.

Hundreds of them have been demolished, and the wind, deprived of its industrial employment, blows aimlessly across the polderland. Admirers of the picturesque mills, deploring their loss, have formed a society whose aim is to preserve the few intact survivors and to restore the mills that are in ruins. They have founded a museum at Zaandam, a windmill mausoleum, where miniature semblances of the arm-waving giants are on view in lifeless immobility. This is a worth-while enterprise that deserves praise and support, yet I would rather look at an abandoned mill whose body, though disfigured by neglect, still stands under the drift of clouds by the windswept polder. For a Dutch mill should be seen in its natural setting, the pasture land crisscrossed by ditches and dotted by cattle; and it needs the whir of the wind in its sails even though they are too stiff through rust and erosion to revolve at its bidding. Mills are near-human, and in former days, when they were still alive with the breath of wind, they were felt to be members of the miller's family and often shared the family name. The mill was shaped and clothed like a man: it had a *body* or *rump;* it wore a cap or coif like a woman in North Holland costume; it was wrapped in a *coat* or *pelt,* and had a *ruff,* a circle-shaped wooden board round the neck of its axis. It even had a *bib* tied to its cap, like children at their meal, a wooden tablet which usually bore in large figures the year in which the mill was built or renovated. These terms are telling proof that the North Hollander invested his mill with a human individuality, as the seaman does his ship. But unlike the skipper, whose ship is a she, the miller spoke of his mill as a male. Every mill was christened and many, it is true, bore women's names such as The Maiden, The Bride, The Housewife, The Beguine, The Princess of Orange, The Queen, The Empress, but when the miller referred to one of these ladies he would include her by means of the personal pronoun among the other sex. "He turns his face towards the master," he would say when a miller had died and his mill was placed in mourning position. For the mill, being one of the family, showed by various devices his participation in their sorrows and joys.

Windmills for drainage purposes were installed in the seventeenth century. Marshes were turned into pasture land, lake after lake reclaimed, and the water that remained within these reclaimed areas was restrained by strait jackets of dikes from which it could escape only by permission of its jailers. These diked-in lands are called polders. When heavy rains have swelled the ditches that crisscross the polders to overflowing, the jailers will open the locks in the dikes to let out the superfluous water into outside receptacles called bosoms. These may be canals, or canalized rivers, or ancient lakes left unreclaimed for this very purpose of serving as reservoirs of discharged polder water.

The planning and execution of these drainages is the work of successive generations. In the year 1641 the engineer Leeghwater drafted a plan for draining Haarlem Lake, but not until 1852 was that wide sheet of water laid dry and turned over to the livestock farmer and the plowman. The winning of more land is a more urgent need today than it was in Leeghwater's time. Then the population of the Dutch Republic barely exceeded a million; it has grown in this century to fourteen times that many, and each day of the year adds six hundred human beings to the number. This alarming growth is one of the most baffling problems that the country now has to solve.

The Dutch hoped to solve it by turning parts of the Zuider Zee into inhabitable land. In the far north lies a string of islands in front of the Friesland coast which once were part of the mainland. The water created even worse havoc here than in Zeeland, for it penetrated deep inland and dug a wide hole there that was known by the name of Zuider Zee. In the past the Zuider Zee was up to all the pranks that its big brother outside used to play. When the North Sea roared and lashed the beaches and dashed against the barrier of dunes, the Zuider Zee joined in the uproar and struck terror into the hearts of the fishermen's womenfolk along its shores. But swells and spring tides can no longer affect it. Its reservoir of water is now fed by the rivers that empty into it. These have turned the salt-water sea into a fresh-water lake, the IJssel Lake, as it is now called; the Zuider Zee is no more. And the IJssel Lake is shrinking in size as more large areas are reclaimed and annexed to the surrounding land.

The success of this enterprise has encouraged the Dutch to undertake an even more difficult task: the closing of the sea gates between the Zeeland islands. The terrors of the 1953 deluge are still vivid in every Zeelander's memory. In the early morning of January 31 a terrific storm from the northwest drove the deep ocean water into the shallow bottleneck of the North Sea. Its impact on the islands of South Holland and Zeeland was disastrous. In a few minutes the sea rose to unprecedented height. It cascaded over the highest dikes and dunes and drowned many towns and villages before the inhabitants had time to escape. Rooftops offered a precarious refuge. It took four days for the rescue squads to reach some of the lost villages and farms and to evacuate the victims of the storm, whose numbers ran into the tens of thousands.

Three hundred and fifty thousand acres of land were inundated, affecting the lives of some six hundred thousand people, nearly two thousand of whom perished in the floods. The Netherlands Minister of Transportation and Waterways immediately appointed a body of experts, the so-called Delta Committee, which recommended the closing of the arms of the sea between the Rotterdam Waterway, which is the main outlet of the Rhine, and the Wester Schelde, which is the open approach from the sea to the port of Antwerp. The effects of this huge operation will be manifold. It will raise the water levels near the points of closure and remove the sand bars now barricading the coast. The North Sea beaches will be widened, navigation will be facilitated in the protected waters behind the dams, and agriculture will benefit from the increase of commercial shipping. The famous oyster banks of Yerseke will be the chief victims of the scheme, but their loss will be amply offset by the gains it will otherwise bring to the country. The New York *Times*, in an editorial comment on the Delta Committee's proposal, said, "The fact that men can plan on this scale and also foresee the consequences of such vast transformations of the earth's surface is one of the marvels of the present age."

Incessant watchfulness is the price that Holland pays for her safety. The water is her friend and ally as long as she keeps it subdued. If it once gets out of hand, it turns from an assistant into an enemy, destroying the homes that it protected, smashing the mills that it set to work, drowning the cattle that it provided with drink, spoiling the crops that it fertilized. "Men's evil manners live in brass, their virtues we write in water," says Griffith in Shakespeare's *King Henry VIII*, deploring the ingratitude of man. The Hollanders, a modest people by nature, have written their own virtues in water, their script being the curving lines of the dikes that shelter what they wrested from the waves by the virtues of industry, persistence, and patience.

CHAPTER THREE

The Dutch Melting Pot

In American usage the name Dutch is somewhat confusing, because it may refer to the language and the people of either the Netherlands or the German *Reich*. Pennsylvania Dutch is a dialectical variety of German, Dutch toys come from Nürnberg, the Dutch butcher on Main Street learned the craft in his native Germany, and a Dutch treat is a form of entertainment unknown in Holland but common among German people. One has to dig deep into the past to find the cause of this vagueness of meaning.

The name Netherlands, or Low Countries, had formerly no clearly defined connotation either. In the Middle Ages the people whose descendants now inhabit the eastern provinces of Holland were not conscious of being nationally different from the ancestors of the people now living across the border line between Holland and Germany. The frontier that now divides the Netherlands from the *Reich* separates people whose medieval ancestors did not look upon each other as foreigners.

In the Burgundian era, the fifteenth century, parts of the Low Countries began to consolidate into a political entity. *Les Pays de par deçà*, the lands over there, was the official name for them in the Burgundian chancelleries. *Les Pays Bas* was another that was in common use. Even the singular Netherland began to crop up,

34

which seems to indicate that they began to be thought of as a closely knit national unit. Albrecht Dürer called the diary he kept of his journey to the Low Countries *Reise in das Niederland.*

Dutch, however, remained the common name for the language of the inhabitants of both the Netherlands under Burgundian rule and the German lands east of them. They all spoke varieties of the same ancient tongue, which was called Dutch, *Deutsch* in German, because it was the speech of the people. For the name Dutch is derived from an old Germanic noun whose meaning was "people." The Christian missionaries, in the Latin reports of their work among the Germanic tribes, called the language they spoke *Lingua Thiodisca,* the peoplish language, and by people they meant pagans, just as in Latin the plural *gentes* was used for the heathen. The new coinage passed from the reports of the missions into the language of the chancelleries and was finally adopted by the people themselves when their conversion to Christianity had emptied the word of its pagan implication. It proved a useful term, for it gathered the many tribal dialects under one head and marked them the common speech of the people as distinct from Latin, the language of the Church.

The name was gradually replaced by the name *Hollands* in the speech of every day, and *Nederlands* became its official name in writing. *Duits* now means German exclusively, and only in English did *Dutch* remain the name of the Hollander's language. When the Briton speaks of the language that is spoken in Dr. Adenauer's republic he calls it *German*, and a lot of confusion would be avoided if Americans would do the same.

The Dutch people do not form a homogeneous race. The North Hollander who lives in the polders between Amsterdam and Alkmaar is a different type from the peasant in the Achterhoek, which is that part of the province of Gelderland that is closest to the German border. The Brabanter and the Limburger in the south show small resemblance to the Frieslander, and the inhabitant of Zeeland is, again, a type apart. These differences are not due to environment but to the survival of prehistoric variations within the race.

Three main groups can be distinguished: the Frisians in the north, the Saxons in the east, the Franks in the west and south; but it is impossible to draw sharp demarcation lines between them. They have mingled along their common boundaries, creating transition groups.

Remnants of another race are living among these Netherlanders. These belong to the Alpine or Celto-Slavic stock which inhabited the Low Countries before they were invaded by the Germanic tribes. In the Zeeland isles, where they were safe from hostile raids behind ramparts of turbulent water, they escaped extinction or absorption, and it is there that one finds a type of people strikingly unlike their longheaded, blond, and blue-eyed Frisian countrymen. They are dark-haired, dark-eyed, shortheaded and less tall. Roelf Pool, the Dutch peasant boy of High Prairie, Illinois, who is the hero of Edna Ferber's early novel *So Big*, is one of these. The author wonders how such an exotic-looking specimen could occur among the stolid settlers of High Prairie. The explanation she offers is doubtless one that she found to be common among the Illinois Dutch themselves: "Some Dutch sailor ancestor or fisherman must have touched at an Italian port or Spanish and brought back a wife whose eyes and skin and feeling for beauty had skipped layer on layer of placid Netherlanders to crop out in this wistful, sensitive boy."

But modern science has measured the skulls and studied the pigments of thousands of blond and dark-haired Netherlanders, and these telling features have taught the biologists a different story. In the Roelf Pools of Zeeland an ancient race survives that in other parts of the Low Countries lost its identity by absorption in the stock of Germanic invaders. South of the Rhine and the Maas, in the provinces of Limburg and Brabant, the effects of this are clearly noticeable. People here are shorter in stature and have darker pigmentation than those farther north in the Netherlands. Another variation of the characteristic Germanic traits can be seen when one travels cross-country from the North Sea coast in an easterly direction, the Saxons along the German border combining the broad skull of the Alpine race with the blond hair and the blue eyes of the Teutons.

The Frisians who live in the province of Friesland have kept their strain pure from alien infiltration. In the province of Groningen they have mingled with the Saxons, in the province of North Holland with the Franks. But Friesland is inhabited by an unadulterated race of tall, blond, and blue-eyed people who speak a language that is a close cognate of English. All Frisians are able to speak Dutch as well, but in the rural districts the spoken language of every day is Frisian. The townspeople speak a mixture of Frisian and Dutch which is known by the name of *Stadsfries*, meaning urban Frisian, but the Frieslander who takes a patriotic pride in his language despises it as a mongrel speech. The literature of Friesland is written not in *Stadsfries*, but in the unadulterated speech of the countryside.

The Frisians cling to their ancient customs and traditions. Many of their womenfolk still wear the gold skullcap and lace hood that have been their distinctive garb for generations. Native tenacity, though, does not make these people impervious to new ideas. Revolutionary thought has often found a fertile soil in Friesland. Menno Simons, a native of Franeker, seceded from the church of Rome in 1536 and became the leader of an heretical sect of Anabaptists who are still known by the name of Mennonites. The Dutch movement for total abstinence originated in Friesland and still has most of its adherents in that province. Frisians have been in the forefront of the Socialistic Labor movement. In 1897 the Labor candidate, Pieter Jelle Troelstra, was elected to a seat in the Second Chamber of the Netherlands Parliament as a representative of Leeuwarden, the Frisian capital. At that time he was the leader of but a small following. But in the year of his death, in 1930, the Social Democratic Labor Party was supported at the polls by

800,000 voters. On the day of his funeral thousands from all parts of the country traveled to The Hague to pay a final tribute to the leader. This son of Friesland was indeed a national figure. His influence was felt even beyond the borders of the Netherlands, for he played an important part in the International Socialist movement. Still, when this Labor leader of international stature expressed himself in poetry it was in the Frisian speech of his native province.

In modern times several alien elements have been added to the original Germanic stock. In the seventeenth century the Dutch Republic, prosperous and more tolerant than most other countries, was an attractive field of enterprise for the adventurous and a haven of refuge for the persecuted from various parts of Europe. Flemings and Walloons from the Spanish Netherlands, Huguenots from France, English dissenters, Scots and Swiss who served as soldiers in the federal army and settled in Holland after their discharge, all these wove many-colored threads through the woof of Dutch nationality. These foreigners seldom settled on the land. They were attracted by the opportunities that Amsterdam and other cities offered them. The infiltration of these alien elements enriched and modified the population of the urban centers. The inhabitants of the rural areas retain the characteristics of the original Germanic stock. The melting pot of Amsterdam has produced a type of Hollander that is different from the peasant type of the polders.

There is one group among the alien newcomers that has maintained its "otherness." The laws of the Netherlands make no distinction between Jews and non-Jews, but socially the Jews have remained isolated from their non-Jewish fellow citizens, partly owing to their affection for Hebrew religion, customs, and traditions, partly owing to inherited prejudices among the Christian community which even Dutch tolerance has not been able to eradicate.

A ghetto in the proper sense of the word never existed in Amsterdam. At no time were the Jews forced to live together in a separate quarter, walled off from the rest of the city, nor were they compelled to wear badges by which they could be recognized as Jews. But they have stuck together voluntarily. The first comers, in the late nineties of the sixteenth century, settled on the right bank of the Amstel, south of the medieval part of Amsterdam. This section of the city has remained the Jewish quarter down to the present day. It was there that Rembrandt built himself a sumptuous house on the Jodenbreestraat, the Jews' Broad Street, in the very heart of their ghetto. On summer days the population, like the Hebrew tent dwellers of ancient Palestine, lived in the open, on stoops and pavements, gossiping and squabbling, transacting business and settling family affairs. The scene in front of his house, which is still standing, was to Rembrandt a resuscitation of New Testament life. He needed but to open a front-parlor window to find suggestions right and left at his own door for scenes from the life of Christ and illustrations of the parables.

The Jews possessed no civil rights under the Dutch Republic. The craft guilds were closed to them, so that they were limited to such professions as were not organized in corporations. First among these was the jewelry industry, in which they retained a virtual monopoly until 1870. About that time the first Cape diamonds were brought to Amsterdam, and the rapid growth of the imports from South Africa caused such a rise in the demand for skilled labor that the cutters and polishers were no longer recruited exclusively from among the Jews. Since the last quarter of the past century Jews and Christians have been working side by side in the mills. A realistic picture of this biracial activity in the diamond industry is given in *Levensgang* (Life's Way), a naturalistic novel by the late Israel Querido, who in his early days was a diamond cutter himself and a sharer in the life and the hardships of the ghetto and the trade.

The jewelry business was not the Jews' only means of livelihood. There were in seventeenth-century Amsterdam Jewish silk merchants, sugar refiners, printers, bookdealers, tobacco merchants, brokers, physicians, surgeons, apothecaries, grocers, innkeepers, moneylenders. Jewish capital was heavily invested in the Dutch West India Company. Civil and political rights were more freely extended to the Jews in the American colonies than they were in the homeland, hence rich Jews became plantation owners in Brazil, Dutch Guiana, and Curaçao, whence many subsequently emigrated to the United States.

The Portuguese Jews, the Sephardim, were the leaders of their race in the Dutch Republic. The Ashkenazim, the Jews from Germany and eastern Europe, still regard them as the aristocracy of their race. They are the heirs of Spanish and Moorish culture; they brought with them refinement, a love of letters, learning, and philosophy which gave them distinction among the Dutch and leadership over the Ashkenazim. The names of these Sephardic families have a musical cadence and sonority that sound exotic in Dutch ears: Orobio de Castro, Mendes da Costa, Lopes Suasso, Teixeira de Mattos, Da Costa Gomes de la Peñha. Men and women bearing such names have been Dutch residents for ten generations and full-fledged citizens for a century and a half. Baruch, or as he later in life signed himself, Benedict de Spinoza, was one of them, the greatest philosopher of his age.

Dutch Jews are loyal subjects of the crown. Their political equality with the rest of the nation, however, does not tend to efface their racial distinctness. It almost seems as if the gradual process of political assimilation were a challenge to the Jews to assert the virtues of their race. The artist Jozef Israels, in his later days, was not unconscious of this tendency. From the portrayal of the North Sea fisherfolk at home and on the beach, he turned in his old age to the study of ghetto scenes, such as the ragged pawnbroker on the doorstep of his mysterious store, a Jewish wedding ceremony, a Hebrew scribe, and episodes from the Old Testament.

This turn in the artistic career of Israels coincided with the rise of a literature that was distinctly and intentionally Jewish. Poets such as Jacob Israel de Haan extolled their martyred race and wrote hopefully of a better future in the new Zion. Still, the work of the aged Israels and the writings of Querido, Heijermans, De Haan and his gifted sister Carry van Bruggen belong to Dutch literature, and they themselves were loyal and patriotic Hollanders. Their proud self-assertion as Jews was not a denial of Dutch citizenship. On the contrary, it was a grateful testimony to the nation whose tolerance accepted them as fellow citizens and left them free to assert themselves as Jews. Without its Jews the Dutch nation would have been much the poorer. They have formed part of it for many generations, not by sufferance but by virtue of the gifts their industry, ingenuity, and talents have contributed to the national life.

CHAPTER FOUR

The Rise of Towns

At the time of the German occupation of Holland in 1940, Adolf Hitler proclaimed that the Netherlands had been reunited with the *Reich,* and later on he informed the world that the new order he was creating was destined to last for the next one thousand years. That was, to put it mildly, not a very pleasant prospect, but there was comfort in the reminder that such promises of a coming millennium had often been made in the past. The millennium that preceded Hitler's advent covers the larger part of the entire history of the Low Countries.

In the early tenth century they were the prey of invaders as barbaric and ruthless as Hitler's hordes. The mighty empire of Charlemagne had fallen apart after his death. The central power was lacking that could maintain its unity. The new order that the great ruler of the Franks had established in western Europe had turned into chaos a century after his death. Danish pirates raided the seacoasts of France and the Netherlands, sailed up the rivers, laid inland towns in ashes, carried the inhabitants off into slavery, and left smoldering homes, famine, and death in their trail. A Viking dynasty, that of Heriold and his successors, ruled over the Netherlands for half a century, treating the subject people as slaves. Early Frisian laws contain provisions that clearly reflect conditions under the Norman terror. It is written there: "The first need is, if a child is taken and bound, northward across the sea or southward over the mountains, then may the mother put up and sell her child's heritage and ransom her child to save its life."

The chroniclers of that period paint a harrowing picture of the depth of demoralization to which the people of the Low Countries had sunk in their serfdom. "This region," wrote Thietmar of Merseburg, "is justly called the Low Countries, for justice, obedience, love for one's fellow man sink low as the sun."

But, like the sun, they rose to a new dawn. Out of the welter a new order evolved. Not at the dictate of a tyrant. The citizens of the fortified towns created that order. Hereditary lords, indeed, held sway over them. But in order to maintain their political power they needed the financial support of the burghers, who were willing to be taxed only in return for freedoms and privileges in the grant of their overlords. The lords ruled by the grace of God, as the saying was, but they actually ruled by the grace of their urban subjects, who held the purse strings.

These burgher towns had grown up spontaneously. They were a mushroom growth that dotted the land in such numbers that by the end of the fourteenth century they had become the chief characteristic of the Netherlands. Some of them were of ancient origin. These had grown from fortresses built by the Romans. Nijmegen is perhaps the most ancient of them all. When one approaches it from across the river it looks impressive on its high embankment, and as the ferryboat brings one closer to it, the town seems to rise higher and higher. Its elevation gives it an un-Dutch character. Nowhere else in Holland do people climb into town.

The steepness of the riverbank at this spot was no doubt the reason for its early selection for settlement. The Romans built a fortress on the hill which they called Noviomagus. Some seven centuries later Charlemagne built a castle probably on the foundation of the old Roman stronghold. Its name, handed down by tradition, was Valkhof—that is, Falcon Court, which seems to imply that he came here to hunt, but he also held court here, combining business with pleasure. Nijmegen remained a fortress until the eighteenth century. The old citadel was long ago dismantled and the ramparts transformed into pleasant promenades.

Maastricht, the capital of Limburg, is equally old. The Romans settled here and fortified their settlement with a *castellum*. The town, thus protected, offered greater security to Servatius, the Bishop of Tongeren, who moved to Maastricht in the last decade of the fourth century. Servatius was revered by his converts as a holy man. His miracle-working relics made the church that bears his name, and where he lies buried, a popular shrine for pilgrims in search of health and consolation. In the days of the Carolingian rulers Maastricht became the center of artistic activities, and in the twelfth century the city was famous for its skillful painters. Jan van Eyck, the greatest painter of the Netherlands in the Middle Ages, was born, two hundred years later, in that same art-productive area.

In the late twelfth century there lived in Maastricht a knight and minnesinger named Heynrick van Veldeke. As far as we know, Heynrick was the first man to write verse in Dutch, a speech whose forms until then had been passed on by oral tradition alone. The earliest specimen of his art was a rhymed legend of Servatius, the local saint of Maastricht.

The city of Utrecht is a rival of Nijmegen and Maastricht in antiquity. The Romans had a trading post in this spot. The Anglo-Saxon missionary Willibrord, who made many converts among the pagan Frisians, built a church here—a modest structure, but one which was the beginning of greater things to come. For Willibrord was made Bishop of Utrecht, and his successors have retained the leadership of the Roman Catholic Church in the Netherlands down to the present day.

Willibrord, a native of Northumbria, was able to preach to his converts in his Anglo-Saxon speech, as Frisians and Northumbrians were of one race and spoke languages that came from a common

THE RISE OF TOWNS

stock. He understood the Frisian temper, which resembled his own, and that was probably the secret of his success.

In the county of Holland Dordrecht has always been honored as the oldest of its cities. It was a thriving port in the Middle Ages, thanks to the transit trade between Germany and England that brought many a merchantman to its quays. Rotterdam was a young upstart compared to Dordrecht, and so was Amsterdam, which grew in the late Middle Ages from a straggling fishing village at the confluence of the Amstel and the Y into a prosperous port and market town. By the end of the fifteenth century Amsterdam must have been a wealthy community. When the Emperor Maximilian was seized and imprisoned by the rebellious citizens of Bruges, and other parts of the Low Countries were causing him no end of trouble, the town on the Amstel came to his assistance with money and ships. He was never able to repay Amsterdam what he owed her, but showed his gratitude with a gift that cost him nothing and made its citizens inordinately proud. He gave them the right to surmount their city's escutcheon with the imperial crown. The glory that this privilege won for Amsterdam gave her first rank among her older and rival sisters.

The medieval county of Holland especially was dotted with towns large and small, but none of the other counties and duchies was without them. Most of these towns sprang from trading posts on spots where the chances for commerce seemed good, at the confluence of watercourses, on the banks of rivers, on the seacoast. Where one merchant settled and throve, others came to try their luck.

With the rise of these towns the breakup of the feudal system began. The big manorial estates had been economic units that were sufficient to themselves. The serfs worked and produced for the lord, who owned everything and fed and protected them in return for their labor, but when they saw that the merchants of the neighboring towns were free within their walls from the arbitrary jurisdiction of the rural lord and were subject only to that of the count's representative, they escaped from the manor and sought freedom and a chance of bettering their condition among the trading community. As the merchants prospered and their wants increased, they were only too glad to welcome these handicraftsmen, whose labor they needed. Thus the feudal estates were gradually denuded of indispensable manual labor. The runaway villein, or serf, was emancipated under town law after a year and a day's residence inside the walls. The air of the town gives freedom, as the saying was.

Although the burghers within their ring of walls and moat were jealous and proud of their isolation, they did not shun communication with the citizens of other towns. When a trading settlement had received from the count the right to immure itself, the burghers copied its legal setup from an older, more experienced commune. The towns of Holland and Zeeland derived their law from outside the county—those of Holland from Brabant, those of Zeeland from their neighbors in Flanders. This sharing of municipal law created a bond between the towns, the giver standing to the receiver in the relation of mother to daughter. In the Bishop of Utrecht's territory, the ancient city of Utrecht was mother to all the other towns of the diocese; in Gelderland, Zutphen on the IJssel River was mother to all the other towns in the duchy.

There are certain features that all Dutch towns have in common. Each was fortified in former days. It had its ramparts to defend it against attacks, and these were surrounded by a moat. In the early nineteenth century nearly all these ramparts were transformed into parks. Trees were planted where the cannon had stood, the walls were demolished, and lawns and flower beds laid out along the edge of the moat. The Dutch name for the moat is *singel*, which means belt, and there is hardly any Dutch town that has not its *singel* and pleasant promenades along either side. Since this transformation took place, all these towns have expanded, in some cases to many times their former size. More homes had to be built for more people, and there was room for these only outside the old ramparts. Thus the *singel,* once the belt that encircled the town, became itself enclosed by the town. But everywhere it retained its old name, and if you walk through the parks along the *singel* you make a circuit around the original town, the old medieval fortress within its moat.

Another feature that Dutch towns have in common is the market square with its ancient town hall. Yet no square resembles any other. Leiden is exceptional in that it has no market square. Its town hall stands on the main street which, though its name is Breestraat, meaning Broadstreet, is so narrow that the quaint architecture of the sixteenth-century façade does not show up to advantage. The city hall of Amsterdam does not stand on the market square either. But that is due to the removal of the municipal administration to another building early in the nineteenth century. The city hall did dominate the square in former days, but it is now in use as a royal palace.

And finally canals are common to all Dutch towns. Even on Manhattan Island the Hollanders who settled New Amsterdam found it necessary to dig one, which gave its name to Canal Street. Each town built its canals in its own way. In Utrecht the streets on either side of them rise high above the water level; in Delft they are extremely narrow, so that the trees that line them form an arch of foliage above the water; in Dordrecht the houses rise out of the water, as in Venice; in Amsterdam the canals run in a semicircle around its medieval center. The *singel* is one of them and, of course, the innermost of these concentric crescent-shaped canals. It was the city's limit until 1610. In that year the *Heerengracht* was dug, and this outer belt was in course of time surrounded by two others, the *Keizersgracht* and the *Prinsegracht,* which together offer a perfect example of seventeenth-century city planning that made Amsterdam one of the most beautiful cities of northern Europe.

CHAPTER FIVE

The Seeds of Revolution

The IJssel is an arm of the Rhine that runs northward into the Zuider Zee. It flows through fertile land past Zutphen, Deventer, Zwolle, and Kampen, four prosperous market towns that in the late Middle Ages carried on a busy trade with the German Hanse.

This region was the scene, in the late fourteenth century, of a religious revival that had a profound influence on the life and manners of the Dutch people. It is known by the name of Modern Devotion, and the men who took an active part in it were called Brothers of the Common Life. Their apostle was Gerard Groote.

The brotherhood of which Groote was the founder did not live according to any monastic rule. They dwelt together under one roof in the leader's native town of Deventer. Their piety, industry, and exemplary conduct set an example to the citizenry and proved that the new Devotion that Groote preached was a way of life worth imitating. It spread its influence up and down the IJssel Valley and to the Hanse cities along the Rhine and the coast of the Baltic Sea. Groote did not live to see its full development. He died of the plague in 1384. His work was carried on by Florentius Radewijns, who turned his house at Deventer into a home for the community of young men whom Groote had gathered around himself and employed as coypists of manuscripts.

Thomas a Kempis, the reputed author of *De Imitatione Christi*, was one of them in the nineties of the fourteenth century. He later moved down the river and found seclusion in the monastery of Mount Saint Agnes near Zwolle, where he composed the little book that made him famous throughout the world. It is the purest expression of the ideals that Groote had instilled into the minds of his brotherhood, ideals that imperceptibly leavened the life and manners of the educated burgher class in the Netherlands. Erasmus also went to school at Deventer, and his insistence on the virtuous life as being more valuable than obedience to dogma was doubtless an effect of his early training in the classroom of Radewijns.

While Thomas and the Brothers of the Common Life were copying manuscripts, a new invention was gaining popularity that made their monkish labors obsolete. Which of the two, Laurens Coster of Haarlem or Johann Gutenberg of Mainz, invented the art of printing is still a matter of controversy, but the question of the inventor's identity is of slight importance. Important is the revolutionary effect of his invention. It changed the medieval into the modern world by turning man into a type-devouring animal and the printed word into his common prey.

The evolution of the book is one from settled to nomadic life, the very reverse of that of man, his creator. In the so-called "dark" Middle Ages, when not the streets but the books were illuminated, the volume was chained to the desk. It did not cheapen itself by going to meet its readers; it waited for them to come to its lectern. In the town of Zutphen a medieval library has been preserved whose greatest treasures are still chained to the desks. Zutphen lies away from the beaten track of the sightseeing foreigner, but the independent and intelligent traveler who prefers to find his own way instead of following Thomas Cook's will be rewarded by a visit to that ancient place. The books are kept in a vaulted room built onto the church of Saint Walburga, which apart from its library possesses another attraction for the aesthetic sightseer in several medieval frescoes. These had been covered under layers of

whitewash by Protestants of the Reformation era and have been
rescued from their plaster graves by Protestants of the present,
more tolerant, age. A medieval manuscript needs for its setting a
scene and an atmosphere such as one finds in this ancient library.
Seclusion, quietude, a lectern of massive oak, the sun falling upon
it through the panes of a Gothic window, the hushed sounds of the
town life outside, and at the hours the voices of the carillons sprin-
kling their music from the top of the church tower.

The chained book won its freedom when the printing press began to multiply its kind and the overflow was relegated from the
desk to the shelf. That development was a slow, gradual process.
In the early days of printing, books were not common and were
chiefly bought by learned scholars. They were supplied by a small
number of printers, who were at work in the Netherlands before
the end of the fifteenth century. Books printed before 1500 are
called incunabula, a Latin name formed of the word *cunae*, meaning cradle. They are specimens of the art of printing in its infancy,
but the beauty of many of them proves that the infant soon developed great efficiency and skill. They came from workshops in
Deventer,'sHertogenbosch, Zwolle, Utrecht, Gouda, Delft, Haarlem, Leiden. Even in a small village such as Saint Maartensdijk,
Peter Werrecoren ran a printing press. On the final page of his
first publication he naïvely admitted that his pioneering was far
from perfect: "I Peter Werrecoren pray those who will see or read
this work that they criticize it not too severely, for it is the first
sample of work that I never did before. I hope to do better in time
by the grace of God."

These early printers, who were at the same time the publishers
of their output, specialized chiefly in editions of classical authors
and in devotional books. The circulation of the latter also pro-
moted the spread of heretical doctrines among the educated Dutch
burghers, for few citizens were without a knowledge of reading.
Hence heretical tracts were widely read and both the civil and
Catholic Church authorities helped to stimulate their popularity by

Netherlands National Tourist Office

Terschelling, viewed from a boat on the Waddensee.

A polder. These fertile reclaimed areas lie below sea level, so ship canals are higher than land.

Carel Blazer, Amsterdam, Netherlands Information Service

A dike, with road and canal at left much higher than polder at right.

Netherlands Information Service

Tulips and windmill, familiar sights in Holland.

Erasmus, famed sixteenth century scholar, was born in Rotterdam. His statue stands in the marketplace.

Venerable volumes chained to desks in library of St. Walburg's Church, Zutphen, built in 1562.

The Night Watch, Rembrandt's controversial masterpiece, now in the Rijksmuseum in Amsterdam.

The Peace Palace in The Hague.

Amsterdam. Skating on the Keizersgracht in winter.

Amsterdam. The Keizersgracht in springtime.

Secret stairs behind this bookcase door, now open, lead to hideout where Anne Frank lived and wrote her diary.

Netherlands Information Service

The Hague. Vijverberg, overlooking canal.

Netherlands National Tourist Office

Ironically titled "Lieverd" (the darling), this statue of a mischievous urchin enlivens an Amsterdam street corner.

Modern school design in Amsterdam provides plenty of space, air and light for study and play.

ANP-Foto, Amsterdam

Emmy Andriesse

Dunes with wide soft-sanded beaches stretch the length of Holland's North Sea coast.

This neat thatch-roofed home at Giethoorn typifies the rustic charm of Holland's rural areas.

Families on holiday at Zandvoort, popular beach resort.

Netherlands National Tourist Office

Wives and daughters of fishermen take time out from net-mending for a coffee-break, as (below) the herring fleet leaves from Scheveningen harbor on the first day of the fishing season.

Netherlands Information Service

Windmills at Kinderdijk in South Holland. Water levels in this area are controlled entirely by such mills.

The cheesemarket at Alkmaar.

Prince William of Orange, 1533-1584.

The Weeper's Tower in Amsterdam. Here wept the sailor's wife when ships left from this point in former times.

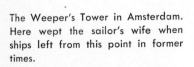

The Oude Gracht (Old Canal) and Dom Tower in Utrecht.

La Berceuse, a portrait of Mme. Roulin, painted in 1889 by Vincent van Gogh. From the collection of the Kroller-Muller Foundation, Wassenaar. Reproduced by permission of the Kroller-Muller Foundation.

prohibiting their sale. Forbidden fruit is always in demand, and the rumor that a new book was put on the Index whetted the public's curiosity and appetite for the wicked fare.

It reached the countryfolk as readily as the townspeople. The cheap religious tracts were carried along among the stock that itinerant hawkers sold to the rural population. Thus the teachings of the reformers were known even among isolated farmers and simple tillers of the soil. The seeds of the Reformation were sown throughout the Low Countries by means of the printed word.

The spoken word, too, helped to spread them. In the fifties and sixties of the sixteenth century Calvinist preachers traveled around and taught the crowds that gathered to hear them the tenets of the new faith. They assembled in deep secrecy in barns and stables, for these meetings were forbidden and the teachers and their proselytes, when caught, were severely punished.

Lutheran tracts were less popular than those that the Calvinists circulated. Luther, who rejected the authority of Saint James, could not win the adherence of the Dutch masses. The teachings of the Anabaptists, on the other hand, appealed to the Dutch. The senseless tortures inflicted on these harmless creatures during the Inquisition did not immunize the Low Countries against the infection of heresy. But the chief danger to the Church of Rome came from the side of the Calvinists. They were the militant force that turned the struggle for religious freedom into a fight for national liberty. Calvin's democratic church organization appealed to the Dutch: church authority emanating from the congregation, which exercised it through its chosen representatives, the board of elders; the minister selected and appointed on behalf of the congregation by the board of elders, though subject to approval by the classis. The classis was an assembly of delegates from several churches in a given area, and all the classes were represented in the national synod, the highest authority of the Reformed Church. Thus an organization was built up that derived its structure and discipline from below and not, as in the Church of Rome, from above.

The first national synod was held on foreign soil. Fear of the Inquisition had driven the heretics abroad, to the harbor towns of England, to the Rhine Province and Cologne, to Emden in East Friesland, and it was in the latter city that the refugees, in order to give cohesion and discipline to the dispersed, started a Dutch Reformed Church in exile on the basis of Calvin's presbyterian policy.

Emden thus became the cradle of the Dutch Reformed Church, which gave leadership to the Protestants at home and in the dispersal. The former, though suppressed and persecuted, were not inactive. The highest nobility of the land, all Knights of the Golden Fleece and as such entitled to give counsel to the absent ruler, sent petitions to King Philip II in Madrid for cessation of the heresy hunt. They knew the temper of the masses better than the absent monarch. But the king would not listen. At last, one summer day in 1566, the pent-up fury of the population broke out in a riot of destruction. It started in Antwerp and spread like wildfire across the country, the news of the insurrection in one town fanning the smoldering passions of its neighbors. Mobs invaded the churches and wreaked vengeance on Papacy and Inquisition by destroying the visible symbols of Roman worship. Images of the saints, altarpieces, stained-glass windows, priestly vestments were wantonly desecrated and destroyed. In a few days priceless art, the aesthetic harvest of several centuries, was lost forever.

CHAPTER SIX

William of Orange

It is not easy for a foreigner to understand how it happened that a king of Spain came to rule in the Netherlands. In the Middle Ages this territory was a jigsaw puzzle of little states, counties, duchies, and seigneuries, each governed by some petty ruler who was a nominal vassal of the German Emperor. But gradually these lords were supplanted by an outsider, the powerful Duke of Burgundy, who through marriage, intrigue, or conquest came to hold sway over all the Netherlands. The Burgundian dynasty became extinct in the male line when Duke Charles the Bold lost his life in the battle of Nancy in 1477. He left a daughter, Duchess Mary, who became the wife of Maximilian of Hapsburg. In 1493, eleven years after his wife's death, Maximilian was elected German Emperor. He had one son by Mary, called Philip, nicknamed "the Fair," who married Joanna, daughter of Ferdinand of Aragon and Isabella of Castile. In 1500 a son, Charles, was born to them at Ghent. When he had grown to maturity, he became the ruler of a large part of western Europe. Young Charles succeeded his maternal grandparents in Spain and was also elected German Emperor when the imperial throne fell vacant through the death of his father's father, Maximilian. The succession in the Burgundian lands, including the Low Countries, fell to him as a six-year-old boy by the early death of his father, Duke Philip the Fair. He subsequently added to these the territory of the unruly Frisians, the secular lands of the Bishop of Utrecht, and last but not least, the large duchy of Gelderland, which he acquired in 1543.

Although Charles V happened to be emperor, he was anxious, as heir of the Burgundian dukes, to maintain for his Low Countries a virtual independence of imperial obligation. As emperor he invited the Netherlands to send deputies to the imperial diets, and his sister, who ruled there in his absence, refused, not without his approval, to comply with the summons. At the Diet of Augsburg in 1548 he persuaded that assembly to recognize the unity of his Dutch possessions and declare them free from imperial jurisdiction. They were at the same time, it is true, officially incorporated with the empire, of which they were to form the tenth *Kreis*, or circle. This arrangement guaranteed them the protection of the *Reich* against foreign attacks, in return for a certain tribute that the *Kreis* was to pay to the imperial treasury. The Dutch treated it as a scrap of paper. They never sent delegates to the diet, they never paid their share of the imperial tax, they never asked to be protected by the *Reich*. As far as they were concerned, the bond with the empire did not exist. When the Dutch Republic, by the Treaty of Westphalia of 1648, obtained its independence, the tenth *Kreis* was officially dissolved. It had never been more than a name, but in that year the empire solemnly relinquished its nominal hold on the Netherlands.

In 1555 Charles V abdicated in favor of his son Philip, who thus became Philip II, King of Spain. Charles's favorite courtier had been Prince William of Orange, who was destined to become the leader of the Dutch revolt against Philip. William was not a native of the Netherlands. He was the eldest son of a count of Nassau-Dillenburg. On the death of a cousin, Count René, in 1544, William became heir to extensive possessions in the Low Countries and also inherited the princedom of Orange in the south of France.

William at that time was only eleven years old. His mother had reared him as a Lutheran. Charles V would not permit the young heretic's succession to René's wealth and titles unless William's father surrendered his guardianship and consented to the boy's being brought up at the court in Brussels as a Catholic member of the Netherlands nobility. The boy's charm won the aging emperor's affection, and the latter, at the abdication ceremony, gave public demonstration of his love for him by entering the Assembly at Brussels supported on the arm of his young favorite.

There was no love lost between Philip and William. They did not see eye to eye in matters of policy. The Low Countries were important for Philip as the northern vanguard of his world power, but William of Orange and the other Netherlands nobles would not have their country treated like a pawn of the Spanish king on the chessboard of Europe. Though William of Orange governed three of the provinces in the sovereign's name, he chose the side of the rebels against their legitimate overlord.

It was an extreme step to take, and he did not take it until all his other attempts to protect the Dutch people had failed. In 1566, shortly after the outbreak of the iconoclastic riots at Antwerp, a united front was accomplished, all parties agreeing on a petition to the King of Spain for a grant of religious liberty, in return for which he was offered the payment of three million gold florins. But Philip would not listen. His reaction to the wanton destruction of church property was the mission of the Duke of Alva, the iron-fisted commander of the best-drilled army in Europe. The Dutch revolt against Spanish cruelty was to be quelled with worse cruelty.

The Spanish Duke soon felt himself master of the situation in the rebellious Netherlands. He levied taxes that had no precedents in the country's history. Commerce was paralyzed, tens of thousands fled the country and sought refuge in the harbor towns of England and East Friesland or on board the Dutch privateers, called the Sea Beggars, that were scouring the Channel and the North Sea. It must have seemed reckless folly to attempt resistance against the power of mighty Spain. Yet Prince William of Orange

dared the impossible and assumed the leadership of an armed revolt. And thus began the heroic struggle of which the American
historian John Lothrop Motley (1814–77) told the stirring tale in
The Rise of the Dutch Republic. This book, published in 1856,
became very popular and was translated into Dutch, French, German, and Russian.

The marvel of that story is that, although Prince William saw
nearly all his endeavors end in failure, the cause he championed
triumphed ultimately. Twice he levied an army to come to the
rescue of his people and twice he saw it dispersed. Two of his associates among the high nobility were beheaded on the scaffold.
The towns that dared fly his colors after the Sea Beggars had made
a successful raid on the seaport of Brielle were sacked in punishment without his being able to come to their aid. Three of his
brothers fell in battle, uncrowned by victory that might have re-
deemed the sacrifice. His greatest achievement, the conclusion of
the Pacification of Ghent, a union of all the rebel provinces in defense of their freedom, proved a Pyrrhic victory, owing to the
successes of the Spanish forces in the south. And his ideal of religious liberty was not embodied in the Union of Utrecht, which
contained a provision, not approved by him, expressly recognizing
the monopoly of Calvinism in Holland and Zeeland. Help from
outside proved unreliable and more often a source of fresh danger
than a guarantee of safety.

And yet the victory was his, although he left his people in the
direst need when he was murdered at Delft in 1584. The assassin
could not destroy the living thought that he had bequeathed to his
people and to the world. The Dutch Republic was becoming a
reality.

CHAPTER SEVEN

Sailing the Seven Seas

The failure of the Treaty of Ghent was a shattering blow to the policy of Prince William of Orange. He had hoped to bind all the Low Countries into a strong federation, free from control by the King of Spain. He had to be satisfied with the substitute that the Union of Utrecht offered him.

William's son, Prince Maurice, aged only fifteen at the time of his father's death in 1584, succeeded him as stadholder and commander of the young Dutch Republic's military forces. The office of stadholder was, of course, an anomaly, for the word is the Dutch equivalent of lieutenant, a substitute or vice-regent for the absent sovereign, but since the States-General had renounced their allegiance to their overlord, declaring Philip II to be undeserving of their obedience, there was no sovereign whom the stadholder could represent in the provinces.

There were, indeed, attempts to circumvent this difficulty: the States-General offered Philip's vacant place to one foreign prince after another, even to the King of France and Queen Elizabeth of England. They both declined the honor, which was less great than the burden it involved.

Henceforth the Dutch dispensed with outside help. They had the good fortune to possess a political leader of outstanding ability.

Johan van Oldenbarnevelt was the statesman whose foresight and political sagacity steered the newly created confederacy through the stormy period that followed Prince William's assassination to safety and undreamed-of prosperity and power.

It seems a miracle that a republic born only recently and under trying conditions almost at once assumed a position of prominence among the states of Europe. Its very birth was a mystery. The Union of Utrecht had not created it, for in 1579, when it was concluded, the provinces still recognized King Philip of Spain as their overlord. Nor did their rejection of him two years later usher in the republic, as is clear from their offer of the sovereignty to the King of France and the Queen of England. At that time Oldenbarnevelt did not yet look upon the Union as an independent commonwealth. Yet by 1609 the King of Spain negotiated with the Dutch provinces as if they were a free and sovereign state, and signed a twelve-year truce with them.

Much had been accomplished in those thirty years. Young Prince Maurice, son of William of Orange, had scored military successes with a thoroughly reorganized army. He built up a well-disciplined force of foreign mercenaries, mostly Germans and Swiss, whose striking power was demonstrated in the campaigns of 1590 and following years, which cleared the united Dutch provinces of Spanish troops before the close of the century.

While Maurice was driving the Spanish garrisons out of one fortified town after another, the seaports of Holland and Zeeland began to send their merchantmen across the seven seas to distant parts of the world, to the Mediterranean, to the arctic north, to the Indian Ocean. In 1596 three ships under De Houtman reached the island of Java, and when they returned two years later the church bells were tolled throughout Amsterdam to welcome them home. It was indeed an important event, for it marked the beginning of Holland's colonial enterprise. By 1600 so many shipowners were competing for the Indian trade that Oldenbarnevelt, to stave off their common ruin, persuaded them to pool their separate interests in a single East India Company. In March of 1602 the States-General granted the new company a charter for twenty-one years.

Seven years later, on April 4, 1609, the good ship *Half Moon* left the quay at Amsterdam under the command of Henry Hudson. The Dutch East India Company sent him out to the arctic to search for a northeast passage to China and the Moluccas, with the order to return to Amsterdam if he failed to make his way through the ice pack beyond Novaya Zemlya; he was on no account to explore any other way to the Far East. Yet that is exactly what he did do, and his disobedience earned him immortal fame. On every map of North America the memory of him survives in Hudson River, Hudson Strait, Hudson Bay.

The map of the world still bears witness to the Hollanders' ubiquity in that age of exploration: Spitsbergen, in the arctic north, was named by its discoverer, Willem Barents; Cape Horn, at the southern extremity of the Western Hemisphere, by Willem Schouten for his native town of Hoorn on the Zuider Zee; Tasmania preserves the memory of Abel Tasman, the Dutch skipper who circumnavigated Australia and thereby proved it to be an island; Staten Island reminds one of the States-General, which gave the West India Company its charter.

These voyages were trying tests of endurance. The ships that sailed every year in the track of De Houtman carried a crew twice as large as was needed, for the directors of the company counted on the loss of fifty per cent of their men. Even the most robust found it hard to subsist for a year on dried meat, salted fish, and hard biscuits. Scurvy exacted its toll, and the logs became a monotonous record of dead bodies thrown overboard. It was finally realized that a halfway port of call was needed, where the ships could take in fresh vegetables and the sick could be cared for. The site that was selected was on Table Bay at the Cape of Good Hope, and here, in 1652, a settlement was made that was the origin of Cape Town.

Soon afterwards the port of call became for many on board the ultimate goal. From 1670 on the East India Company encouraged emigration of settlers to South Africa. These were birds of many feathers, but chiefly of Dutch, Low German, and Huguenot stock. They were the pioneers of the white race in South Africa, called the Boers in earlier days and now known by the name of Afrikaners.

There were Dutch settlements too in South and North America, along the coast of Brazil, and along the banks of the river that Hudson discovered. These were enterprises of the West India Company, which received its charter from the States-General in 1621. They were lost before the end of the seventeenth century, the Brazilian one to the Portuguese, the other, called New Netherland, to the English, who changed the name of the Dutch town on Manhattan from New Amsterdam to New York. In exchange for the latter colony the British ceded to the West India Company their settlement at the mouth of the Paramaribo River on the east coast of South America, and this, called Surinam, is still a part of the Netherlands realm.

The defeat of the Spanish Armada in 1588 had made these nautical exploits possible. It put an end to Spain's sea power and made the sea-borne commerce of Spain a helpless victim of the English and the Dutch. These invaded with impunity the Spanish colonies in America and the Orient, expelled the Spaniards from their possessions, and in course of time reduced King Philip's once mighty empire to a power of the second rank. Financially exhausted by her wars on land and sea, Spain was glad to arrange a twelve-year truce in 1609.

It was a signal victory for the young Dutch nation. But as soon as hostilities were suspended and no external danger threatened, internal dissension broke out. The two leaders who had led the provinces on to victory became the standard-bearers of the two opposing factions. Oldenbarnevelt was for strengthening the power of the individual states, Prince Maurice, the commander-in-chief of the federal forces, for centralization and greater power for the union. Passions ran high and rose to such a pitch that the faction which triumphed could not be satisfied with less than the death of its chief opponent. Prince Maurice won, and Oldenbarnevelt was beheaded on the scaffold.

CHAPTER EIGHT

Science, Letters, and the Arts

The entire population of the Dutch Republic in the early seventeenth century did not exceed a million, and six hundred thousand of these lived in the province of Holland. It was the energy of that small number that accounts mainly for the greatness and wealth of the Dutch Republic.

Golden Age is the name that the Dutch give to this period. There was plenty of gold in the country, but it was not the gold that can be weighed and counted and put away in coffers that gave the age its name. Gold is the noblest metal, and Holland was rich at that time in men of noble mettle, who accomplished great things in science, letters, and the arts.

They had predecessors who had shown them the way. In the late Middle Ages the towns of the maritime Low Countries were busy centers of industrial activity. Weavers, clothmakers, dyers, potters, wood carvers, carpenters, blacksmiths, goldsmiths, sculptors, painters plied their tools in yards and workshops. One does not wrong the painters and sculptors by mentioning them in the same breath with potters, weavers, and blacksmiths. They were craftsmen pure and simple, and the potters and weavers were artists in their crafts, each turning out a product that bore the stamp of his individual taste and of his love for the work of his hands.

The skill of these workers was the fruit of the accumulated experience of successive generations. The son grew up in his father's workshop and inherited with the shop the old man's technique. Apprentices came from all parts of Europe, attracted by the fame of Dutch workmanship. They brought not only their energy but also new ideas that tended to improve traditional skills and stimulate the growth of new ones. Albrecht Dürer's father was one of these. He came to the Netherlands from his native Hungary to work as an apprentice in a goldsmith's workshop before he settled for good in Nürnberg. These itinerant craftsmen spread among foreigners the praise of Dutch workmanship. As a consequence, buyers and collectors came to the Netherlands to buy pictures and prints. Antwerp in the early sixteenth century and Amsterdam in the seventeenth were important art markets that attracted the connoisseurs.

After the fall of Antwerp in 1585 many craftsmen emigrated to the north and settled in the free province of Holland where, thanks to the wealth that the commercial ventures in the Baltic, the Mediterranean, and the East Indies poured into its ports, they found ready employment and an ever expanding market for their output.

An age-old technical tradition alone cannot account for the excellence of that output. Other contributory factors came into play. The painters were such fine craftsmen thanks to the fact that they acquired their skill at an age when the mind is most malleable and receptive. A boy whose fingers itched to ply the brush was usually apprenticed to a local master at the age of ten or, if he was a painter's son, was taught in the father's workshop. By that time he knew the three Rs, and that knowledge was all he needed from school. Life would complete his general education. By not striving for versatility, these early artists attained perfection within their limited range. Each was a specialist excelling in one narrowly circumscribed field. Among the still-life artists were painters of breakfast tables, of fowl, of fish, of venison, of fruit, of flowers; among the landscapists, painters of winter scenes, of river and city views, of woodland and mountain scenery.

Landscape painted for its own sake and not as a background to a portrait or a scene of human activity was a Dutch innovation. The English word "landscape" reveals its Dutch origin, for the English equivalent of the Dutch suffix -schap is -ship, as in township, not -scape. The word was borrowed from the Dutch landscape painters with the genre that they introduced into England. Even the names of some of the tools of their craft were imported from the Netherlands. The Dutch painter calls the support of his panel *ezel*, meaning donkey, his dumb beast of burden; the English artist who calls it easel is probably not aware of its actual meaning.

Most Dutch artists came from the working class. Rembrandt was the son of a miller; Frans Hals, his great rival in portrait painting, of a linen weaver; Pieter de Hoogh, the painter of patrician homes, of a mason, and as craftsmen they did not rise above the class they were born in. The Dutch painters of that age who were received in high society can be counted on the fingers of one hand.

Being sons of the people and men of little book learning, they painted by preference the simple, humble life they knew best. Italian artists filled huge canvases with scenes of ancient history and mythology, taking their subject matter from the poetry of Homer and Virgil or from the Bible. The Netherlanders did not illustrate literature, but portrayed the real life around them. Even when they tried their hand at biblical scenes they did not care to be historically correct, but painted the Bible story as some happening in a Dutch setting. These simple painters discovered beauty and poetry at their own doorstep. They made it clear that the beauty of a painting was not in the subject, but in the artist's vision and his manner of portraying it. They were painters of the common man, the peasant at work in the field or drinking with his fellows in the alehouse, the old woman at her spinning wheel, the beggar asking for alms at the door, the burghers skating or feasting or listening to a sermon in church, the fishwife behind her booth in the market place, the doctor visiting his patient, children in school and at their games, the young lady strumming on the clavichord, the craftsman in his workshop, the painter at his easel, the scholar at his desk. This democratic character of its art is the distinctive merit of the Dutch school of painting.

Hieronymus Bosch in the fifteenth century and Rembrandt in the seventeenth were notable exceptions. They also portrayed on occasion the daily life around them, but their fancy often strayed beyond it into the realm of imagination and dreams. Bosch was little-known in America before the advent of Salvador Dali. It was the recent vogue of the Spanish painter's fantasies that awakened interest in the fantasies of the early Dutch master. Bosch was proclaimed the precursor of our latter-day surrealists, and the fame the early artist had won for himself acquired new luster from his inclusion in their fraternity.

The similarity between Dali's paintings and those of Bosch (whose name, by the way, is pronounced Boss, not Bosh) exists only on the surface. Misshapen creatures—half human, half something else, be it fish or bird or beast, or jug or shell, dead and hollow tree trunks, carcasses and skeletons, all symbols of death and decay —figure in the compositions of both artists, but there the resemblance ends. Bosch was a moralist who confronted his generation with a visual indictment of its sins; Dali is clearly not prompted by any moral indignation at the shortcomings of his contemporaries. He laughs at them and enjoys the spectacle of their gullibility, at their discovering deep meaning where there is none.

Puzzlement and snobbish pretense at understanding Bosch was not the feeling with which his contemporaries in the Netherlands looked at his work. They knew what he was driving at, for he spoke—subtly, yet comprehensibly—their everyday language. The supposedly surrealistic creatures that people his compositions are illustrations of the racy idiom that had been theirs from early childhood. Bosch was a medieval philologist who instead of making the picturesque locutions of his people readable in book form, gave them visible shape in paintings. It was no accident that Bosch was a contemporary of Erasmus, the collector and editor of *Adagia*, and of the anonymous compiler of *Proverbia Communia*, the first extensive collection of proverbs in a Germanic language, which appeared in print at Deventer about the year 1480. A scholar armed with a copy of that collection of common proverbs will be able to solve many a riddle that Bosch has posed for us.

This mystifying artist had yet other sources from which he drew suggestions for his weird imagery. He did not live and work in a vacuum; he followed a tradition that had a long and varied history. He had anonymous precursors in Dutch craftsmen who gave their fancy free play in grotesque sculpture, with which they decorated cornices of church pillars and the nether side of pew seats; in moralists who ransacked the animal world for symbols of human characteristics; in limners who adorned the margins of manuscripts with bizarre fantasies; in mummers on the popular stage who accoutered themselves as amphibious monsters, half man half beast, to act the parts of demons and devils. The medieval craftsmen reveled in the deformities their fancy created, and Bosch found in the jumbling of discordant things an effective means of satirizing the deformity of his discordant age.

Rembrandt, who lived almost two hundred years later than Bosch, during Holland's Golden Age, amazes one by the diversity of his works. We think of him first and foremost as the painter of soul-searching portraits, but there was nothing in the world around him that his brush did not re-create on panel and canvas: landscapes, either realistic or imaginative; still life to which he added movement by painting some human figure in the background; biblical scenes for which the Jewish quarter of Amsterdam, where he chose to live, supplied the types; stories from Greek mythology; episodes from Netherlands history. But he amazes also by the diversity of his technique. Never satisfied with his latest achievement, he tried to do differently and better next time. He was a restless explorer of untrodden tracks, a tireless seeker of pictorial effects never before attained, a heretic unafraid of the charge that he sinned against convention and tradition. His unshakable faith in himself has been justified by the acclaim of posterity.

His father, a miller living in Leiden, was aware that his fifth child had something uncommon that distinguished him from his older brothers. These were trained for a handicraft, but Rembrandt was sent to the Latin School and in his fourteenth year enrolled as a student in the university. But the boy knew better what he was destined for: he said farewell to the lecture room and entered the workshop of Jacob van Swanenburgh. The pupil soon excelled the master. He left Leiden for Amsterdam and studied for a time under Pieter Lastman. But Lastman could not teach him much, either, and after half a year Rembrandt returned to his native city and, together with his friend Jan Lievens, set up a studio and took in pupils.

It was there, in that simple workshop, that Constantijn Huygens, the private secretary of the Prince of Orange, came to see them and inspect their work. The extravagance of the diplomat's praise for his early work is eloquent testimony to the wonder Rembrandt's precocity aroused among the connoisseurs.

Little is known of the home in the Weddesteeg where he was born in 1606 and grew up, except what he tells us in some of his etchings and paintings, and these are unmistakable expressions of his devotion and love for his mother. At her knee he listened to her reading of the Scripture, and when he grew up he loved to paint her bending an aging face over the Book and holding onto it with wrinkled hands. One of Rembrandt's portraits of her was acquired three years before her death by England's King Charles I and now hangs in Windsor Castle, where it passes for a portrait of the Countess of Desmond.

Rembrandt never kowtowed to the great. He never aspired to a future of social eminence such as the artists Anthony Van Dyck and Peter Lely, both natives of the Netherlands, attained in England during the same period. The wealthy patricians of Amsterdam never realized that an intimate friendship with the artist would have done them honor. They employed him as a first-class craftsman; they did not treat him as a social equal. Rembrandt did not care. He felt drawn toward the weak and the humble. Christ comforting the sick, the Holy Family in a simple home or resting on the flight to Egypt were subjects that he loved to paint.

It is not true that Rembrandt's art was not appreciated in his own lifetime. He was the best-paid portraitist in Amsterdam, and inventories in the notarial archives prove that appraisers valued his paintings highly. That he landed in the bankruptcy court was not due to indifference of the connoisseurs and collectors. He was an improvident spender, and the final years of his life were darkened by poverty and the loss of his dearest ones. But the artist in him suffered no decline. In the depth of his misery he painted two of his greatest canvases, both of which are now on view in the Rijksmuseum at Amsterdam, "The Syndics" and the so-called "Jewish Bride."

Dutch art of the seventeenth century had its patron in the citizenry. In pre-Reformation days the Church and the court of the Burgundian dukes were the chief employers of the craft, and in their service the painters produced a limited range of subjects, mostly religious and historical scenes. The insurgents despoiled the places of worship of all works of art and established a Reformed Church in which God was worshiped without the allurements of painting and sculpture. But art, though banned from their houses of prayer and deprived of court patronage, did not become an outcast. The burghers of the new democracy welcomed her to their homes. There was hardly a Dutch interior without a picture on the wall, and there were rich burghers who owned small picture galleries. The people themselves had become the patrons of the painting craft.

Dutch literature of that era did not mirror the life of the burghers as faithfully as did the art of the painters. Writers were not trained in a workshop but in school, and the school gave them a deep respect for the Greek and Latin classics. An exception to that rule was Gerbrandt Adriaenszoon Bredero, a shoemaker's son of Amsterdam who was, as a young boy, apprenticed to an artist; and when he exchanged the brush for the pen and began to write verse and comedies and farces, he wrote poetry that is a literary counterpart of the painters' output. He knew no other book, he wrote, than the book of usage, and he apologized with mock humility for any errors he might have committed "through ignorance of outlandish tongues. For I have as a painter been guided by the painter's maxim that the best artists are those who come nearest to life."

The Dutch language was but a clumsy tool when the scholar Erasmus chose to address Europe in Latin. The nobility, if they expressed themselves at all on paper, wrote French, the language of the Burgundian court. With the scholars and the aristocrats disdaining to cultivate their native speech, the care of it in the sixteenth century was left to the small fry of middle-class rhymesters and scribblers whose speech was plastic enough, but who lacked a literary model in their own idiom.

The successful revolt in the early seventeenth century against the foreign ruler in Madrid stimulated a national fervor and a proud love for the native language. The poets of the young Dutch Republic did not share the indifference that Erasmus had shown to his mother tongue. But they shared his veneration of the classics and, except for Bredero, strove to create a literature whose character was less Dutch than Roman. Pieter Corneliszoon Hooft (1581–1647), an Amsterdam burgomaster's son, wrote nationalistic drama in the classical manner and a history of the first twenty years of the war against Spain in a style modeled on the prose of Tacitus. And Joost van den Vondel (1587–1679), the leading poet of the age, strove to become the Christian Seneca of Holland. His drama is a late survival of the medieval mystery play, cast in the form of classical tragedy.

Vondel was not the most popular poet of his era. That distinction belongs to Jakob Cats (1577–1660), who was affectionately called Father Cats. It was not the beauty of his verse that won him the title, but its somewhat pedestrian philosophy; the blessedness of family life, courtship, marriage, childbirth, school, work, prayer, sickbed, death were his favorite topics. He was a master of gnomic lore. Proverbs strike home by the picturesque wording of a common truth, and Cats knew how to make a commonplace sound uncommon by his plastic expression of the truism. He was but a minor poet, but a poet who struck a personal note that made him unique among his contemporaries.

Hooft and Cats belonged to the ruling class. They were patricians; Vondel was a businessman, a dealer in silks and hosiery. But that difference in social position did not reveal itself in the verse that they wrote. That of Cats, in fact, is more folksy than Vondel's. Another aristocrat, Constantijn Huygens, the private secretary of the Prince of Orange who was often employed on diplomatic missions, wrote poetry that in its artificial diction reveals him as a man of refined culture, but in its subject matter is as homely an expression of a bourgeois outlook as that of Cats. Class distinctions counted for little in the literature of the Dutch democracy.

Vondel, Hooft, Cats, and Huygens wrote only for their age, but the artists who painted the people's home life continue to charm three centuries after their death. One glance at a sunlit parlor scene painted by Johannes Vermeer or Pieter de Hoogh helps us to understand what attracted Descartes to the Dutch Republic and held him there for more than twenty years. It was the atmosphere of peace and tolerance and freedom that kept him there. "What other country could you choose in all the world," he wrote to a correspondent, "where you can enjoy such perfect liberty?" It was there that Spinoza, the Jew, though accused of being an atheist by the Calvinist ministry, was able to live and write in peace and win followers of his thought by conversation and correspondence. There Joost van den Vondel continued to live unmolested and honored, though he had outraged the feelings of the orthodox Reformed by leaving the faith for which his parents had suffered persecution to return to the Church of Rome.

The laws that these free citizens of the Republic obeyed were laws of their own making and were, consequently, obeyed without grudge or demur. They were framed, it is true, by the ruling class, an oligarchy of the best families. But the members of that class knew the temper of the masses and had learned by experience that the best safeguard of their authority was the approval of the multitude. Pieter Corneliszoon Hooft, himself a member of the ruling patriciate, wrote in his *Netherlands Histories*, "In this country the greatest changes have been brought about through the instigation or, at any rate, through the active compulsion of the common man, and in these days not the least art of municipal government consists in managing and placating the multitude." The legislative power was not in the hands of the masses, but no laws were passed that the masses would not tolerate. For the freedom of utterance was granted to all, and the murmur of discontent was a danger signal that few magistrates dared disregard.

Spinoza (1632–77) was undoubtedly the wisest man of his age in the Republic, but he never taught in a university. Philosophy was his hobby, the grinding of lenses his profession. There were other original thinkers among his contemporaries for whom the pursuit of learning was a sport rather than a means of earning a living. The most original was Anton van Leeuwenhoek (1632–1723), a simple burgher of Delft who earned a modest salary as usher at the city hall. In his leisure hours he pursued a hobby that revealed to him the existence of a world of whose existence his fellow burghers had no suspicion. He was as good a grinder of lenses as Spinoza and constructed himself the microscopes that he needed for his research. With these he discovered living creatures that were invisible to the naked eye. He found that a drop of the water he drank was inhabited by crawling little monsters; he saw that the remnants of food he had eaten and scraped off his teeth were alive with tiny creatures. "Little beasties," he called them. Van Leeuwenhoek lived to a ripe old age and had the satisfaction of seeing his findings accepted by the learned of his day, though they did not consider him one of their number, as he was ignorant of Latin, then the hallmark of scholarship. But even Czar Peter the Great, who lived in Holland for a time to study the art of ship-building, traveled by barge to Delft and called on its famous citizen.

Another original investigator was Jan Swammerdam. He proved that insects were not creatures of spontaneous generation from mud, manure, and putrid matter, as was commonly believed in those days; he described insect life as a circular course from egg to egg, and classified insects on the basis of their various metamorphoses.

And there was Christian Huygens (1629–95), a son of the poet Constantijn, who declared that probability was the nearest that man could come to truth. The skeptic in him would not conform to any religious creed beyond the negative confession that he did not exclude the deity from the probable that he believed to be attainable.

Freedom from the tutelage of the Church of Rome had created a daring spirit of exploration. Established truths were no longer accepted by inquisitive thinkers. The mathematician Simon Stevin (1548–1620) searched for a reign of law in the bewildering diversity of nature and rejected belief in miracles as a denial of the cosmic order.

Calvinist orthodoxy saw serious danger in this widespread questioning tendency. But it could not win the support of the civil authorities for its suppression. The burgomasters of Amsterdam were unwilling to interfere with heterodoxy. A wise policy, aiming at the city's economic welfare, was the basis of their tolerance. Intellect, enterprise, and labor which other countries recklessly ejected enriched Amsterdam in return for its hospitality. Victims of tyranny and intolerance found refuge and asylum there. The city rulers were not to be cowed by the fulminations of the ministers from the pulpit. The Calvinist divines called themselves the watchmen on the tower, but the tolerant burgomasters were the rulers over the people's life at its foot.

CHAPTER NINE

The Periwig Period

Oldenbarnevelt's tragic death had not settled the dispute over state rights as against federal rights. On the contrary, it left a bitter memory in the hearts of his adherents and gave rise to an anti-Orange faction among the merchant-rulers in the cities of Holland. Their opposition did not come into the open while the war with Spain lasted. But when the Dutch Republic, by the peace treaty of Westphalia of 1648, obtained the Spanish king's recognition as a free and independent state, the anti-Orangists moved to the attack. They accused William II, who had succeeded his father, Prince Frederick Hendrick, in 1647, of military ambitions and of intriguing for a resumption of the war against Spain in conjunction with France. Before the party conflict had come to a head, Prince William suddenly died of smallpox in his twenty-fourth year. He left a little son, also called William, who was still a baby in his mother's arms. This gave the anti-Orangists an unexpected opportunity to rule without political and military interference by a meddlesome stadholder.

They were fortunate in having for their leader one of the greatest statesmen of that age. Jan de Witt held the same high office that Oldenbarnevelt had occupied half a century earlier. The title had been changed from Lord Advocate to Pensionary, but the

Pensionary's chief function was still the management of the Republic's foreign affairs. De Witt remained in office for twenty years. It was not a period of uninterrupted peace. Oliver Cromwell had seized power in England. The English Parliament issued in 1651 the Navigation Act, which forbade the importation into Great Britain of foreign goods in other than English ships or in ships from the country of origin. It declared the carrying trade between England and her colonies a monopoly of the English merchant marine and prohibited foreigners from selling in the English market any fish they had illegally caught in English waters.

This act struck a blow at the Hollanders' remunerative carrying trade. The commercial rivalry between the two sea powers led to a series of naval wars in which the Dutch fleet, though not always victorious, scored many a triumph. In 1666 De Ruyter sailed to the Thames with a fleet of over eighty ships. He occupied the mouth with his main force and sent admiral Joseph van Ghent up the Medway. Van Ghent broke through the chain with which the river had been blocked, destroyed several English men-of-war, captured others, including the flagship *Royal Charles*, and created a panic in London.

The shock to English prestige had its effect on the peace negotiations that were proceeding too slowly to satisfy De Witt. Five weeks later the peace of Breda was concluded, which gave commercial advantages to the Republic and a welcome modification of the Navigation Act.

The leadership of Holland in the foreign affairs of the Dutch Union had its dangers. The province, and especially its metropolis, the city of Amsterdam, was chiefly concerned with the maintenance of sea power. Holland's delegates to the States-General saw England as the Republic's most menacing enemy. They failed to see the greater danger that lurked in the imperialistic designs of King Louis XIV of France. A strong, efficient fleet and a neglected army were the results of this one-sided policy.

De Witt was not blind to its dangers, but his efforts to balance the defense system were thwarted in the States-General. The Orangists in the assembly, most of them from the land provinces, refused to vote appropriations for a larger army unless the Prince of Orange, then a mere stripling, were appointed commander-in-chief. De Witt could not consent to that. How could he entrust that high office to an inexperienced boy? Frustrated in his attempts to build up the land force, De Witt had to rely on his statecraft to keep the ambitions of Louis XIV in check.

In 1672 the King of France succeeded in forming an anti-Dutch coalition with England and the archbishops of Münster and Cologne. Attacked from three sides, the Republic seemed doomed. The population in panic clamored for the Prince of Orange as their savior. De Witt had to yield to popular pressure and consent to young William's appointment as stadholder and commander-in-chief of the federal army. But the man in the street, always passionately devoted to the House of Orange, was not satisfied with the statesman's defeat. De Witt and his brother were brutally butchered at The Hague by a riotous mob as scapegoats for the country's misfortune.

The mob that committed this atrocity gave vent in barbarous fashion to an instinctive feeling that only the Prince of Orange could bring salvation and the man who had kept him out of power had to atone for that offense. Young William fully justified the people's trust in him. He showed himself a good strategist. He soon cleared the country of enemy troops, aided by a fortunate turn in the weather. The French had penetrated deep into Holland across the ice that covered the inundated polders. A sudden thaw forced the invaders to retreat, pursued by William's troops across soggy terrain, on which the French were out of their element. At the same time a spectacular high tide, such as occurs only once or twice in a hundred years, flooded the coast line of Holland, making it inaccessible from the sea and safe from any danger of a British landing.

The war was not popular in England. Many a Briton felt

ashamed of his country's alliance with France's Catholic majesty against the Dutch Protestant Republic. Peace between the two naval powers was restored in 1674 and four years later the Republic concluded a satisfactory peace treaty with her other enemy, the King of France.

Prince William's brilliant leadership established him firmly in the saddle. The states of Holland, Zeeland, Utrecht, Gelderland, and Overijssel made the office of stadholder hereditary in William's family, thereby reversing the policy of the state of Holland, which had voted six years earlier to exclude forever the Prince of Orange from the stadholderate. William had married Mary Stuart, daughter of James, Duke of York, a younger brother of Charles II, whom he succeeded in 1685. King James II was ousted by his own subjects for favoring the Catholic religion, and his Dutch son-in-law ascended the British throne in his place.

William's marriage remained childless. At his sudden death in 1702, due to injuries suffered in a riding accident, he was succeeded in England by his wife's sister Anne and as stadholder in the Republic by a distant cousin, Count John William Friso.

William III was the last Prince of Orange directly descended from William the Silent. That noble line passed out in glory. The first William had been outlawed and murdered by order of the King of Spain. The third, as leader of the republic the earlier William had founded, headed at the time of his death a European coalition that would decide the partition of the decayed Spanish Empire. There was poetic justice in that course of events.

John William Friso was a descendant of the Silent's younger brother John, Count of Nassau, and stadholder of Friesland, as his father and grandfather had been before him. He was accidentally drowned when the ferryboat by which he crossed the Moerdijk capsized on a stormy night. He left a posthumous son who inherited his political offices in Friesland and Groningen, but in the other provinces the oligarchs seized power again and ruled without a stadholder.

They managed well until 1747, when danger from abroad, just as in 1672, aroused popular clamor for the restoration of the Prince of Orange. A French invasion threatened, and under pressure of the general discontent the young prince, Friso's son, was reinstated in his father's high functions.

Neither he nor his son and successor, William V, was a strong link in the chain of the Orange lineage. They were not any better than the age they were born in. The eighteenth century was far inferior to its immediate predecessor. The Republic's vitality had been sapped by repeated bleedings in the wars unchained by Louis XIV, and the weakened body needed a long rest to recover from its exhaustion.

When the Golden Age of the Netherlands went into its decline, the painter Gerard de Lairesse published a theory of the art of painting. Though he belonged to the seventeenth century, he was in taste and mannerism a typical representative of the eighteenth. Nature, he said, is the same as she was a thousand years ago: woods, fields, mountains, rivers remain forever unchanged. Hence Nature is modern—that is to say, imperfect—but she is antique and perfect when the landscape is fitted out with beautiful buildings, tombs, and suchlike remains of classical antiquity. He wanted to see Nature dressed up in what he thought was the Greek and Roman manner; he found perfect beauty in the unnatural.

His theory was widely accepted in the eighteenth century. The Dutch of that era were strangely blind to the beauty of the landscapes that Ruisdael from the tops of dunes had painted of bleaching fields and pasture land under a towering sky of sunlit clouds. As a result the art of landscape painting passed out in the eighteenth century. The artificiality that De Lairesse preached as perfection corroded not only the painter's but also the poet's art. It suffered from the striving for perfection through adornment. The landscapes that the rich collected, the verse that they admired, even the gardens they laid out around their country places were travesties of nature's simple beauty.

The Dutch call this era the periwig period. The human head, too, was perfected by an artificial coiffure, a manufactured mass of powdered hair that in stiff permanent waves rolled down upon men's shoulders. To succeeding generations which had returned to simplicity, the periwig was the most typical symbol of that unnatural era. It marked, in their judgment, an effete generation no longer capable of bold, heroic action.

Indeed, in comparison with the Golden Age, the Republic in the eighteenth century was in the doldrums. But the mass of the people should not be judged by the appearance of their periwigged rulers. And even these were not as effete as they seemed under their absurd hairdos. They went about their work in office, warehouse, and workshop with traditional punctiliousness and industry, but they moved by routine; the inner drive was gone. They were satisfied with their accumulated wealth and preferred its quiet enjoyment to the busy pursuit of greater riches.

They vied with each other in the building of stately summer homes, they dabbled in science and philosophy, and turned their town houses into little museums. The proud owner of such a collection was always glad to show his paintings or rare books or curios to connoisseurs who called on him with reliable credentials. Scholars from abroad found patrons in Holland who were willing to finance their research. The Swedish botanist Linnaeus was the guest for a time of the banker Clifford, who owned a beautiful garden in the neighborhood of Haarlem. He arranged his host's botanical collection and published a scientific description of it in 1737.

The universities of Leiden and Utrecht retained their international fame. Since the vehicle of instruction was Latin, foreign students who were versed in that language could understand what the Dutch professors taught them. The most famous among these was Herman Boerhaave, whose textbooks on the practice of medicine, translated into several European languages, spread his fame abroad and attracted young physicians from all parts of Europe to his classes.

The urge to explore was not entirely extinct. It survived in Albert Schultens, who was the first to perceive the unity of the Semitic languages and to interpret the Hebrew of the Old Testament by comparing it with Arabic and other related idioms. And Lambert ten Kate, a native and lifelong resident of Amsterdam, brought proof that the infinite variation of word forms was subject to laws as strict and inescapable as those which all things in nature had been proved to obey. He found such laws to be inherent in the structure of all Germanic languages by a painstaking comparison of Dutch with its Germanic sister tongues, and he proceeded to write an etymological dictionary of Dutch on the basis of the vowel shift in the so-called strong verbs. The study of the Indo-European ablaut, thus called by Jacob Grimm a century later, has made great progress since Ten Kate's day, but to him belongs the honor of having been the first to reveal its function as a wellspring of word forms.

The man who was responsible for the Republic's foreign policy at this time was Simon van Slingeland, Pensionary of Holland. He was not a typical representative of the periwig period. He proved himself an able, forceful statesman who could diagnose the ailments from which the Union was suffering and dared propose a treatment for their cure. The antiquated machinery of the federation was in need of repair. The ruling families in towns and provinces had gradually become closed corporations that admitted no outsiders into their fenced-off domain. They filled by co-option all vacancies in the town councils, disposed of all offices within the grant of the government, divided them among themselves and sold the minor jobs to relatives and protégés. Such a system did not encourage the rise to power of the best minds. Men of character and courage were feared rather than favored and were kept out of office by the conspiracy of ensconced mediocrity.

Prompt disposal of questions relating to the conduct of foreign affairs was impossible. The provincial state assemblies were so anxious to preserve their independence that they did not allow their delegates to the States-General to use their own judgment in casting their votes. The entire deputation had to travel back to get instructions before any matter could be settled in the States-General. The slowness resulting from this roundabout procedure was a laughingstock among the foreign diplomats at The Hague. "Which is better," asked Van Slingeland, "to let the state perish or to apply remedies for its salvation which somewhat circumscribe provincial freedom?" He pleaded in vain. His recommendations were read in manuscript by successive generations of oligarchs; they were published in print in 1784, nearly seventy years after they were proposed, but nothing was done to turn their wisdom into practice. The vested interests of the best families blocked all attempts at reform.

If William IV, who was stadholder of all the provinces, had been as strong and courageous as his ancestors had been, he could have used his power to curb provincial freedom and strengthen the federation. Unfortunately he was temperamentally disinclined to forceful action. The clamor of the multitude had brought him to power, but his native timidity made him suspicious of popular movements. A conservative by nature, he felt a closer affinity to the class that had barred him from power than to the masses to which he owed it.

He died in 1751, leaving a three-year-old son, for whom his English widow, Anne, daughter of King George II, acted as regent. When the son came of age he proved no less timid and irresolute than the father. He humbly requested the states to confirm him in the offices of stadholder and commander-in-chief of army and navy instead of claiming them as his by hereditary right. He retained as his confidant Duke Lewis Ernest of Brunswick-Wolfenbüttel, whom his mother, feeling her death approaching, had appointed his guardian when he was in his early teens. The duke planned and disposed, the prince assented and signed on the dotted line. He was capable of resistance only against the impact of new ideas on his mind. For he was conservative to a degree and feared, as had his father, the ferment of radical thought imported from France.

He was supported in this by the ministers of the Dutch Reformed Church, the watchmen on the tower guarding the nation's spiritual heritage. These succeeded in obtaining from the state of Holland the suppression of Rousseau's *Emile* and *Contrat Social*. The effect of the ban was the opposite of what it was meant to attain: it enhanced the popularity of the forbidden books among an enlightened middle class that strove for freedom from the traditionalism of the Church's theology. They read not only Rousseau but also the English Deists, and with arguments borrowed from these sources opposed intolerance, prejudice, and ignorance which, it was claimed, were fostered by the orthodox ministers.

The truce between the stadholder and the anti-Orange oligarchs came under a severe strain at the time of the American Revolution. Prince William V, son of an English mother, had inherited from his forebears a political tradition of alliance with England and suspicion of France. The oligarchs, headed by the rulers of Amsterdam, received support for their opposition to the House of Orange from heterogeneous elements that had no stake in the vested interests of the ruling families. Radical thinkers among the middle class who had read Voltaire and Rousseau and patriotic burghers who resented the Prince's weak-kneed subservience to British interests were in sympathy with Amsterdam's policies.

These elements formed a loose coalition without clearly defined aims. Claiming to be the sole defenders of Dutch honor and dignity, they arrogated to themselves the name of Patriots. The old conflict of states' rights as against centralization of the federal government was pushed into the background. The Patriots demanded they be given a voice and responsibility in the government of city and province. They objected to the exclusion from city council and state assembly of competent men who did not belong to the ruling families. They hailed the American Revolution as a hopeful sign of the times; and the rulers of Amsterdam, always in the forefront of the anti-Orange faction, negotiated secretly with emissaries of the American rebels. The text of their secret agreement fell by accident into English hands, and the British Government declared war on the Republic, greatly to the distress of the stadholder and the Orangist party.

Thus the Dutch Republic became the ally of her young American sister. The Yankees were popular in Holland. That became clear to John Paul Jones when he ran into a Dutch port with a British prize. He was fêted wherever he went and was made the hero of a popular song, snatches of which linger on in a nursery rhyme that is still being sung throughout Holland.

The Republic was the first European power to follow France's lead in recognizing the United States of America, and the States-General resolved without a dissenting vote to admit and acknowledge John Adams as envoy at The Hague. "The American cause has gained a signal triumph," he wrote to a correspondent, and he quoted—at the risk, he said, of being charged with vanity—the words in which the Spanish envoy to Holland had complimented him on his achievement: "Sir, you have struck the greatest blow of all Europe. It is the greatest blow that has been struck in the American cause and the most decisive." Shortly afterwards he arranged with three Dutch banks the floating of a loan of five million guilders.

The Amsterdam market all through the eighteenth century was a great power in international politics. Though Dutch commerce and industry were on the decline, the financial position of the Amsterdam exchange remained unimpaired. Foreign merchants shipping goods abroad could rely on having their drafts paid promptly in Amsterdam. During the Seven Years' War England's expenditures for her armies on the Continent were for a large part met by loans from Dutch bankers. And when the American Congress, through its spokesman John Adams, appealed to the Dutch bankers for financial support, they did not hesitate to supply it.

The Patriots had small reason to pride themselves on having got the country into war. The carrying trade and territory in India were the Republic's worst casualties. When peace was concluded at Paris in 1784 there was a general sense of relief. Enough had been lost to make any peace preferable to a prolongation of the conflict.

The Patriots shifted the burden of guilt for this disastrous outcome onto the shoulders of Prince William V. They blamed him for the desolate condition of army and navy. His trusted counselor, the Duke of Brunswick, withdrew from The Hague under pressure of a vicious campaign against him and left the country for good. This success emboldened the Patriots to further rebellious action. They formed volunteer corps which clashed in several places with the Orangist populace. The Prince's consort, a sister of King Frederick William II of Prussia, was held up by one of these corps and was refused permission to enter the province of Holland. She wrote an indignant report of the incident to her brother in Berlin. The Prussian king's ambassador at The Hague demanded satisfaction for the insult to the princess, and when the States of Holland refused, the king sent an army of twenty thousand men into the Republic. Patriot resistance collapsed, the Orangists came back into power, the volunteer corps were disbanded, and the princess received assurance from the States of Holland that all who were responsible for her detention would be punished. Thousands of Patriots fled to safety in America and France. But the regime they escaped from was not any the stronger for its triumph. It was a tottering rule that could be stabilized only with the aid of foreign intervention.

Its instability became apparent at the first flare-up of democratic aspirations beyond the border. The storm of revolution that had risen in France soon swept northward across the Low Countries. Patriots who had found refuge in France formed a Dutch legion under Colonel Daendels. He joined the invading forces of General Pichegru, who crossed the frozen rivers into Holland. On January

19, 1795, Daendels entered Amsterdam at the head of what he called his Batavian Legion. The stadholder fled in a fishing smack to England, and a new democratic state, called Batavian Republic, was established on the ruins of the antiquated commonwealth that had been founded by William the Silent two centuries earlier.

The Batavian Republic was a mushroom growth. The instability of its government frustrated the best intentions of the reformers. Repeated interference—first by the Paris Directory, then by Napoleon—in the internal affairs of the new state and passive resistance by the Orangist majority of the nation increased the difficulties of the Batavian rulers. In 1806 Emperor Napoleon, possessed with the ambition to extend the power of the Bonaparte dynasty, made his brother Louis King of Holland. The Patriots had no choice; if they refused to accept Louis as king, the country, Napoleon warned, would be annexed.

Louis had a gentle disposition and actually won the affection of his alien subjects. His imperial brother accused him of courting popularity and of being too lenient with the Dutch. He failed, the emperor complained, to enforce the law against all trade with England, and connived at the lucrative smuggling activities of the Hollanders. In 1809 the English landed on the isle of Walcheren, and although the raid miscarried, it brought proof that the emperor's continental fortress was not impregnable. Napoleon welcomed the incident as a pretext for his brother's removal. He summoned Louis to Paris and forced him to accede to conditions that were humiliating to his pride, and when Napoleon ordered General Oudinot to occupy Amsterdam, which Louis had made his capital, the king resigned on behalf of his second son. But the emperor decided otherwise. He incorporated the Netherlands with the empire.

For three years the Dutch nation possessed no political entity. Their country had become part of the Napoleonic Empire and French officials directed its administration. The Dutch were far from happy under alien rule. As part of the French Empire, their country shared none of its glories and all of its sacrifices. It lost its colonies to England, saw its merchant marine decimated by the British fleet, its people reduced to poverty by unemployment, its youth enlisted in the imperial armies and marched away to the shambles of the battlefield. When rumors reached Holland early in November 1813 that Napoleon had been defeated near Leipzig, there was general rejoicing. The shipyard carpenters in Amsterdam set fire to the customhouses, hated symbols of French rapacity. At The Hague a more dignified demonstration in defiance of the emperor was staged by a triumvirate of aristocrats headed by Gijsbert Karel van Hogendorp. They constituted themselves a provisional government, sent envoys to London to invite the Prince of Orange to return to The Hague, and welcomed him amid popular jubilation when he landed soon afterward. In a proclamation issued on December 2, 1813, the prince declared, "It is not William VI whom the nation has called back. It is William I who as sovereign prince appears among his people."

CHAPTER TEN

The Monarchy

One-man rule had never been popular among the Dutch. But it was not awareness of the traditional aversion to royal authority that made William I assume the title of Sovereign Prince. He knew that Great Britain for her own security would insist on the expansion of his territory, and he postponed the assumption of the royal crown until he could claim it as king of the united Netherlands. The British Government wanted a strong and self-reliant power on the Continent that would counterbalance French ambitions. King William was to be England's sentry on the northern frontier of France.

Thus the southern Netherlands, which had been ceded by Spain to Austria at the Peace of Utrecht (1713), became part of the new kingdom, and the emperor in Vienna was indemnified for their loss with extensive territory in north Italy.

In this way the abortive union of all the Burgundian Netherlands that William the Silent had formed at the Treaty of Ghent in 1576 was restored. Their reunion under King William I was equally short-lived. His subjects in the solidly Catholic provinces in the south revolted against the rule of their Protestant monarch, and the Great Powers that had arranged their fusion in 1815 decided in 1830, at a meeting in London, to dissolve it and turn the southern

Netherlands into a separate monarchy under Leopold of Saxe-Coburg as King of the Belgians. King William withheld his approval for several years, but finally signed the London treaty in 1839.

King William possessed great qualities: tireless industry, a flair for business, a talent for finance, the courage of initiative, a genuine interest in the education and welfare of the masses. But the nation's morale was at a low ebb. The Napoleonic regime had sucked the country empty of resources. The apathy of his subjects made it possible, if not imperative, for King William to assume despotic power. He discarded the Council of State, ruled without responsible ministers, made far-reaching decisions without consulting Parliament, influenced the judiciary, and would not allow any examination of the manner in which he administered the state finances. Finally even his most loyal counselors rebelled.

Opposition against this autocratic one-man rule came from the side of the enlightened middle class, that section of the nation from which in the previous century the Patriots had drawn their strength. The name Patriots was no longer in use; they now called themselves Liberals. They had an able leader in Jan Rudolf Thorbecke, professor of public law at Leiden. He formulated their principles and defined their aims in terse, eloquent prose.

King William II, who succeeded his father in 1840, saw in Thorbecke a dangerous radical and tried to block his efforts toward reform, but the revolutionary storm that raged over Europe in the forties swept the Liberals into power in 1848. A committee of five under Thorbecke drafted a new constitution which laid the foundation for the modern democracy of Holland. The personal rule of the monarch was abolished, his ministers were made responsible for his acts to the assembly of the States-General, the members of the First Chamber, who used to be appointees of the crown, were henceforth to be elected by the Provincial States, and these, as well as the Second Chamber, were to be chosen directly by all persons paying a certain amount in taxation. The legislature was given the right of amending bills submitted on behalf of the crown by its responsible ministers, and obtained the right of passing on the annual budget and scrutinizing the government's expenditures.

Thorbecke realized the imperfection of a suffrage based on property. "There is nothing but irony in legislation that offers citizenship to all under conditions that are accessible only to few," he wrote in 1844. But the principle of universal suffrage had a hard and long struggle for recognition. It was finally included in the revision of the constitution of 1917.

The militancy of the Liberal party in the reign of King William III (1849–90) led its opponents to organize and formulate principles and aims in their turn. Political life became clearly patterned and varied. The conservatives were Calvinists who assumed the name of Anti-revolutionaries. They were opposed to the rationalism of the eighteenth century that had produced the French Revolution, of which modern Liberalism, in their opinion, was a dangerous offshoot.

The Catholics also came to the fore as a distinct political entity. They had always been tolerated, but treated as second-class citizens. Thorbecke proposed in 1853 to give them freedom of organization, guaranteed under the constitution as revised in that year, and the measure was carried over the violent protests of the Dutch Reformed ministry. However, the Anti-revolutionary Abraham Kuyper, made his Calvinist followers' consent to a coalition with the Catholics' party. "As faithful Calvinists," he told them, "you ought to oppose Rome in all dogmatic and religious matters, but to accept their support if you find them willing to fight for your Christian school and for the Christian foundation of the state."

The laboring class, too, became politically articulate under the leadership of the Frieslander Pieter Jelle Troelstra. Proletarians in the sense that ancient Rome gave to the name: "paupers who did not contribute anything to the state except offspring (*proles*)" do not exist any more in Holland. The workman gets a decent wage and is able to pay taxes like any other citizen. The early Socialists were opposed to the monarchy, but during the reign (1898–1948) of Queen Wilhelmina they changed their tactics and became a reform party loyal to the crown. Political co-operation with the bourgeois parties is no longer scorned as a betrayal of Labor's interests. They may still talk about the chains in which they are held by capitalism, but they prefer the chains of their oratory to the doubtful blessings of a Marxian revolution.

Early in March of the year 1937 the Social Democratic Labor Party made a momentous decision. It passed a resolution in favor of abandoning its traditional opposition to all military expenditures. From the very beginning of Labor representation in Parliament, the Socialists had always voted as a man against the War Minister's annual budget. In the first decade of the twentieth century the Labor spokesmen firmly believed that measures of defense were a waste of precious money. The possibility of war seemed remote. The ruler, they argued, who should be so mad as to start a conflagration would find his army paralyzed by the refusal of organized labor to take up arms against their comrades of neighbor countries. They felt sure that the solidarity of the international proletariat was a firmer guarantee of national immunity from war than a costly defense system.

The collapse of that solidarity at the outbreak of World War I in 1914 gave these Socialist dreamers a rude awakening. Still they did not relinquish their opposition to any plans for military preparedness. For in the twenties they began to pin their hopes upon a new kind of shock absorber. Collective security as provided for by the Covenant of the League of Nations was sure to restrain the warmongers, they felt. No nation eager for conquest would dare to satisfy its land hunger in the face of international opposition under the aegis of the League. War was at last officially branded as a crime, and the threat of international punishment for a disturber of world peace was an effective deterrent. And there were many Hollanders outside the Social Democratic Labor Party who shared its optimism.

The experience of the thirties dispelled their day dreams. From the mountains of Abyssinia the smoke of battlefields and burning villages drifted across Europe and threw an ominous shadow over the Continent. The Hollanders realized that international action for the maintenance of peace was a forlorn hope, and that they had to rely on themselves for the preservation of national safety. The Labor party swallowed the bitter pill and approved the war budget.

Labor had come to its senses was the comment of the Liberal press in Holland. But that was a wrong diagnosis. Europe had gone out of her senses, and in a world gone mad and torn by dissension, Labor had taken the only course that it saw open, reliance on national self-defense.

The geographical position of the Netherlands was precarious. The Dutch did not flatter themselves with the hope that their country in the next European war would escape involvement, as it had in the first. Holland is not a natural fortress like Switzerland. Its eastern frontier lies open to invasion, and only a small section can be inundated to impede the progress of an invading army. The Dutch hated to have to make provision for military preparedness, but the hazards of the world situation made them resigned to the sacrifice.

The army, once treated as a stepchild, became the spoiled hopeful of the nation. It got costly presents of fortifications along the eastern and southern frontiers, it was promised an increase in the annual contingent for compulsory military service, and might experiment with new aircraft, artillery material, caterpillars, and armored cars. Its twin brother, the navy, received an equal share of the popular favor. In short, the Netherlands, after a short spell of toying with collective security, had gone back to the old policy of self-reliant neutrality.

The Liberal doctrine that the state must abstain from interference in the lives of the citizens was based on the romantic belief in the self-healing power inherent in the social organism. The

Liberals thought of the evolution of society as a natural process by which the fruits of regeneration were brought forth from the seeds of corruption. But the crass realities of modern life brought accumulating proof that interference was a necessary evil for the prevention or suppression of evils that were infinitely worse.

During the half century of Queen Wilhelmina's reign (1898–1948) the Liberals and the clerical parties, that is the Catholics and Calvinists, vied with each other in passing welfare legislation that made the state a guardian of the poor, the unemployed, the disabled, and the aged. The state owns and runs public utilities that in the United States are private enterprises—not only the postal but also the telegraph and telephone services. The railroads are operated by the state, as well as the coal mines in the province of Limburg. Most museums and picture galleries are owned and administered by either the central or a local government. The cost of primary, high school, and university education is defrayed from the public revenue, no matter whether it be given in public or in private schools; the latter, however, must conform to the standards set up by the government to obtain this support. Only the private universities, the Catholic one at Nijmegen, the Reformed Free University at Amsterdam, the Catholic Economic School of Tilburg, and the Municipal University of Amsterdam are free from state control.

It was an enlightened pattern of life. Most city slums were cleared and replaced by communal dwellings for which the tenants paid a moderate rent. The countryside, especially in the densely populated western section, assumed the aspect of a vast garden city. Co-operatives flourished in the agricultural districts and made it possible for the farmer, however far distant from an urban center, to dispose of his products and receive an ample return for his labor. Compulsory insurance against accident, sickness, and old age created a sense of security among the masses of the working class. They were enjoying more leisure than in former days, and the general health of the nation was good. People with limited incomes joined travel societies that organized excursions to foreign countries, which in earlier days were the exclusive playgrounds of the rich. In summer the beaches along the north seacoast swarmed with bathers; camps for boys and girls were scattered throughout the country, and youth hostels were provided for hikers and cyclists where they found shelter for the night at minimum cost.

With all the social layers contributing their energy as never before to the national effort, Holland unfolded in the first decades of the twentieth century an unprecedented activity. She expanded her commerce, developed new industries; her architects created an original style that gave fresh beauty to her old cities; art and literature found new ways and forms of expression, and her universities regained the international prestige they had possessed in the seventeenth and eighteenth centuries.

CHAPTER ELEVEN

Invasion

Suddenly, on the tenth of May, 1940, Hitler's hordes swooped down upon that happy land and turned it into a waste. The Nazis paid romantic lip service to the sanctity of their German soil, yet they denied the Dutch people's right to similar soil worship. One would think that if any nation had a just claim to its soil it was the Dutch, who created a large part of their land themselves. In as many days as it took them centuries to reclaim their country from the water, the Germans took it from them by force of arms.

A friend of mine in Holland wrote me on September 14 of that year: "Your letter reached me the day before yesterday. I had read more than half of it when I noticed that it bore the date of May 6th. That is to say, a century ago." That remark was more revealing to me than a detailed description of his daily life would have been. He felt as if he had awakened, like Rip van Winkle, from a long sleep during which the familiar face of things had changed beyond recognition. The Holland he had known early in May was his Holland no more.

The people's free country had, as if by some evil magic, become a ghastly prison where no one dared speak above a whisper. Abundance, which they used to take for granted, had gone the way of liberty under the harsh German invaders. The livestock was dec-

imated, the country looted empty of foodstuffs and general com-
modities. Everything was rationed, and many things for which
one held the indispensable ration cards were not obtainable.
Leather became so scarce that many Hollanders had to replace
their worn-out shoes with the wooden clogs of more primitive
days. Malnutrition and undernourishment showed their effects on
the general health. Skin and eye diseases were prevalent. Fuel was
just as scarce as food, and neighboring families assembled on frosty
days around a communal fire. Where bombs had not fallen, the
old town houses and the more modern homes in suburbs and the
countryside still looked like their former selves, but the joy had
gone out of them, and the lack of a fresh coat of paint, once the
pride of every houseowner, was symbolic of that inner lack of
cheer.

Rotterdam was sacked, and the brutal missionaries of Nazi *Kul-
tur* threatened to inflict a similar fate on Amsterdam if the Dutch
did not cease their obstinate armed resistance. Terrorism was the
German short cut to victory. That Amsterdam survived unharmed
was cause for gratitude, but it was not to the Nazis that Holland's
thanks were due. They would have destroyed Amsterdam's beauty
without the slightest scruple if destruction could have served their
end. It was General Winkelman's decision to lay down arms that
saved the city. It was hard for a brave soldier to be beaten by
blackmail tactics. The surrender was on his part an act of bitter
self-sacrifice; to him Holland owes the preservation of a priceless
monument of Dutch history and culture.

After the loss of the official Dutch Army, underground resistance forces took over. One should not take the term underground
in its literal sense. There is no lower level beneath the Lowlands
by the North Sea, nor are there any dense forests and mountain
caves where guerillas could hide and lie in ambush. The forces of
national resistance had to operate in the open, because the entire
country lay open to the sky. The freedom fighters found security
and shelter under the cover of impassive faces. The underground

that was their field of operation was safe from invasion by the Gestapo, for the German police could not pry into loyal Dutch hearts. Those who served in this secret militia formed a force of soldiers whose armor was absolute trust in each other. The discipline maintained among them emanated from a common determination to liberate their country at any cost of suffering and sacrifice. Their clandestine papers were the sole organs of public opinion. The muzzled journals which the Nazis approved had no following. The forbidden press flourished in spite of all attempts of the Gestapo (the *Geheime Staatspolizei*, Secret State Police) to stamp it out. Its writers turned their pens into weapons that the Germans could not match in kind, and they wielded them at the risk of their lives.

Queen Wilhelmina escaped to London, where with her cabinet of ministers she set up a makeshift government in exile. On August 31, her birthday, the cry that spontaneously arose wherever Hollanders met abroad to pay tribute to their queen was, *"Leve de Koningin!"* To every Hollander who joined in the chorus this meant, "May the Queen live to see the day of her return to the liberated fatherland."

In the fatherland itself the day was not celebrated. There it was a breach of Nazi law to make public demonstration of one's loyalty to the House of Orange. The national colors might not be displayed. All visible tokens of allegiance to the royal house were struck by the German ban. "The gathering and having in stock of certain kinds of flowers such as orange-colored blooms, marigolds, white carnations, and forget-me-nots may be considered attempts to provoke forbidden demonstrations," ran an order issued from The Hague over the signature of Dr. Seyss-Inquart, the German Civil Administrator. It was amusing to see the *Herrenvolk* "the master race," in such a quandary over the display of those flowers.

To any human being who was not a Nazi it was obvious that a Hollander's loyalty was due to his own government and to the

House of Orange that for nearly four centuries had shared the nation's destinies. Queen Wilhelmina's son-in-law, Prince Bernhard, though a German by birth, was as bitterly opposed to all that Hitler stood for as the most patriotic Dutchman. Bernhard is the husband of the present Queen Juliana, Wilhelmina's daughter. In a broadcast from London he told his listeners how the Nazi invaders had planned to treat the Netherlands Government and the royal house. On the body of a German general whose plane had been shot down by the Dutch a document was found containing two sets of instructions. One assumed that no resistance would be offered to the German forces, in which case guards should be stationed in front of various specified buildings, including the palaces of the royal family. If, however, the Dutch people should be "disloyal" enough to put up a fight against their German "protector," the other instruction should apply. It ordered the capture of the members of the royal family and the Queen's entire cabinet and their immediate transportation by air to Berlin, where the prisoners would be dealt with in accordance with the resistance offered. The Nazi code of honor did not respect an enemy who resisted attack, but wreaked vengeance on him for fighting back, and the braver the resistance, the harder the punishment.

The Dutch people celebrate the feast of Saint Nicholas Eve on the fifth of December. They call it *Sinterklaasavond*. The feast and the name were brought by the Dutch settlers to this country and *Sinterklaas* became Santa Claus in American pronunciation.

The Dutch word for celebrate is *vieren*. The Hollander does not only veer a feast, he also, if he is a sailor, veers a line; if he drives a horse he veers the rein when relaxing his restraining hold. What is the connection between the two meanings? The basic sense is "to let go, to set free." The sailor and the driver let the line and the rein slip through their hands unimpeded; the celebrants of a feast let the day slip by unimpeded by labor or cares. *Vieren* is an enjoyment of freedom, a release from restraints. The *vierdag* is a free day. There were no free days in Holland in all the years under the tyranny of Hitler and his Gestapo.

The Gestapo saw to it that Saint Nicholas did not ride across the roofs any more. Instead of the holy bishop's presents, it dropped through the chimney flues its own unholy horrors upon the hearths: suspicion, fear, anxiety, fright, distrust. One could not let slip anything, no presents through the chimney, no words across the lips. One could not let oneself go.

Yet the Gestapo was powerless against Saint Nicholas himself. Though the monster could drive the bishop's white horse off the roofs and prevent the Dutch people from celebrating his feast, it could not desecrate the saint. For Saint Nicholas is a spirit who is stronger than all the physical force that Hitler's fury could unchain. Saint Nicholas has known and has triumphed over enemies who fought him with stronger weapons than Hitler wielded, spiritual weapons such as are needed for fighting a spirit. The ministers of the Dutch Reformed Church in the seventeenth century attacked him with the insidious weapon of anti-popish prejudice. The Dutch people, who had freed themselves from what the ministers called the misbelief of Rome, might not revere a saint of the Roman calendar, they told their flocks from the pulpit. But fortunately the flocks did not obey them. They had an aversion to Rome, but that aversion was not stronger than their love of Saint Nicholas. In spite of all thundering from the pulpit, the Reformed people of Holland remained faithful to their Roman saint.

That Roman saint is older than the Roman Church. The Church christened the spirit Saint Nicholas, but before that christening his name was Wodan. Wodan was to our pagan ancestors the god of fertility, the personification of the divine life force that is the source of our existence and all its blessings. The rod with which the bishop's black servant threatens the naughty children was not originally destined for punishment. It was the magic wand of the spirit of fertility. According to the popular belief of heathen times, a stroke with that rod could fertilize the stricken one, were it man, beast, or plant. In short, the spirit we call Saint Nicholas is the imperishable life force implanted by God in his creation. It is the force from which all blessings flow, also the blessing of being able to give and being willing to give. Everyone who distributes presents on Saint Nicholas Eve is himself an agent of that divine life force.

How then could the Gestapo outlaw Saint Nicholas? The will to give is ineradicable in man, as it is in this fertile earth of ours. The stores in Holland were plundered empty, the bank accounts of Dutch burghers had been depleted by taxes, fines, and extortions. But that did not mean that there was nothing for the Dutch to give on Saint Nicholas Eve. In times such as those which the Hollanders had to endure under the Gestapo, insignificant actions acquired great value. One gave one's friend a wink of understanding; one gave a word of comfort to the mourning; one gave an encouraging smile to the disheartened; one gave one's Jewish neighbor whom Hitler had reduced to a pariah a cordial handshake. The need of the times turned such gifts into valuable presents. The poorest could be as generous in such giving as the richest, for there is often greater wealth of heart in those who are least blessed with earthly goods.

The Jews especially were in need of such gifts. The misery to which the Nazis, in their sadistic fury, condemned them was testing the strength of those long-suffering people beyond endurance. They shared with their non-Jewish countrymen all the hardships of the German occupation—loss of personal liberty, harsh treatment at the hands of the Gestapo bullies, extortion, searing indignities, hunger, cold—but on top of these they were subjected to crueler torments such as only the diseased minds of Hitler and Himmler could devise. Jewish families were torn apart, thousands of boys and men were taken from their homes in the dead of night and herded together near the German border to be transported, like cattle bound for the slaughterhouse, to the occupied areas of Russia. There they had to slave for the German war machine, to be starved to death or murdered by gas when the hardships of slavery made them unfit for further labor. And this treatment was not limited to men and boys. The diary of Anne Frank is a revealing document in which an innocent young girl has described the hidden life of a few Jewish families in their Amsterdam hiding place. Her innocence could not shield her against Nazi cruelty. She too suffered capture, deportation to Germany, and death.

At the time of the massacre of German Jews that was engineered by the Nazi Government after the assassination of Vom Rath in Paris, a young Dutch poet, Hendrik Marsman, wrote a noble protest against that outrage and the withering shame of its impunity. *Despair* he entitled his outburst. It is a nightmarish vision of the world turned into wasteland, of cities burning and silhouetted against a lurid background of a sky in flames, of nations perishing in orgies of murder.

> Should not our hearts rot away
> With shame and remorse because
> This is done with impunity?
> For none of us has done aught
> To prevent with his very life
> That blood stains clot the hands
> And the spawn of the underworld
> Sit on volcanoes enthroned.

That was written before the outbreak of the second World War. What would he have said if he could have witnessed how the Nazis, having seized his native land, scourged the Dutch Jews with unimaginable horrors? That evil sight was spared him. Shortly after the invasion he sailed for South Africa. His ship was torpedoed in the English Channel, and Marsman was not among the saved. The finest tribute that was paid to his memory was a national protest against the deportations of Jews, a protest that surpassed his own in nobility and power, as it was uttered in the face of Nazi tyranny, in the very teeth of the oppressor whose ruthless wrath might punish such a protest with death.

It first briefly summarized the story of the increasingly cruel measures against the Jews that culminated in the wholesale order for the deportation of some hundred thousand Jewish Netherlanders. "This is a cool résumé of the facts," the writers of the protest declared, "which in harshness and businesslike efficiency are paralleled only by the orders of the Egyptian Pharaoh. . . . Holland has been hard hit and deeply humiliated. Now we shall have to prove that even under pressure we have not lost our honor or silenced our conscience. We trust that everyone in a position to do so will sabotage these sadistic Nazi measures, especially State officials, policemen, and railroad personnel, and we ask all Netherlanders to address a protest to the Commander-in-Chief of the German armies in the Netherlands, Air General Friedrich Christianse."

The protest may have given relief to the conscience of those who signed it and of those who actively responded to it, but it did not bring relief to the Dutch Jews. They were decimated. When the war was over only 15,000 were left of the 150,000 who were Dutch citizens in 1940.

Other religious groups also suffered under the Nazi invaders, especially the leaders of the churches, for they never wavered during the German occupation in their steadfast resolve not to submit to the dictates of iniquity. They had the courage to protest again and again when Nazi orders violated concepts of decency and Christian charity, and many a priest and pastor paid with his life or his freedom for following Christ rather than Hitler. To cite only one instance out of many: Early in September, 1941, Nazism was denounced in a pastoral letter signed by the five bishops in protest against German interference with Catholic trade unions. The Workers Union had been ordered by the Nazis to affiliate with the National Socialist Party, and since the Church took the stand that membership in that party automatically excluded Catholics from the sacraments of the Church, the clergy could not remain silent when so arbitrary a measure confronted Catholic workers with the choice between loss of livelihood or excommunication. "Openly and loudly we raise our voices," the bishops wrote, "against the injustice done to these tens of thousands by robbing them of their social status. We protest against the moral constraint and the attempt to force upon them a conception of life conflicting with their religious convictions."

The men who, at the danger of their freedom, dared vindicate the rights of their flocks had thereby won the right to warn them, when the tide of war finally turned, against the evil of vengeance. None more so than Archbishop Jan de Jongh, the head of the Catholic Church in the Netherlands. He was fined a few times by the Nazis, but they never dared imprison him. Intrepidity and determination were expressed in the lines of his face. Most Dutch Catholics are natives of the southern provinces of Brabant and Limburg, but De Jongh was of Frisian ancestry. His father was the local baker of the village of Nes on the island of Ameland in the far north of Holland, a windswept and sea-menaced strip of land where nature's inclemency breeds a hardy race. The people of Friesland are proverbially obstinate. *Koppige Friezen,* headstrong Frisians, they are called by their countrymen of the other provinces. The Nazis discovered, to their vexation, that the Frisian archbishop did not deviate from the type. They did him an inestimable service, for their persecution helped him to rise to impressive stature in the eyes of his countrymen, both Catholics and Protestants, a revered embodiment of the people's will to live their own lives in freedom of conscience.

CHAPTER TWELVE

Modern Authors
and Artists

The medieval winter with all its terrors was brought back to Nazi-ridden Europe. The homes were cold and cheerless. If the fuel rations sufficed, they were enough for one home fire only. The entire family lived and worked in the one room that could be heated and lighted. The medieval lack of privacy came back to Holland with Hitler's winter. The blackouts turned the streets at night back into the trackless wastes that our ancestors took for granted. Starvation stalked the homes of the poor, like a wolf looking for prey in the track of the German looter. The Dutch and their fellow Europeans under the Nazi's heel shivered and hungered and huddled together and stumbled through the darkness, and longed with aching hearts for light and warmth and cheer and space.

But Hitler, hacking at the rock of time, could not carve it into the shape of his grandiose imaginings. His pickax struck unsuspected veins from which torrents rushed forth, followed by landslides, and under the impact of forces beyond his control the would-be molder of the new Europe went down with his millennial dream into chaos.

Hitler's defeat by the Allies and the return of Queen Wilhelmina to Holland were the occasion of nationwide rejoicing. The queen was acclaimed wherever she went with moving demonstrations of the people's loyalty and love. They knew that hers had been the strongest and most determined will among the Netherlands Government in Exile. But the jubilation was a surface joy. Underneath was a mood of sadness and mournful remembrance. The war had taken a heavy toll of Holland's population. Many innocent men had been executed as hostages, others had fallen in the underground war of resistance, and thousands had died in German concentration camps. In the book of Holland's martyrs two names will stand out in golden letters: that of Dr. J. Eijkman, a leader of the Christian Youth Movement, and of Dr. J. Huizinga, professor of history in Leiden. Eijkman had the courage, soon after the invasion, to denounce in bold print all attempts at collaboration with the German enemies. "Judas, the betrayer of Christ," he wrote, "must not be allowed to join our work of reconstruction. For the Judas in our midst has made false idols his saviours: the soulless State, Race, Blood and Soil. We Dutch Christians cannot build anew on those foundations, nor join in the work of reconstruction with such Judases as helpers." He was promptly sent to a concentration camp and died there a few weeks before Germany's defeat.

Huizinga published before the invasion a withering indictment of Nazism. He entitled the book *In the Shadows of Tomorrow*. It predicted the doom that was coming over Europe and painted the future in somber colors. His life was blotted out by the shadows when they fell over Holland. The country lost in him one of its greatest and noblest sons, an original thinker, a loyal patriot, a bold champion of right and justice and decency in human relations. In retaliation for his bold defense of academic freedom, he was imprisoned in the concentration camp at Saint Michielsgestel. Thanks to Swedish intervention in his behalf, he was released in October 1942 but was not allowed to return to his home in Leiden. In 1945 he became ill, weakened as he was by the shortage of food and fuel, and died before he had seen his country liberated from the oppressor's rule. The Nazis did him the honor of dreading the leadership that he wielded over his countrymen, but by silencing him as an academic teacher they could not kill the powerful word through which he wielded it.

The loss of individual lives, however precious, could be borne with resignation; heartbreaking was the loss of a large part of the Netherlands realm. The East Indies, which are now called Indonesia, were the heritage of Holland's Golden Age. The Dutch began trading with the Malay Archipelago in the closing years of the sixteenth century. Among the many products they brought home from those parts, the spices of the Moluccas were then the most coveted. Their first trading post in the archipelago was established on one of these Spice Islands. But in the twenties of the seventeenth century Jan Pieterszoon Coen, Governor General of the Dutch East India Company, a man of vision and great administrative ability, removed the center of Dutch interests in the Far East to West Java, much nearer to the European homeland. There he founded the city of Batavia, which became the capital of the Netherlands East Indies.

The Hollanders went to the Indies as traders. The East India Company was a commercial concern, not a political body. But they soon found that it would be to their commercial advantage if they could exercise political authority. The native princes were often warring among themselves, crops in the fields were destroyed, and trading was hampered by the general unrest. The company intervened and restored order by force of arms. In this way it came to be a political power. When the Dutch Republic, as has been told above, was replaced by the Batavian Republic, the East India Company was dissolved, and the Malayan territories were henceforth governed as colonies owned by the state.

Until 1877 the native labor of Java was employed to produce wealth under a system of forced cultivation. The tillers of the soil were required to place at the government's disposal a certain proportion of their land and one fifth of their labor time. The advantage of this system was that the government could prescribe what crops should be cultivated instead of having to accept the rice which the natives grew to the exclusion of nearly everything else.

It was not a bad plan, for it encouraged experimentation with new crops, but in practice it did not work so well. It discouraged private enterprise; the officials strove to distinguish themselves by stimulating production, and as a result the people were overworked and underpaid. As the administration of the colonies was held to be the personal concern of the king, the Dutch public was kept in ignorance of conditions in Java.

Public opinion was aroused at last by the publication of *Max Havelaar*, an autobiographical novel by Multatuli, pen name of Eduard Douwes Dekker (1820–87). The story explained why he had reason to call himself by that self-pitying pseudonym, "I have suffered much." It established his fame as an author and inaugurated reforms in the methods and practices of colonial administration.

In the course of Queen Wilhelmina's reign the East Indies ceased to be colonies. The Netherlands constitution no longer regarded them as such. They were parts of the realm, equal in standing with the kingdom in Europe; in other words, the former mother country was considered their elder sister.

During the twentieth century the Dutch governed this tropical part of the realm with skill and conscientiousness. They built roads, fought disease, spread education, enlisted the aid of science for the improvement of agricultural methods and crops, and increased the number of products by importing new ones from other regions, such as cinchona and rubber from South America.

The deletion of the word "colonies" from the Netherlands constitution was proof of the Dutch people's realization that the days of colonial governments were over. They did not foresee in the thirties that the end of their rule was close at hand. The universal upheaval brought on by the second World War accelerated the course of events. The islands were invaded by the Japanese and made a part of what the government in Tokyo chose to call the Great East Asian Co-prosperity Sphere. Japan's defeat and her withdrawal from the islands was followed by an upsurge of nationalistic fervor. The Javanese, under the leadership of Sukarno, rose up in arms supplied to them by the Japs and proclaimed their independence. Nationalism was the fruit of Dutch education, and the insurgents who refused to submit again to Dutch rule were turning into practice what their guardians had taught them.

The guardians considered it premature and ill-advised, but world opinion, especially public sentiment in America, was on the side of the Indonesians. On December 27, 1949, the Queen of the Netherlands signed and handed to Mohammed Hatta, Premier of the United States of Indonesia, the Act of Transfer and Recognition, and thus a new nation came into being, one that is destined to play an important part in the near future of the Far East.

Multatuli was a pioneer not only in the field of colonial rule but also in the field of letters. His revolutionary temper fired the young writers of the generation that followed his. He died in 1887 in voluntary exile in Germany, at a time when in Amsterdam a group of young authors whose outlook on life was akin to his were editing a new monthly which became the organ and rallying point of a literary revival. They shared Multatuli's contempt for Holland's bourgeoisie, its narrow-mindedness and smugness, and they resumed his onslaught on the stereotyped diction of nineteenth-century poetry. "I do my best," he wrote, "to write living Dutch, although I have been to school." The sarcasm was prompted by a deeper feeling than mere pleasure in paradox. A rebel by temperament, he hated school for its choking grip on originality, and by shaking off the grip of the literary standard upon the language, which squeezed all expression into stereotyped forms, he started a revolutionary movement whose impetus launched *De Nieuwe Gids*. "Word Art" was the name by which these youthful writers chose to call their new style. Each strove for a strikingly individual form of expression, believing with Guy de Maupassant and Flaubert that "whatever one wishes to say, there is only one word to express it, only one verb to animate it, and only one adjective to qualify it." New words were coined and old words were given new syntactic functions. This hunt for the one exact phrase often led to mannerism and extravagance of diction, but even their severest critic cannot deny that these "Eightiers," as they were called, transformed and permanently enriched the language.

Willem Kloos was editor-in-chief and published sonnets in *De Nieuwe Gids* that assured him at once a high place in Dutch literature. Readers of the present day may still find them beautiful but no longer defiant. What sounded revolutionary in the late eighties set the style for ensuing generations, and their modernism became convention in the twentieth century.

The success of the Eightiers was followed by dissension in their ranks. Kloos's colleagues became more and more interested in social rather than literary reform. His younger colleague Albert Verwey became convinced that true poetry has a higher vocation than to express individual moods and emotions in musical and picturesque words. He founded a new monthly which he called *De Beweging* (The Movement). This became the rallying point of a group of younger poets who recognized in Verwey their mentor and master. His talent as a literary critic and essayist, which he demonstrated by his contributions to *De Beweging*, won him in his later years appointment to the chair of Dutch literature at the University of Leiden, in which function he was succeeded when he reached the age of retirement by P. N. van Eyck, the most brilliant of the *Beweging* group.

Frederik van Eeden was coeditor with Kloos and Verwey of *De Nieuwe Gids*. In it he published his beautiful fairy tale *De Kleine Johannes*,* the story of Johannes' longing for the Great Light, an allegory of Van Eeden's search for God. The search

* Transl. *Little Johannes* (1895) with an introductory essay by A. Lang.

leads him to "the great, dark city of humanity and its misery." The most versatile author of his generation, Van Eeden was a poet and essayist, novelist and playwright. Perhaps his best novel is the one that in its English translation is called *The Deeps of Deliverance*, his best drama *The Witch of Haarlem*. In a long philosophical poem in *terza rima* he gave the fullest exposition of his perspective of life and the world. He felt himself a solitary stranger among his contemporaries, but the next generation clearly realized his worth and founded a society for the study of his works, a form of recognition that was not given to any other of the Eightiers.

The most classical poem of that self-centered generation was *Mei* (May) by Herman Gorter. He did not belong to the *Nieuwe Gids* group but they hailed him as one of them when his poem appeared in 1889. He soon became dissatisfied, as did Van Eeden, with their cult of art for art's sake and embraced the cause of the world's proletariat. His later verse did not fulfill the promise of his youth.

The internationally known novelist Louis Couperus belonged to that same generation, but neither he nor his friend Marcellus Emants identified himself with *De Nieuwe Gids*. Both were of The Hague, the elegant resort of diplomacy, of military display, of the idle rich, of retired men of business and officials on half pay. Couperus is the charming interpreter, Emants the stern critic, of that life of leisure where woman reigns supreme. Woman as the embodiment of insincerity, selfishness, vanity, and folly is the theme of most of Emants's plays and novels. Couperus's opinion of his fellow man is scarcely much higher, but he accepts life as an artist enamored of its colors, though they be the allurements of corruption. He possesses, unlike Emants, a saving sense of humor. In *Van en over Myzelf en Anderen* (Of and Concerning Myself and Others) he smiles with gentle irony at his own idiosyncrasies, and these delicate little sketches of mocking self-revelation are perhaps his most precious contributions to literature.

Dutch art did not produce anything startling for nearly two hundred years after the death of Rembrandt and his great contemporaries. But in the middle of the nineteenth century a renascence in art occurred that coincided with the appearance of Multatuli on the national literary scene. Jozef Israels was the leading figure among a group of artists known by the name of the Hague School. Jacob and Willem Maris belonged to it, Jacob a versatile craftsman who turned his hand with equal skill to landscape, figure, and portrait, Willem more limited in his range, a painter of pasture with grazing cattle and of ducks among the reeds along the edges of a ditch in the polder. It was not the cattle nor the ducks that fascinated him, but the play of the sunlight upon white skins and feathers. He painted light, he used to say, not animals. And Jacob, too, studied light effects in clouded skies and on dimly seen towns and villages that glittered in the distance. Another member of this so-called school was Anton Mauve, who won fame with his canvases of the Drente heath, where flocks of sheep in the twilight straggle toward the fold. And Johannes Bosboom belonged to this group at The Hague, a master draftsman who did beautiful sketches in sepia of church interiors and peasants' homesteads, and magnificent oil paintings of similar subjects.

Mauve was related to Vincent van Gogh, and for a short time in 1881 the latter worked under Mauve's encouragement and guidance, when Vincent was badly in need of both, feeling distrustful of himself and his fellow men. He received small recognition from the public, which did not care to buy his paintings, and if his brother Theo, who was an art dealer in Paris, had not supported him financially, he might have perished of starvation. When Vincent van Gogh died by his own hand in 1890, he was little-known in his native country.

Van Gogh himself was the best propagandist for his art. He wrote the tragic story of his own life in letters to Theo. Week after week, for seventeen years, he poured out his soul to him. Theo treasured the letters, and his widow made it her life's task to edit this intimate autobiography. They appeared in Holland in

1914 and have recently been translated into English and published in the United States. The publication revealed an artist who had been as great a master of the pen as of the brush, and a noble soul who had striven in all humility to give the best that was in him to his fellow men.

The artist would have been gratified by the growth of the small but distinguished elite that admired his work into a less distinguished multitude of tens of thousands. Not because he shared the naïve American delusion that bigger and better are synonyms. But he loved the simple folk far better than polite society, and he liked to believe that his art would appeal to the undistinguished many. "It is very true," he once wrote, "that the common people who are content with chromos and melt when they hear a barrel organ, are in some vague way right, perhaps more sincere than certain men about town who go to the salon." Madame Roulin, the postman's wife who was the model for the "Woman Rocking a Cradle," was one of those common people who had the true artistic instinct. Van Gogh did three portraits of her and let her choose one as a present. "She had a good eye," he wrote, "and chose the best."

To capture the direct and simple taste of the Roulins and their like Van Gogh used his colors in the arbitrary way he did. If art is a symbol, not a copy of reality, that symbol which does not seem or pretend to be a copy will be more easily understood as art. One might compare his style with the style of primitive literature. To the primitive mind that language alone is poetry which by its rhythm and its uncommon vocabulary is far removed from the common speech of every day. Color to Van Gogh expressed something all by itself. The fierce dissonants of red and pink and yellow and green of his "Night Café" expressed, he said, "that this is a place where one can ruin oneself, where one can turn mad and commit crimes." Of his "Bedroom in Arles" he wrote, "Here color is to do everything, and, giving by its simplification a grander style to things, is to be suggestive of rest or of sleep."

It was his hope that his colorful paintings would delight the common people and give them something better to look at than the chromos that they loved. For his art was to be a gift to the poor. Art, which the Renaissance had taught us to adore as a mystic god revealed only to the initiated, was to come down to earth and become human, as God had become human in Christ, to bless the simplest and the poorest.

People speak of the tragic life of Vincent van Gogh and they think of his poverty, his lack of appreciation, his consciousness of the mental derangement that darkened his final days. But those were not the real tragedy. The real tragedy is that when recognition and fame did come at last, a generation after his death, his pictures attained values that made them accessible only to the very rich and the speculators, the very people he never thought of in painting them. Fortunately there are generous, public-spirited owners. One was Mrs. Hélène Kröller-Müller, whose superb collection of modern art is now on view, thanks to her gift of it to the nation, in the museum that perpetuates her name at Otterlo, near Arnhem. It contains the most exquisite Van Goghs that one can see anywhere. And the artist's nephew, Theo's son, possesses another rich collection of his uncle's works which is on permanent loan to the city of Amsterdam and on view in its Municipal Museum.

Across the street from the Municipal Museum stands the Amsterdam Concertgebouw, which is known by name at least among music lovers all over the world. Willem Mengelberg became the conductor of its orchestra in 1895. He gave up a promising career in Switzerland to accept the call to Amsterdam, and Holland owes him a debt of gratitude for building up an orchestra which now ranks among the world's chief exponents of music. He lost the people's favor in the second World War, when he showed himself an overzealous servant of the Nazis. He was forced to leave the country and went to live in Switzerland, where he died. The loss of his leadership did not impair the artistic quality of the orchestra.

It has maintained its high standards under his successors, and no celebrity who is on a European tour fails to play for the Amsterdam audience.

Through their interest in the arts—in painting, music, and literature—the Hollanders are in close touch with the outside world. Their men of letters form a strong and enthusiastic center of the international P. E. N. (International Association of Poets, Playwrights, Editors, Essayists, and Novelists).

In the summer of 1931 the international congress of P. E. N. assembled at Amsterdam, where Dutch authors acted as hosts to their fellow poets, essayists, and novelists from all over Europe. "We are gathered here," said Mr. John Galsworthy, the president, in replying to speeches of welcome by the Netherlands Minister of Home Affairs and the Dutch poet P. C. Boutens, "because the world leaves much to be desired and Holland, so far as our observation goes, practically nothing to be desired. . . . In an age when the tendency is all towards standardization and the leveling of forms, it is refreshing to find oneself in a country which has preserved its atmosphere and the dignity thereof, as a man should, but I fear does not always, preserve the dignity of his soul. The sturdy individuality of Holland is like an island in the rising sea of cosmopolitanism."

It was pleasant for a Hollander to hear this and to believe that it was more than a mere compliment such as a visiting stranger is expected to pay to his hosts. But if there is truth in the flattery, one cannot help wondering how Holland has been able to maintain that dignity of soul. For there is no more cosmopolitan nation upon God's earth. The Dutch are fond of travel and can indulge in it at small cost of time, as a few hours' ride by train or auto will take them from Amsterdam or The Hague across the border, and a plane will carry them to foreign territory in a matter of minutes. The different speech of their neighbors does not scare them away, for they all have been taught at least a smattering of French, German, and English, sufficient to help them along in the unavoidable altercations with railway porters, hotel clerks, waiters, and chambermaids. The educated read foreign books in the original and prefer them, I am sorry to admit, to their own Dutch literature. They follow foreign fashions, Paris models being no less popular among the ladies at The Hague and Amsterdam than they are among their sisters in New York. Their scholars are steeped in German learning, and some of them write an involved sort of Dutch that reflects a German trend of thought. The national sports are all imports from England, and their own extinct *kolf*, a popular Dutch game in the seventeenth century when it was exported to Scotland, has come back to them as *golf* from across the North Sea. Various creeds from abroad are received with open minds; Theosophy, Free Catholicism, Christian Science, the Star of the East, Mormonism have devout adherents among the Dutch. Storekeepers are fond of decorating their windows and signboards with inscriptions in French, or in what they believe to be French.

How is it, then, that in spite of this willingness to follow foreign models the nation has been able to resist the tendency of which Mr. Galsworthy spoke toward the leveling of forms? It may be that, since there is safety in numbers, the Dutch have saved themselves by being accessible without discrimination to influences from England, France, and Germany. But I do not believe that this all-round hospitality is the right explanation. If the desire to imitate foreign models is a disease, as chauvinists claim it to be, then the Dutch, thanks to age-long exposure to its ravages, have ceased to suffer from its effects. For Holland has never been insulated. The waves of foreign influence have always washed her lowlands no less persistently than the sea has invaded her shores. There was French penetration in the Middle Ages and again in the age of Louis XIV and in the Napoleonic era; there was German penetration in the nineteenth century so persistent and thorough as to make Bismarck convinced that Holland would ultimately annex herself with the German Empire. And English literature and sports and fashions for men have been widely popular since the days of Lord Byron.

Yet the nation has sturdily maintained its peculiar identity. The disease of imitation leaves only superficial, skin-deep marks. It does not harm the health of the body national, which has become immune to its infection by chronic exposure. That which is essentially native lies too deep to become adulterated, and the creative faculties of the soul, drawing inspiration from those depths, will express the nation's inner life in terms of beauty that no one can mistake for anything but Dutch.

It is not easy to define the nation's Dutchness. It has so many facets that glitter and attract the observer's mind. He is tempted to false generalizations by seizing on one sparkling surface and declaring that to be characteristic of the whole. The language is the mirror that best reflects the people's mentality; another is the painter's art. Both reveal the Dutchman's tendency to notice detail. There was little in everyday life that escaped the attention of Jan Steen and his fellow craftsmen. They painted the little things of their small world with loving care. One of them, Otto Marseus van Schriek, painted lizards, newts, and efts, little snakes and adders, insects, and butterflies fluttering over the grass through which he watched them crawl.

In the Hollander's speech this affection for smallness is evident in the profusion of diminutives that he uses. The suffixes *-je*, *-tje*, *-etje* are audible in nearly every sentence that he utters. They do not serve exclusively, though, to describe little things. They also serve to express moods and emotions, from love and compassion to contempt and indignation. When father has been generous to his dear little daughter she will call him *Vadertje*, a pious old woman will speak of God as *Ons lieve Heertje* (our dear Lordikin), two angry fellows will sarcastically call each other *mannetje* and *ventje*, and the man who comes home soaked to the skin will vent his disgust with the exclamation *Wat 'n weertje* (what weatherkin).

There is a close relationship between this microscopic observation of life and the Dutch housewife's insistence on cleanliness within the home. The Dutch word for little is *klein*, which is etymologically identical with the English word *clean*. "Don't overlook the little specks of dust and you'll keep your place clean of dirt," she seems to imply. And cleanliness, which the English claim to be next to godliness, is in her eyes identical with beauty. The Dutch word for beautiful is *mooi*, and *mooi* has a synonym in *schoon*, which also means clean. *Een schoonmaakster* is a cleaning woman, *een schoonheid* is a beauty.

Dutch speech is pictorial. It is a language of people who use their eyes and paint what they see in plastic phrases. A Hollander's talk sparkles with imagery, though he himself may be unaware that his words conjure up pictures. Sight, not insight, is his forte, clarity his aim, not profundity.

Being so clear-sighted in noticing little things, the Hollander is apt to overlook the wood for the trees and the underbrush. He sees the differences that divide instead of the similarity that overarches and unites. To him the whole is less important than the parts. That makes him in politics the very reverse of the American. A two-party system would be unthinkable in Holland. There are parties galore, and this profusion makes the formation of a party government impossible. No one faction is numerous enough to form a cabinet entirely composed of its own members. The man who is entrusted by the monarch with the task of selecting the colleagues who must head the various ministries needs the support of other parties. Coalition governments are the only solution that can break the deadlock resulting from the multiplicity of factions.

Native moderation and tolerance lessen the bitterness of dissension. Sir William Temple, who was the British envoy at The Hague in the sixties of the seventeenth century, noticed with surprise that in Holland all sects were tolerated and yet religious strife was less bitter than elsewhere. "It is hardly to be imagined," he wrote, "how all the violence and sharpness which accompanies the differences of religion in other countries seems to be appeased or softened by the general freedom which all men enjoy." And this self-restraint that tempered the heat of religious controversy in the distant past is still characteristic of the Dutch people in this politically-minded modern age.

CHAPTER THIRTEEN

The Youngest Generation

Queen Wilhelmina, after completing the fiftieth year of her reign, resigned the throne in 1948 in favor of her daughter, Juliana, and withdrew into retirement on her country estate, Het Loo, in the province of Gelderland. She resigned also her royal title and expressed the wish to be called not Queen Mother but Princess Wilhelmina. She had always played her part with quiet dignity and restraint. Big words and boastful utterances never crossed her lips. In that she was a true daughter of her country. The braggart is a social outcast in Holland. Dutchmen feel nothing but scorn for the self-advertiser and respond to his barrage of self-praise with mocking silence or a sneer. A mob mind enslaved, as in Hitler's Germany, by a controlled press supplies but a dull sounding board to the dictator. He must shout and thunder to impress. In Holland the quiet voice of Wilhelmina found clearer resonance in the hearts of a free people.

A sincere believer in the tenets of the Calvinist faith, Wilhelmina scorned ostentation and the pomp and pride that are vanity to the deeply religious. Not splendor but aloofnes was the mark of her regal status. She lacked that captivating ease of manner by which King Edward VII and his grandson won the hearts of their British subjects. Yet, though she seemed to have shunned rather than sought popularity, she was, fifty years after her inauguration, no less close to the hearts of her people than when she had appealed to their loyalty as a winsome young girl just come of age. For her people knew that they had been years spent in devoted service to the country. A constitutional monarch's task, self-effacing though it be, is nevertheless no sinecure. Wilhelmina insisted on being kept informed by her ministers on all affairs of state, and devoted laborious hours of study to the problems submitted to her attention. The law is the royal will defined with the co-operation of the States-General, and that being so, the Queen never shirked her share in the partnership. Posterity will speak of her reign as the Age of Wilhelmina, and the phrase will not be an empty flattery. She stamped her personality on the nation's accomplishment. Her earnest devotion to duty and the example she set in stressing spiritual above material values informed her reign with a dignity which the breath of vulgarity could not touch.

By the name that was given her at the font, Juliana's life was linked to the life of one of the noblest women among her ancestors, Juliana of Stolberg, the mother of William the Silent. The present-day Queen Juliana was married to Prince Bernhard of Lippe-Biesterfeld on Thursday, January 7, 1937. The ceremony took place in the city hall at The Hague, for the law of the Netherlands does not recognize any marriage that has been solemnized only in church, and the parson, priest, or rabbi who should presume to bind two in marriage before the civil ceremony had been performed would commit an unlawful act and run the risk of being sent to prison. There was issued no special license to Her Royal Highness. She appeared with her fiancé at the city hall, where both signed the register in token of their intention to be married. Prince Bernhard signed it as a Netherlands citizen. A Dutch girl marrying a foreigner loses thereby her Dutch citizenship, so a couple of weeks before the prince signed the marriage register he was naturalized by a special act of Parliament.

The couple have four children, all daughters. One of them was born on foreign soil, in Canada, but thanks to a proclamation by King George declaring and directing "that any place in Canada within which Her Royal Highness Juliana of the Netherlands may be confined shall, for the period of the lying-in and to the extent of actual occupation for such purposes, be extra-territorial," little Margriet Francisca was not born a British subject but, as a daughter of Dutch parents, a citizen of the Netherlands.

Juliana had fled to Canada after Hitler's invasion of Holland, and she remained there with her daughters until, after the liberation, it was safe for her to return to the fatherland. She took up her residence in the palace of Soestdijk in the Province of Utrecht. Rapid means of communication by auto along modern speedways make it possible for her to live at some distance from The Hague, the seat of government.

When she came back from North America the country was in a sorry state. The traces of devastation were visible everywhere: yawning holes in the center of once prosperous cities, mangled village churches, burned-out farmhouses, windowless railway carriages, broken bridges, poor countryfolk living in makeshift shelters—in lean-tos, canalboats, stables, pigsties—the stores depleted of merchandise, and the people in all stages of life complaining of physical and mental fatigue that made them averse, they claimed, to any kind of exertion. Yet the labor of reconstruction that was started at once belied that self-diagnosis.

Five years later the country presented a scene of general well-being. The holes in the cities were still gaping, but the rubble piles had been cleared away and masons and carpenters were busy building. The broken bridges had been restored, the railway service was back at its high prewar level, the homeless had been rescued from their miserable shanties, and the many houses in town and country that used to stand paintless and with boarded-up windows had recovered their good looks and their eyesight, thanks to a fresh coat of paint and new panes.

The Marshall Plan deserves credit for this miraculous improvement, but also the government's wise policy in subjecting the nation to a program of strict austerity. Mr. Lieftinck, the Minister of Finance, was the most criticized and best-hated member of Her Majesty's Cabinet, but when his unyielding policy of iron control proved to have raised the country out of the morass of dejection and insolvency and restored the nation's self-confidence, his critics grudgingly admitted that he had been right.

Yet there is little confidence in the future among those who have known prewar days. The loss of Indonesia, the Russian menace, the general jitteriness of Europe, and the growing problem of overpopulation create a sense of uneasiness and insecurity which cannot be dispelled by the return of general prosperity and private well-being. The young, however, who were born and are growing up in this postwar world accept these changed conditions as a matter of course. They knew no other and are not plagued by vain regrets. To an old-timer these children seem courageous and amazingly skillful in adjusting themselves to the new order of things, but they think nothing of it and claim no credit for their adaptability. They are the products of the present age and are naturally able to thrive in it. A man who remembers what he calls better days is apt to be sorry for them, but they will laugh at his compassion; they do not feel worse off than he was in his youth. They enjoy, indeed, a freedom of movement that was denied to their parents. By motorcycle and auto they travel across the Continent and learn with ease to speak in the market place foreign languages which their elders tried with difficulty to acquire in the schoolroom.

The boys and girls of the poor cannot so easily wander into foreign lands, but they, too, find freedom from the restraints of home on the streets of towns and cities. Juvenile delinquency is a social problem also in Holland, but the Dutch do not take it tragically. In Amsterdam, where the young street Arab is sarcastically called *de lieverd* (the darling), a statue of the darling was unveiled in 1960 by the burgomaster's wife on a busy thoroughfare in the center of the city. There he stands, with arms akimbo and an impertinent grin on his face, as a symbol of the youth of Amsterdam and a visible assurance to the young delinquents that they are not looked upon as criminals.

University students are better-behaved individuals. They do not stage political riots such as disturb academic dignity in France. They gave a telling demonstration of good manners in 1960. It happened during the debate in Parliament on the government's bill for the revision of the higher-education law. It contained a proposal that aroused the students' anger. This would have given the professors the right to bar from the classrooms students who had failed to pass their first exam within twice the normal period. The universities have been confronted since the end of the second World War with increasing numbers of enrollments, and the offensive article was aimed at removing from the campus those boys and girls who were incompetent or would rather be loafers and pleasure seekers than scholars. One night the windows of the Minister of Education were plastered with posters showing two manacled hands. Next morning the perpetrators called up and offered to come and clean the windows, but the Minister's wife replied that the posters had already been removed. Shortly afterward two coeds called and presented her with a bouquet of roses by way of apology for the nocturnal misdemeanor. And more than 15,000 written protests were addressed to the members of the Second Chamber, who, impressed by the students' indignation, amended the bill by deleting the offensive provision.

The universities in Holland differ in many respects from those in England and America. They came into existence when monasticism had been stamped out in the northern Netherlands. They owed their genesis not to the private devotion of a pious founder, but to the collective initiative of a young democracy. That gives them their peculiar character, so different from Oxford and Cambridge. The college with its quadrangle and its cloister, its chapel and its dining hall is here unknown. The Calvinist burghers of the

Dutch Republic would not admit such monkish relics into their modern schools of learning. They were to be schools exclusively, not hostels for a monastic brotherhood. It was scholarship alone which was to constitute the brotherhood of students, not the community of roof and board. Hence the care for the student's physical well-being was his own concern. The university supplied him with the knowledge that he sought and for the rest let him shift for himself.

Hence householders in university towns made an industry of letting rooms to students. For the freshman the new life in his diggings was an exciting experience. It gave him the thrill of total independence from parental control. That independence, however, was sadly restricted in the first three weeks succeeding his enrollment. Being a greenhorn just released from Mother's apron strings, he had to go through the process of de-greening. There was no way of escape from the trial: what his seniors, the members of the older classes, ordered him to do was law to him.

Not every freshman was thus initiated into the mysteries of student life. No one who entered the university was compelled to join the students' *Corps*. The Corps is the social bond between the students; the university constitutes their scholastic unity. The latter includes the entire student body, the Corps only those students who believe that knowledge alone does not make men. Friendship, conviviality, games, the luxury of loafing, the romance of nightly escapades also add an indispensable element to the stuff a real man is made of.

A century ago it was a matter of course that enrollment in the university automatically meant initiation into the Corps, but the students in those days were few in numbers and mostly sons of well-to-do families. A university education then was the gentleman's prerogative; it is now a privilege obtainable by any boy with brains. It was formerly a shame not to be in the Corps; now the number of those who stay out of it exceeds its membership list. Yet the real student life remains centered in the Corps, and those who want and can afford not only to study but to be students will join it when they enter the university.

The four universities mentioned so far are not the only institutes of higher learning in Holland. A private corporation, the Society for Higher Education on a Calvinist Basis, founded in 1880 the Free University at Amsterdam. A similar one for Roman Catholic students is at Nijmegen. A state institute of technology was founded at Delft in 1842, which at its reorganization in 1905 received the official name of Technical University. Its student life has been modeled on that of Leiden and Utrecht and resembles it in nearly all particulars. There is, further, a veterinary university in Utrecht, an agricultural university in Wageningen, both maintained by the state, and a commercial university founded in 1913 by a private corporation in the city of Rotterdam. These are young institutions, lacking the stamp of dignity which the four older ones derive from age and an inherited devotion—now unfortunately on the wane—to the study of Latin and Greek, a knowledge of which is still required from freshmen wishing to enroll in the faculties of law, theology, and letters.

Student life in these younger institutions is still in the making. It has not had time to mature and develop a revered tradition whose very essence is its age. It is this tradition which really constitutes the student life. Without it there would be no tie between the classes, nor any devotion to the Corps. Tradition or, as the students call it with a Latin name, the *Mos*, saves the Corps from being a continuous experiment in democracy.

Steadily increasing enrollment since the late war has caused a drastic change in the students' way of life. Since the number of rooms for rent is not sufficient to accommodate all newcomers, the problem of housing them had to be solved in the American way. The University of Leiden has built dormitories for boys and for girls, and the communal life in these appears to be more attractive to them than the hermit existence in private rooms. The United States is shaping more and more the face of things in the Netherlands. Many Dutch professors have lectured at American universities, and scholarships of various kinds have enabled thousands of students to spend a year or more at a college in the United States, and both groups have suggested adaptation to American models.

The rapid growth of the student body is an unavoidable result of the alarming increase of the country's population, which has more than doubled during the past century. That growth has changed not only the manner of Holland's student life, but also the face of the Dutch landscape. Its general aspect a hundred years ago was not much different from what it was when Jan van Goyen and Jacob van Ruisdael painted it. It was a beautiful country then, not marred as yet by the noisy rush of motor traffic, by the destruction of woodland and pasture for the building of voracious highways that must facilitate that rush, by the rise of huge apartment houses on the outskirts of towns and cities that have turned the charm of rural environs into a dreary waste of steel and stone.

This creeping invasion of the countryside by mechanized city life is causing deep concern to all nature lovers in the Netherlands. They have started a movement for its conservation that is winning supporters by leaps and bounds. The man who conceived the organization of the Society for the Protection of Nature Monuments was Pieter Gerbrand van Tienhoven (1875–1953), a native and lifelong citizen of Amsterdam, of which his father at one time was burgomaster. Holland is deeply indebted to him for the tireless persistence with which he fought to save precious woodland and wildlife for future generations. He was a lover of birds, and thanks to him there are now several sanctuaries where his winged friends can live free from persecution and the peril of extinction. In 1905 his native city planned to purchase Naarden Lake, a favorite haunt of water birds south of Amsterdam, and use it as a dumping ground for its garbage. Van Tienhoven and fellow conservationists protested against this outrage, and, thanks to the public indignation they aroused, the city fathers heeded their protest and abandoned the scheme. The danger that had threatened Naarden Lake was a warning signal. The calamity that was narrowly averted in this case might occur again in other places. Nature lovers clubbed together and organized the society under Van Tienhoven's presidency. For fifty years he directed its activities and succeeded in saving many other equally precious beauty spots. It now owns nearly sixty protected terrains, scattered all over the country.

The society's signal success stimulated the foundation of provincial organizations, all intent on protecting precious scenery from encroachment by urban expansion and industrial development. The islands along the northwest coast are less exposed to that menace. They have long retained their virgin solitude, but in this century they, too, have been invaded by business enterprise, especially Terschelling, which during the past decades has become a popular seaside resort. Fortunately its beaches are so wide and stretch out to such length that the bathers seem mere specks on the sand to the lover of solitude on top of a high dune. Here one can forget for a moment Holland's two most serious problems: lack of room for a steadily increasing population, and the eternal danger of the sea. The stillness here is broken only by the distant roar of the breakers and by the shriek of gulls and terns and other kinds of sea birds that seem to be in sole possession of the scenery.

INDEX

According to Dutch custom, family names which are preceded by *de*, *ten*, *ter*, or *van* are listed under their initials, not under *d*, *t*, or *v*.